Becoming a Grand Reiki Master: Skill, Spirit & Service
Copyright © 2025 by Dr. Constance Santego.

Copy Editor & Interior Design: Constance Santego
Book Layout: ©2017 BookDesignTemplates.com

Ordering Information:
Quantity sales. Special discounts are available on quantity purchases by corporations, associations, and others. For details, contact the "Special Sales Department" at the address above.

Trade Paperback ISBN: **978-1-997907-10-7**
eBook ISBN **978-1-997907-11-4**
Created and published In Canada. Printed and bound in the United States of America

First Edition
Published by Maximillian Enterprises
Kelowna, BC
Canada
www.constancesantego.ca

BECOMING A GRAND REIKI MASTER

Skill, Spirit & Service

DR. CONSTANCE SANTEGO
Grand Reiki Master

Maximillian Enterprises
Kelowna, BC

Dedication

To the One who whispered,
"You will join in."
To Spirit,
who lifted me into a calling I did not seek,
yet could not ignore.
To every student who stepped into my classroom
and unknowingly became part of my initiation.
You were the mirrors through which I saw my own
awakening.
To the healers, teachers, and seekers
walking their own path of faith, courage, and
surrender—
may this book help you recognize
the moment Spirit calls your name.
And to the unseen hands that drew the symbols
above us all,
on the day my life changed—
this book is my offering in service to You.
— Grand Reiki Master
Constance Santego

ALSO BY DR. CONSTANCE SANTEGO

NOVELS
Illegitimate Grace
Ashcroft Hollow

Okanagan Trilogy:
Beneath the Vineyards
Under the Okanagan Sun
Guardian of the Lake

The Nine Spiritual Gifts Series:
Journey of a Soul – (Vol 1 Michael)
Language of a Soul – (Vol 2 Gabriel)
Prophecy of a Soul – (Vol 3 Bath Kol)
Healing of a Soul – (Vol 4 Raphael)
Miracles of a Soul – (Vol 5 Hamied)
Knowledge of a Soul – (Vol 6 Raziel)
Wisdom of a Soul – (Vol 7 Uriel)
Faith of a Soul – (Vol 8 Pistis Sophia)

NONFICTION
The Intuitive Life, The Gift Of Prophecy, Third Edition
Fairy Tales, Dreams And Reality… Where Are You On Your Path? Second Edition
Your Persona… The Mask You Wear
Archangel Michael's Soul Retrieval Guide
Tesla And The Future Of Energy Medicine
Beyond Tesla: Advancing The Science Of Energy Healing
Tesla's Code: Mastering Energy, Frequency, And Creative Power
Beyond The Mind: Harnessing The Power Of Astral Projection For Creative Awakening
Bend, Don't Break: Finding Your Way Back To Abundance
Ring Therapy: A Guide To Healing And Balance
Ring Therapy Pocket Guide
Floraopathy™: The Art And Science Of Vibrational Healing With Essential Oils
Dear Older Me: A Memoir… Of Sorts
It's Just Like Poker: A Spiritual Guide To Playing The Cards Life Deals You

Signs And Meanings: What The Feet Reveal About Health, Stress, And The Body's Story
Auricions: Unlocking Subconscious Healing Through Quantum Medicine
Quick Fix Acupressure Method
Manifestation – The DREAM Method in 5 Steps
Confidence- Mastering the Dream Method
The New Paradigm: Conscious Healing In The Age Of Ai

REIKI WISDOM, SERIES:
Angelic Lifestyle, a Vibrant Lifestyle
Angelic Lifestyle 42-Day Energy Cleanse
Reiki and the Power of The Joint Points: Unlocking Energy Pathways for Healing (Vol I)
Reiki and Karmic Healing: Releasing Patterns From Past Lives (Vol II)
Reiki and the Five Elements (Vol III)
Secrets of a Healer, Magic Of Reiki
The Reiki Master's Manual *(In English, German, Spanish, French, Portuguese, Russian, Hindi, and Mandarin Chinese)*

CHAKRA SERIES:
Heart Chakra 101: The Bridge
Root Chakra 101: Building Safety, Survival, Foundation
Sacral Chakra 101: Creativity, Pleasure, Emotions
Solar Plexus Chakra 101: Power, Confidence, Will
Throat Chakra 101: Truth, Voice, Self-Expression
Third Eye Chakra 101: Intuition, Vision, Insight
Crown Chakra 101: Spiritual Connection, Transcendence.

SECRETS OF A HEALER, SERIES:
Magic Of Aromatherapy (Vol I)
Magic Of Reflexology (Vol II)
Magic Of The Gifts (Vol III)
Magic Of Muscle Testing (Vol IV)
Magic Of Iridology (Vol V)
Magic Of Massage (Vol VI)
Magic Of Hypnotherapy (Vol VII)
Magic Of Reiki (Vol VIII)
Magic Of Advanced Aromatherapy (Vol IX)
Magic Of Esthetics (Vol X)
The Reiki Master's Manual (Vol XI)

ADULT COLORING JOURNALS
SERIES-ZEN COLORING:
Quantum Energy and Mindful Living Journal (Vol 1)
Reiki Energy Journal (Vol 2)
Nine Spiritual Gifts Journal (Vol 3)
I Forgive Journal (Vol 4)

FOR CHILDREN
I am Big Tonight. I Don't Need the Light
The Magic Elf Book: 25 Days of Surprises

COOKBOOK
My Favorite Recipes, with a Hint of Giggle

BUISNESS
How To Use ChatGPT For Authors: From Idea To Published Book
Scaling Beyond 6 Figures: Strategies For Health & Wellness Professionals
The Academypreneur's Playbook: Turn Knowledge Into A
Revenue-Generating School

HUMOR/GIFT BOOK
How Do You Like Your Eggs? Crack Into Your Personality, Yolk and All

Contents

Note to Reader..xxi

What I Mean by "Spirit"...............................xxiii

How to Use This Book..................................xxv

Introduction — The Book I Was Meant to Write 1

Why This Book Is the Capstone of My Teachings 6

The Distinction Between a Reiki Master and a Grand Reiki Master...................................9

Why Spirit — Not Humans — Elevates the Grand Master..................................14

How the Spiritual and Practical Sides Merge 21

✦ Chapter 1 — What Reiki Really Is: The Universal Life Force..28

The Vibrational Reality of Healing..............35

The Soul's Relationship to Energy..............41

Healing Through Relationship: How Reiki and the Soul Work Together 47

✦ Chapter 2 — The Three Human Levels of Reiki ..53

Level 1 — Self-Healing..............................54

Level 2 — Practitioner 58

Level 3 — Master/Teacher..........................63

✦ Chapter 3 — Level 4 - The Spiritual Appointment
....68

Why Grand Mastery Cannot Be Taught.....68

The Moment Spirit Steps In.........................76

The Moment Spirit Choose Me 81

Human Teachers Recognize Grand Masters;
They Do Not Create Them 86

Signs, Synchronicities, and Spiritual
Confirmation 91

The Shift from Doing Reiki to Being Reiki .98

✦ Chapter 4 — The Intuitive Awakening 105

Understanding Energy as Communication 105

Developing Intuitive Perception 112

Listening to Spirit 119

Energetic Discernment 126

Becoming a Clear Channel...........................136

Spirit-Guided Knowing: When Messages
Arrive Without Effort 144

When Intuition and Reiki Merge Into One
Consciousness 150

The Intuitive Responsibilities of a Grand
Reiki Master 149

✦ Chapter 5 — The Prophetic Senses 145

Developing Spiritual Sight, Hearing, and
Knowing...145

Dreams, Visions, and Symbols....................175

Energetic Timelines 182

Prophetic Clarity for Healing 191

✦ Chapter 6 — The Nine Spiritual Gifts as Energetic Tools 199

Faith as the Central Frequency 199

Healing, Knowledge, Wisdom, Miracles 208

How the Gifts Awaken Along the Reiki Path 215

The Merging of Gifts at the Grand Master Level 224

✦ Chapter 7 — Soul Refinement 234

Karmic Purification 234

Emotional Transmutation 242

Ego Dissolution 251

Spiritual Ethics 261

The Responsibilities of True Service 270

✦ Chapter 8 — The Higher Dimensional Reiki Stream 280

Expanding Beyond Symbols 280

Working in the Quantum Field 288

Reiki as a Consciousness Field 248

Aligning With Divine Intelligence 305

✦ Chapter 9 — The Symbols Revisited at the Grand Master Level 314

Dai Ko Myo as a State of Being 314

Hon Sha Ze Sho Nen Beyond Time............322

When Intention Becomes the Symbol........330

Advanced Symbol Combinations 328

When Spirit Removes the Need for Symbols
....346

✦ Chapter 10 — Holding the Field of a Grand Master
....354

Energetic Container Creation 354

Activating the Morphic Field......................363

Leading Healers and Students....................371

Reading Multidimensional Energy 381

Channeling Higher Beings 348

✦ Chapter 11 — Working with the Higher Realms 358

Archangels (Michael, Raphael, Gabriel, Uriel, Pistis Sophia, etc.)..............................358

Ascended Guides 368

The Spiritual Lineage Behind Reiki...........378

Receiving Transmissions and Teachings ...387

✦ Chapter 12 — The Tests: The Gateways Every Grand Master Must Pass 397

The Loneliness of the Path 397

Loss, Surrender, Faith.................................445

Shadow Work..453

Discernment..460

The Call to Step Forward...........................464

✦ Chapter 13 — The Moment Spirit Chooses You 477

The Initiation That Cannot Be Planned, Predicted, or Earned 477

What Changes Energetically 486

What You Begin to "Know" 475

Spiritual Signs of Ascension 479

How to Recognize the Calling 484

✦ Chapter 14 — The Grand Master Attunement 503

Preparation of the Soul 503

The Ceremony 502

The Silent Energetic Moment 507

What Is Passed On by Spirit 513

What Humans Can and Cannot Do 519

Post-Initiation Transformation 526

✦ Chapter 15 — Becoming the Teacher of Teachers 533

How Grand Masters Teach Masters 533

Activating Lineage 540

Passing on the Deeper Teachings 546

✦ Chapter 16 — Service, Humility & Leadership .. 552

The Ethics of Spiritual Authority 552

Maintaining Purity 559

Leading Communities 565

Guiding Global Healing Movements 577

✦ Chapter 17 — The Future of Reiki 584

   Global Expansion of Energy Medicine 584

   The Merging of Science & Spirit 592

   Your Role in Shaping the Next Generation
  599

✦ Conclusion — The Grand Master's Prayer 606

✦ Appendix 610

   Appendix A — Signs You Are Being Called to
   Grand Mastery 610

   Appendix B — Meditations for Spiritual
   Elevation 618

   Appendix C — The Grand Master Self-
   Assessment 625

   Appendix D — Dr. Constance's Lineage 632

   Appendix E — Journal Reflections for the
   Grand Master Path 633

   Appendix F — Glossary of Reiki Wisdom
   Terminology 639

✦ Bibliography 649

✦ Message From The Author 654

✦ About The Author 657

Preface

There are certain thresholds in a healer's life that cannot be crossed until the soul is ready. They are not marked on calendars, nor are they reached through linear progression. They unfold in divine timing, often when we least expect it, and always with a guidance that feels both intimate and absolute.

This book was born from such a threshold.

For decades, I taught Reiki the way it had been passed to me—level by level, symbol by symbol, initiation by initiation. Each class brought new students, new stories, and new experiences that affirmed the profound healing power of Reiki. Yet throughout those years, a quiet truth lived beneath the surface: that Reiki is not simply a system. It is an evolving consciousness, one that continues to reveal deeper layers as we grow in spirit.

The moment Spirit initiated me into Grand Mastery did not occur in a ceremony, nor through another teacher, nor during any planned event. It arrived in the stillness of a meditation, in a classroom filled with students who had come seeking their own healing. I was guiding them—yet Spirit was guiding me.

When the voice within said, *"You will join in,"* everything I understood about Reiki, teaching, and initiation shifted. The structure I had relied on dissolved, and a higher wisdom stepped forward. In that moment, I became both teacher and receiver, leader and vessel, student and servant. The attunement I received was not drawn by human hands but woven by the Divine.

It took years to fully understand the magnitude of that moment.

I came to realize that Grand Reiki Mastery is not a role.
It is not a rank.
It is not something one can claim.

It is a spiritual appointment.

It is given in silence, through grace, to those who have surrendered to the deeper work of intuition, prophecy, healing, faith, service, and soul alignment. It is a doorway that opens when Spirit decides the time is right—and not a moment before.

This book is for those who feel that door stirring within them.

For the healers who sense a deeper calling.
For the practitioners who feel Spirit drawing closer.
For the teachers who know they are meant to guide at a higher level.
For the souls who have walked through fire and still choose love.

This book is not meant to teach you how to *become* a Grand Reiki Master in the human sense.
It is meant to prepare your soul for the moment Spirit chooses you.

May these pages offer clarity where there was confusion, affirmation where there was doubt, and peace where there was searching. And may they remind you that the true path of a Grand Reiki Master is not found in the mind, but in the heart—and not walked alone, but with Spirit ever beside you.

Note to Reader

This book is more than information.
It is an energetic transmission.

As you move through these pages, you may feel sensations, emotions, memories, or intuitive insights rising within you. This is natural. When we speak of Reiki at the level of Spirit, we are not merely discussing concepts—we are awakening frequencies.

Please read this book the way you would approach a sacred teaching:

- slowly
- with openness
- without rushing
- allowing space for reflection

Some passages may speak directly to your mind.
Others may speak only to your heart.
And a few may bypass both entirely, entering you at the level of the soul.

There will be moments when you recognize something—
not because you've learned it before,
but because you've *always known it.*

That recognition is your initiation beginning.

If at any point the energy feels intense, simply pause.
Breathe.
Place your hands over your heart or your abdomen.
Allow your body to integrate.

This book is not meant to convince you of anything.
It is meant to awaken what is already within you.

Whether you are a practitioner, a teacher, or someone drawn
to the deeper spiritual current of Reiki, trust that you were
guided here for a reason. Your presence in this moment is
part of your path—your unfolding, your preparation, your
becoming.

May these pages offer clarity, comfort, and truth.
May they remind you of your infinite connection to Spirit.
And may they open a doorway—one you will step through
only when you are ready.

With gratitude for your courage and your light,
Grand Reiki Master, Constance Santego

What I Mean by "Spirit"

In this book, you will see me use the word *Spirit* often.
Because at the level of Grand Reiki Mastery, Spirit becomes central—not as a doctrine, but as a Presence.

When I say *Spirit*, I am not referring to any one religion, deity, or belief system.
I am speaking of the universal intelligence that moves through all life:

- the Source of Reiki
- the consciousness behind intuition
- the wisdom within the quiet inner voice
- the higher guidance that calls us forward
- the unseen hands that initiate, heal, and transform

Different traditions give this force different names:

God
Source
Creator
Universe
Higher Self
Divine Intelligence

The Holy Spirit
The Field
Life Force
Love
Light

Each is valid, and none is excluded.

Reiki itself is universal.
It belongs to no religion and yet flows through all of them.
It is accessible to anyone who approaches with sincerity,
humility, and an open heart.

When I use the word *Spirit*, I mean:

**The greater, benevolent intelligence that guides healing,
awakens gifts, and calls a soul into alignment with its highest
purpose.**

You do not need to follow a specific spiritual path to read this
book.
You do not need to adopt new beliefs.

You need only be open to the possibility that:

- Life communicates with you
- Energy responds to intention
- Your soul has a purpose
- Guidance arrives in many forms
- Healing is both personal and universal

Grand Reiki Mastery cannot be understood without
acknowledging the role of Spirit—because it is Spirit, not
humans, who elevates a Master to Grand Master.

As you read, take "Spirit" in whatever way feels true to you.
The name does not matter.
The Presence does.

How to Use This Book

How to Use This Book

This book is not meant to be read the way you would read a typical Reiki manual.
It is not a collection of steps, techniques, or linear lessons.
It is a **spiritual companion**, meant to walk beside you as you evolve in skill, sensitivity, and service.

Here are a few ways to get the most from your journey through these pages:

1. Read Slowly, Not Quickly

Many teachings in this book are experiential.
They are meant to be *felt*, not just understood.

Move at a pace that allows the wisdom to settle into your body, your energy, and your awareness.

If a section feels dense or powerful, pause.
Let your intuition catch up with your mind.

2. Pay Attention to What Resonates

You may find certain chapters feel familiar, even if you've never learned the content before.
This is often a sign of:

- spiritual memory
- soul-level recognition
- or an initiation beginning internally

Make note of these feelings. They are meaningful.

3. Use the Reflections as Integrations

Throughout the book, you'll find moments where you are invited to reflect, journal, breathe, or tune inward.

These are not optional.
They are part of your energetic development.

A Grand Reiki Master is not formed through information alone, but through integration.

4. Let Spirit Guide Your Timing

You do not need to read this book in one sitting.
Or even in order.

Some readers will move from cover to cover.
Others will be guided intuitively to chapters based on what they need most in that moment.

Trust your instinct.
The right teaching will always call you at the right time.

5. Keep a Journal Beside You

This book will likely stir insights, memories, symbols, synchronicities, dreams, or intuitive messages.

A journal provides a place to capture:

- awakenings
- questions
- energetic sensations
- guidance
- moments of clarity
- signs from Spirit

This becomes your own record of becoming.

6. Revisit Chapters as You Grow

Some teachings in this book will make sense immediately.
Others will reveal themselves only after you've deepened your
practice, healed certain wounds, or stepped into greater
service.

Return to the chapters again when you feel called.
This book is designed to teach you differently each time you
read it.

7. Let This Book Support Your Path — Not Define It

Reiki is a living consciousness.
Your journey will be unique to your soul, your lineage, and
your purpose.

This book offers guidance, clarity, and truth, but your
relationship with Spirit will always remain your greatest
teacher.

8. Read This with an Open Heart

Grand Reiki Mastery is not achieved through effort alone. It is awakened through:

- readiness
- humility
- surrender
- devotion
- faith
- and service

Approach this book with openness, curiosity, and sincerity.

Your heart will know what your mind cannot yet comprehend.

This book is a lantern, not a staircase.
It illuminates the path,
but you will walk it with Spirit.

BECOMING A
GRAND REIKI
MASTER
Skill, Spirit & Service

DR. CONSTANCE SANTEGO
Grand Reiki Master

Introduction — The Book I Was Meant to Write

Becoming a Grand Reiki Master: Skill, Spirit & Service
by Dr. Constance Santego

There are books we choose to write, and there are books that choose us.

This is the latter.

For years, I taught Reiki with the same devotion and consistency I had given to every part of my spiritual work. I taught Level 1. Level 2. Level 3 Master/Teacher. I taught intuition, prophecy, energy medicine, spiritual gifts, the nature of the soul, and how Spirit communicates through signs, symbols, and subtle knowing. I wrote novels that expressed spiritual truths through story, and nonfiction that gave readers the practical pathways to awaken their own gifts.

Each book felt like another step on a staircase I couldn't yet fully see.

Only now, looking back, do I understand that everything I created—every class, every manuscript, every meditation, every initiation—was preparing me for *this* book. The one that gathers all the threads and weaves them into the tapestry of Grand Reiki Mastery. The one that explains what cannot be taught in a classroom. The one that reveals the spiritual path behind the technique.

Because becoming a Grand Reiki Master is not a result of completing levels.
It is a result of completing a transformation.

To understand that truth, I must begin with where my path began.

My Journey Through Reiki

Like many healers, I began with curiosity and a deep inner knowing that energy was more than theory—it was relationship. Reiki became the language through which I first understood universal life force, not as a concept, but as a presence.

Level 1 taught me to listen to my own body.
Level 2 taught me to feel beyond time and space.
Level 3 taught me to lead others into the light of their own awakening.

But something in me always sensed that there was more—another layer, another calling, another frequency waiting behind the veil. I could feel Spirit guiding my path long before I ever had the language for it.

My Journey Through Intuition

Years before I became a Grand Reiki Master, intuition opened within me like a door that would never close again. I learned how energy speaks:

- in whispers
- in impressions
- in knowing
- in the sudden clarity that comes without explanation

I taught students how intuition behaves like a sense— perceiving what is unseen in the same way the eyes perceive light and the ears perceive sound. Intuition became the foundation on which all my spiritual work was built.

It prepared me to hear Spirit when the moment came.

My Journey Through Prophecy

There is a spiritual hearing—different from intuition—that speaks from beyond the edges of linear time. In my teachings on prophecy, I explored how Spirit communicates through dreams, visions, and inner messages that guide us toward our highest path.

I never imagined I would one day be asked to step into a higher calling through this very ability. That the same spiritual hearing I had taught to others would be the voice that whispered the words that changed my life forever:

"You will join in."

Those four words altered my path more than any training ever could.

My Journey Through the Spiritual Gifts

Through my spiritual gifts books and the Nine Spiritual Gifts novel series, I explored the gifts described in 1 Corinthians 12—not as ancient concepts, but as living energies that move through modern life.

I saw how the gifts awaken one by one:
faith, healing, wisdom, knowledge, prophecy, discernment, and more.

I learned that the gifts are not tools we use.
They are frequencies we embody.

And I learned that when the gifts align, they converge into a higher consciousness—one that prepares the soul for service, humility, and spiritual leadership.

All of these teachings were preparing me for what came next.

The Book That Brings It All Together

Even before I understood the title, this book lived inside me.

It is the bridge between:

- intuition and healing
- prophecy and teaching
- Spirit and service
- the human levels of Reiki and the divine calling that elevates them

It is the book that explains what truly makes a Grand Reiki Master:

Not the certificate.
Not the level.
Not the role.

But the moment Spirit steps in and says, **"Now."**

This book is the culmination of decades of healing, teaching, writing, listening, serving, and surrendering. It is a map for those who feel the stirring of something deeper—something calling them into a higher expression of their soul's work.

This is the book I was meant to write.
And if you are holding it now, it is likely the book you were meant to find.

Why This Book Is the Capstone of My Teachings

Every teaching path has a summit — a point where all previous lessons rise, gather, and merge into a higher understanding.
For me, this book is that summit.

For over twenty-five years, I have taught Reiki, intuition, prophecy, energy medicine, healing arts, and the nine spiritual gifts. Each topic seemed separate at first, as if they belonged to different chapters of my life. But over time, a deeper truth revealed itself:

These teachings were never meant to stand alone.
They were pieces of the same whole.

Reiki taught me how energy flows.
Intuition taught me how Spirit speaks.
Prophecy taught me how guidance arrives.
The spiritual gifts taught me how the soul awakens.
My novels taught me how Spirit weaves wisdom through story.
My students taught me how healing transforms a life.

And my initiation into Grand Mastery taught me why all of it mattered.

It became clear that every class, every chapter, every book, and every experience was quietly preparing me for a larger purpose — to articulate the path that lies *beyond* Reiki Mastery.

To explain the level that cannot be learned from curriculum alone.
To reveal the moment when Spirit, not humans, elevates a soul into deeper service.

This is the book that ties everything together —
the threads of energy, intuition, prophecy, gifts, faith, soul evolution, and divine calling.

It is the culmination of all my teachings because:

- It brings Reiki back to its spiritual origin.
- It honours the role of Spirit in true initiation.
- It unifies everything I have studied, practiced, and lived.
- It reflects the truth I have witnessed in myself and in my students.
- It expresses the lesson Spirit waited for the right time for me to share.

Without Reiki, I would not have understood energy.
Without intuition, I would not have heard the calling.
Without the spiritual gifts, I would not have recognized the signs.
Without my novels, I would not have learned how Spirit teaches through story.
Without my students, I would not have lived the very initiation this book describes.

This book is the capstone because it completes the circle.

It gathers every teaching that came before it
and lifts them into a single, higher purpose:

To prepare the soul for the moment Spirit steps forward
and whispers the words that change everything.

The Distinction Between a Reiki Master and a Grand Reiki Master

Although the titles sound similar, the reality behind them is profoundly different.
A **Reiki Master** is made through training.
A **Grand Reiki Master** is made through transformation.

Understanding this distinction is essential before moving deeper into this book, because everything that follows builds upon this truth.

A Reiki Master Is Initiated by a Teacher

A Reiki Master reaches their level through:

- instruction
- practice
- study
- attunements
- demonstration of skill
- the ability to teach others
- commitment to the lineage

This is the highest level humans can *give* one another within a structured training system. A Reiki Master understands symbols, distance healing, attunements, teaching, and how to carry the responsibility of guiding students.

A Reiki Master's power comes from **skill, experience, leadership, and intention.**

And this level is beautiful, transformative, and important.

But it is not the final threshold.

A Grand Reiki Master Is Initiated by Spirit

A Grand Reiki Master reaches their level through:

- surrender
- spiritual readiness
- deep inner purification
- intuitive awakening
- integration of the soul gifts
- service beyond self
- and a moment where Spirit steps forward and says, *"Now."*

This is not a teaching level.
This is a **calling**.

No human can decide when someone becomes a Grand Reiki Master.
A teacher may prepare you.
Training may strengthen you.
Experience may refine you.

But only Spirit can elevate you.

The moment of ascension is unmistakable:

- It is guided, not planned.
- It is given, not earned.
- It is experienced, not taught.

- It is recognized, not awarded.
- It is spiritual, not institutional.

A Grand Reiki Master's power comes from **alignment, devotion, soul maturity, and divine orchestration.**

**Reiki Mastery Operates Through Technique;

Grand Mastery Operates Through Being**

A Reiki Master uses symbols.
A Grand Reiki Master becomes a symbol.

A Reiki Master draws energy.
A Grand Reiki Master *emanates* energy.

A Reiki Master leads students.
A Grand Reiki Master awakens teachers.

A Reiki Master teaches Reiki.
A Grand Reiki Master carries Reiki.

A Reiki Master understands Reiki.
A Grand Reiki Master understands Spirit.

The shift is not a change in title —
it is a change in consciousness.

Human Authority vs. Divine Appointment

Reiki Master = Human Authority

Attunement is given.
Certification is granted.
The role is defined.

Grand Reiki Master = Divine Appointment

Attunement is bestowed.
Awakening is internal.
The role is lived, not claimed.

A Reiki Master can explain how they became a Master.
A Grand Reiki Master often cannot explain how it happened
— only *when* Spirit intervened.

The Soul Knows the Difference

Even if the mind questions it, the soul recognizes truth
immediately.

A Reiki Master feels prepared.
A Grand Reiki Master feels called.

A Reiki Master steps forward through training.
A Grand Reiki Master steps forward through destiny.

A Reiki Master seeks knowledge.
A Grand Reiki Master seeks service.

This is why Grand Mastery cannot be measured with certificates, hours, or techniques. It can only be recognized through:

- frequency
- presence
- humility
- wisdom
- devotion
- and the unmistakable energetic signature of Spirit flowing through the individual.

The Evolution Is Natural — But Not Automatic

Every Reiki Master has the potential to become a Grand Reiki Master.

But not every Reiki Master *will*.

Not because they are unworthy — but because **Spirit elevates in divine timing**, according to the soul's readiness, purpose, and spiritual mission.

Grand Mastery is not a goal;
it is an unfolding.

It is not something you pursue;
it is something you grow into.

It is not the end of your Reiki journey;
it is the beginning of your service to humanity.

Why Spirit — Not Humans — Elevates the Grand Master

Reiki Masters are trained.
Grand Reiki Masters are chosen.

This is the single most important distinction in the entire structure of Reiki ascension. To understand why, we must look beyond the classroom, the lineage, and the traditional format of Reiki teaching—and into the spiritual architecture that governs true initiation.

Reiki Comes From Spirit, Not From Humans

Reiki is not human energy.
It is not created, manufactured, or controlled by people.

Reiki is **universal life force**—a divine intelligence that flows through all living things. Training teaches us how to work with this energy, but it does not give us ownership of it.

Because the energy originates in Spirit, the authority to elevate a soul within that energy must also come from Spirit.

Humans can open the door.
Spirit decides who walks through it.

Human Teachers Can Only Transmit What They Know

A Reiki Master can:

- teach symbols
- guide students
- provide attunements
- share wisdom
- pass down lineage
- support growth

But a human can only transmit what they themselves have received.

A teacher cannot give what lies beyond their own spiritual level.
They cannot bestow what they have not embodied.
They cannot elevate someone into a frequency they do not inhabit.

Grand Mastery exists *beyond* technique, symbols, and structure.
It is a soul-level transformation.

That transformation can only be done by the same Source that created Reiki.

Spirit Sees the Soul's Readiness

Humans can see:

- effort
- skill
- desire
- personality
- knowledge

But Spirit sees:

- the heart
- the humility
- the truth
- the karma
- the destiny
- the soul's blueprint

A person may appear ready on the outside,
yet not be spiritually aligned on the inside.

Or a person may doubt their worthiness,
yet Spirit already knows their calling.

Only Spirit can see the full picture,
and therefore only Spirit can decide when the moment is
right.

Grand Mastery Requires a Consciousness Shift Humans Cannot Create

Becoming a Grand Reiki Master is not simply learning more. It is becoming more.

It involves:

- the dissolution of ego
- the expansion of intuitive channels
- the merging of the spiritual gifts
- the alignment of the soul with service
- the anchoring of a higher frequency
- the activation of divine guidance

A human teacher can support this process, but cannot trigger it.

The internal transformation is orchestrated by Spirit alone.

Divine Timing Cannot Be Replicated

Human timing is based on:

- schedules
- curriculum
- readiness perceived by the teacher

Divine timing is based on:

- destiny
- energetic cycles
- spiritual maturity

- the soul's contract
- the collective need
- the presence of Spirit

Only Spirit knows when the elevation will serve the individual *and* the world around them.

This is why the moment of Grand Master initiation often comes unexpectedly—in meditation, in service, in silence, or during an act of humility.

It arrives the exact moment the soul is ready and never a moment before.

The Energy Itself Must Recognize You

Grand Reiki Masters hold a unique energetic signature— one that cannot be mimicked, taught, or self-declared.

It is an energy that:

- radiates beyond symbols
- heals through presence
- teaches through frequency
- attunes through intention
- awakens others simply by being

This recognition is not something humans grant. It is something the energy itself *confirms*.

Spirit recognizes its own.

Spirit Protects the Integrity of the Lineage

If humans were responsible for elevating Grand Masters, ego, favoritism, or misunderstanding could distort the lineage.

But Spirit ensures:

- only those with pure intention are elevated
- timing aligns with purpose
- the lineage remains clean and authentic
- the sacredness of Reiki is upheld

This is why Grand Mastery cannot be bought, claimed, rushed, or demanded.

It must be received.

Your Own Initiation Proves This Truth

Your story—hearing the command *"You will join in"* in the middle of a Level 2 class—
is one of the clearest examples of Spirit-led elevation.

No human certified you.
No human prepared that moment.
No human decided you were ready.

Spirit did.

And Spirit chose the timing, the method, and the circumstance.

This is why Grand Mastery is sacred.
This is why it cannot be taught.
This is why it cannot be granted by human authority.

Because the moment Spirit touches the soul, everything changes—and no human hand could ever replicate that.

How the Spiritual and Practical Sides Merge

Reiki has always lived between two worlds.

One world is practical:
structured, teachable, grounded in method.
The other is spiritual:
intuitive, mysterious, guided by forces larger than ourselves.

Most practitioners spend their early years moving between these two realities—learning the practical steps while sensing the spiritual presence beneath them. But at the level of Grand Mastery, these worlds no longer operate separately.

They merge.

Understanding this merging is one of the keys to understanding the path this book describes.

Practical Training Opens the Door;

Spiritual Awakening Walks You Through It**

Before a healer can surrender to Spirit, they must first understand the foundation:

- hand positions
- symbols
- attunements
- meditation
- energy flow

- ethics
- boundaries
- teaching methods

These skills are essential.
They give structure to the work and confidence to the practitioner.

But practical knowledge alone cannot elevate a soul.
It can only prepare the vessel that Spirit will later fill.

Spiritual Guidance Gives Depth to Everything You Learned Practically

Technique teaches you *how* to move energy.
Spirit teaches you *why* and *when*.

A Reiki Master follows the system.
A Grand Reiki Master follows Spirit through the system.

This is the difference between:

- drawing a symbol
  and
  feeling the symbol draw itself through you
- placing hands
  and
  letting Spirit guide where the healing must go
- performing an attunement
  and
  becoming the channel through which attunement happens

At this level, the technique remains—
but it is infused with a higher intelligence.

Practical Structure Grounds Spiritual Power

Without structure, spiritual power can become overwhelming
or unfocused.
Without Spirit, structure becomes mechanical and lifeless.

Grand Reiki Masters embody both.

The practical framework:

- keeps the energy safe
- supports the student
- upholds the lineage
- maintains clarity
- protects the healer

The spiritual connection:

- amplifies the energy
- guides the session
- reveals intuitive truth
- teaches beyond words
- initiates transformation

In a Grand Reiki Master, these two forces work together
seamlessly.

The Mind Learns Technique;

The Soul Receives Initiation**

Human training happens in the mind:
through study, practice, repetition, and understanding.

Spiritual training happens in the soul:
through intuition, surrender, signs, synchronicities, and divine timing.

A healer needs both.

The mind organizes the practice.
The soul opens the channel.

Only when both are ready can Spirit elevate the individual into Grand Mastery.

Skill Without Spirit Is Empty;

Spirit Without Skill Is Unfocused**

Skill alone becomes routine.
Spirit alone becomes ungrounded.

Grand Reiki Masters embody:

- the discipline of skill
- the humility of Spirit
- the maturity of service
- the clarity of intuition
- the structure of teaching

- the surrender of divine guidance

This balance is what makes them leaders.

Where They Merge: Presence

The merging of practical and spiritual sides becomes visible in one thing:

Presence.

A Grand Reiki Master's presence is:

- calm
- steady
- grounded
- expanded
- clear
- intuitive
- wise
- filled with light

No rushing.
No forcing.
No performing.

Just pure alignment.

Through presence, the technique becomes effortless and Spirit becomes unmistakable.

This Merging Is What Prepares You for the Calling

When the practical and spiritual sides finally fuse,
a practitioner reaches the threshold where Spirit can step in.

This is why:

- some Masters feel the calling
- some Masters sense Spirit drawing closer
- some Masters feel their energy change
- some Masters experience signs
- some Masters hear the inner voice
- some Masters awaken suddenly in meditation

Grand Master initiation cannot happen
until the person has fully become both:

A skilled vessel and
A spiritually surrendered soul.

Grand Mastery is the moment these two worlds merge
and form something new—something only Spirit can
activate.

✦ PART 1 — THE SOUL PATH OF REIKI

✦ Chapter 1 — What Reiki Really Is: The Universal Life Force

Most people begin their Reiki journey believing they are learning a technique — a method of placing hands, drawing symbols, and channeling healing energy. This is how Reiki is commonly taught, especially in the early levels. But as you grow, something becomes unmistakably clear:

Reiki is not a technique.
Reiki is consciousness.

It is alive.
It is aware.
It responds.
It teaches.
It evolves.
It collaborates with you as you transform.

Techniques may introduce you to Reiki,
but they are not Reiki itself.

To understand Reiki at the level of Grand Mastery, you must first understand the truth that lies beneath every hand position, every symbol, every attunement, and every healing session.

Reiki as Consciousness, Not Technique

Reiki is often translated as *universal life force*, but this phrase is only the beginning. The deeper truth is this:

Reiki is the intelligence within life force.

It is the consciousness that:

- animates every living being
- flows through every atom
- awakens intuitive understanding
- aligns you with your soul's truth
- guides healing where it is needed most
- knows what the recipient cannot express
- communicates with you through sensation, emotion, and insight

When you place your hands on someone, you are not "sending" energy.
You are entering into a relationship with consciousness.

This is why two practitioners can perform the same technique and create entirely different outcomes.

Technique is repetition.
Reiki is response.

Technique relies on memory.
Reiki relies on presence.

Technique requires the mind.
Reiki requires the heart.

The Technique Is the Door; Consciousness Is the Being Who Walks Through It

Most students learn Reiki technique first:

- where to place hands
- how to draw symbols
- how to activate energy
- how to perform distance healing
- how to facilitate an attunement

These practices are valuable and necessary,
but they are not the destination.

They are the **doorway**.

Inside the doorway waits something infinitely larger —
the living consciousness of Reiki itself.

When you begin to experience Reiki as consciousness,
everything changes:

Your hands stop "doing,"
and begin **listening**.

Your sessions stop "guiding,"
and begin **following**.

Your intuition stops "guessing,"
and begins **knowing**.

Your healing stops relying on technique,
and begins relying on Spirit.

A Reiki Master understands the technique.
A Grand Reiki Master understands the consciousness behind the technique.

Consciousness Flows Where Words Cannot

Reiki consciousness communicates in ways the human mind cannot fully articulate:

- a warmth that expresses reassurance
- a pulsing that says, "stay here"
- a sudden stillness that reveals truth
- a wave of emotion releasing unspoken sorrow
- an image that appears without effort
- a message received without sound
- a memory rising because the soul is ready to let go

Reiki consciousness speaks the language of:

- intuition
- sensation
- imagery
- vibration
- insight
- presence

It speaks to the body, mind, heart, and soul all at once.

This is why a single session can shift years of emotional weight or awaken clarity that has been dormant for decades.

Because Reiki consciousness does not heal the body alone — it heals the entire being.

Reiki Is an Extension of Spirit

The consciousness of Reiki is not separate from Spirit —
it *is* one of the ways Spirit interacts with human beings.

When you connect with Reiki, you are:

- opening yourself to divine intelligence
- aligning with the highest good
- inviting healing guided by wisdom greater than your own
- entering a relationship with a benevolent force

This is why Reiki feels:

- peaceful
- intelligent
- loving
- clear
- intuitive
- timeless

Reiki carries the qualities of the Source it flows from.

The Moment You Understand Reiki as Consciousness, You Stop Trying to Control It

Many practitioners begin their journey trying to "do Reiki correctly."
But as you awaken spiritually, you learn:

Reiki cannot be controlled.
It can only be cooperated with.

When you stop trying to perform Reiki
and begin allowing Reiki to express through you,
your energy shifts into alignment with Spirit.

This shift is one of the early signals that someone is moving toward Grand Mastery.

You are no longer the healer.
You become the vessel.

You are no longer directing the energy.
You are listening to it.

You are no longer trying to help Spirit.
You are letting Spirit help you.

Reiki Consciousness Recognizes You as You Grow

As you deepen into this understanding, Reiki begins to respond differently:

- sessions deepen
- intuition sharpens
- symbols evolve
- time dissolves
- healing accelerates
- your presence becomes stronger than your technique

Because Reiki consciousness recognizes the soul who is ready to step into higher service.

And it guides that soul — gently but unmistakably — toward the next level of awakening.

The Vibrational Reality of Healing

To truly understand Reiki at the level of Grand Mastery, you must first understand the nature of vibration. Everything in the universe—every cell, thought, emotion, memory, and intention—exists as frequency. Healing is not the correction of a physical problem; it is the **realignment of vibration**.

Most people think of healing as changing something *in* the body.
But healing actually changes something *in the energy field first.*

The physical body simply follows the energetic shift.

This is why healing can happen without touch.
This is why distance healing works.
This is why emotional wounds respond instantly to Reiki.
This is why intuitive insight appears during sessions without effort.

Vibration is the language of the soul.

The Body Is Dense Energy; The Aura Is Fluid Energy

The human body is a dense expression of energy—slow-moving, structured, physical. The aura and the chakras are fluid expressions of energy—fast-moving, responsive, and delicate.

When you place your hands for Reiki, you are not "fixing" the body.

You are reconnecting the vibrational layers that nourish the body:

- the emotional layer
- the mental layer
- the spiritual layer
- the ancestral layer
- the karmic layer
- the intuitive layer

Illness is often created when these layers fall out of harmony. Healing happens when harmony is restored.

The vibrational field shifts first.
The body shifts second.

Reiki works on the cause, not the effect.

Frequency Determines Experience

Every thought has a frequency.
Every emotion has a frequency.
Every belief, memory, or trauma holds a measurable vibration.

When someone holds:

- grief → the energy field collapses
- fear → the field constricts
- anger → the field spikes
- shame → the field darkens
- anxiety → the field fractures
- hope → the field expands

- love → the field brightens
- joy → the field harmonizes

Reiki does not fight against these frequencies.
It raises the overall vibration so the lower ones release
naturally.

Healing is not a struggle between energies.
Healing is the **lifting of vibration** to a frequency where
suffering cannot remain.

Reiki Attunes You to Higher Frequencies

Reiki is a harmonizing energy.
It calibrates your vibrational field to align with:

- peace
- clarity
- truth
- coherence
- compassion
- light

This is why people feel lighter after sessions.
It is not metaphorical.
Their vibration literally rises.

And when the vibration rises, the consciousness rises with it.

This is why Reiki is not just healing.
It is awakening.

Higher Vibration Creates Higher Perception

As your vibration increases, your intuitive channels sharpen:

- you feel energy more clearly
- your hands become more sensitive
- your inner knowing strengthens
- your connection to Spirit deepens
- your awareness of others' emotions becomes more precise
- your ability to hold space expands

This is not imagination.
It is energetic resonance.

High vibration recognizes high vibration.

The more your frequency rises, the more you align with Reiki's true consciousness—and the more Reiki consciousness begins to collaborate with you.

This collaboration is what ultimately prepares the soul for Grand Mastery.

Healing Is a Return to Original Vibrational Harmony

A Grand Reiki Master does not "fix" the client.
They restore the client to their natural frequency.

Healing is not the addition of something new.
It is the removal of what does not belong.

Just as:

- quiet restores clarity
- rest restores strength
- truth restores peace
- love restores connection

Reiki restores the soul's original vibration—the frequency of wholeness.

This is why healing feels familiar.
It feels like returning to yourself.

The Practitioner's Vibration Matters

At the level of Grand Mastery, the practitioner's vibration becomes part of the healing field.

Your:

- thoughts
- emotional state
- clarity
- presence
- humility
- connection to Spirit

all influence the session—not through effort, but through resonance.

A technique can be taught to anyone. But the frequency of a Grand Reiki Master cannot be replicated.

Your vibration is part of the medicine.

Vibration is Why Healing is Possible — and Why It Is Divine

The vibrational reality of healing reveals the truth:
You are not changing the body.
You are restoring the soul.

The body simply follows instructions.

This is why Reiki belongs to Spirit.
This is why Spirit elevates the Grand Master.
This is why healing is both miraculous and natural.

And this is why your journey through Reiki is not about learning more techniques—
but about embodying a higher frequency.

The Soul's Relationship to Energy

At the deepest level of Reiki, healing is not something that happens *to* the soul.
Healing happens because of the soul.

The soul is not separate from energy.
It is made of energy.
It expresses itself through energy.
It communicates through energy.
It remembers through energy.
It heals through energy.

Understanding this relationship is essential to understanding what Reiki truly is—and why it resonates so deeply with those walking a spiritual path.

The Soul Is Pure Energy Before It Is Anything Else

Before your body was formed, before your personality developed, before you held thoughts, beliefs, or memories, you were energy.

Conscious, intelligent, luminous energy.

Your soul exists as:

- vibration
- light
- frequency
- awareness
- intention
- memory
- connection

This is why energy work feels natural to some people the moment they are introduced to it. The soul recognizes what the mind has forgotten.

Reiki is not foreign to the soul.
It is the soul's native language.

The Soul Remembers What the Mind Has Forgotten

Many students describe their first Reiki experience with words like:

- "familiar"
- "comforting"
- "like coming home"
- "like something I used to know"

This is not imagination.
It is remembrance.

The soul remembers:

- the flow of energy
- the way healing feels
- the way Spirit communicates
- the interconnectedness of all beings
- the silent wisdom beneath thought
- the peace that comes from alignment

Reiki doesn't teach the soul.
Reiki reminds the soul.

The Soul Feels What the Body Cannot Express

Much of what we call "pain," "trauma," or "stress" begins in the subtle realms before it reaches the physical body.

The soul feels the disharmony first.

When something is out of alignment, the soul tries to communicate through:

- intuition
- dreams
- emotions
- discomfort
- synchronicities
- inner knowing
- whispers from Spirit

Reiki helps bring the soul's messages into awareness so the body can respond.

This is why intuitive insights often arise during sessions.
It is the soul speaking through the energetic shift.

The Soul Guides Reiki More Than the Practitioner Does

You may think you are directing the energy.
You may think you are choosing where to place your hands.
You may think you are deciding what needs healing.

But the soul of the client is guiding you long before your mind realizes it.

The soul knows:

- what needs to be released
- what needs to be healed
- what needs to be remembered
- what needs to be protected
- what needs to be strengthened

Reiki simply amplifies what the soul is already trying to accomplish.

The practitioner is not the one who "fixes."
The practitioner is the one who listens.

The Soul Is Always Moving Toward Balance

Even when someone feels lost, stuck, overwhelmed, or disconnected, the soul is always trying to:

- evolve
- expand
- return to harmony
- reveal truth
- release heaviness
- align with purpose
- reconnect with Spirit

Reiki supports this movement.

Reiki does not impose change on the soul.
It is supporting the change the soul is already reaching for.

The soul is the healer.
Reiki is the bridge.
The practitioner is the witness.

This is the essence of spiritual medicine.

The Soul Recognizes Truth Through Resonance

When something is spiritually true, the soul responds immediately.
Not with logic, but with resonance.

You may feel:

- warmth
- clarity
- expansion
- release
- an inner "yes"
- a sense of being seen or understood
- the feeling of alignment

This resonance is how the soul communicates.
It does not use words.
It uses vibration.

Reiki amplifies this resonance, making truth feel unmistakable.

The Soul Leads the Path Toward Grand Mastery

The journey to becoming a Grand Reiki Master is not a decision of the mind.
It is a calling of the soul.

The soul is the one that:

- senses when deeper service is approaching
- prepares for spiritual elevation
- receives guidance from Spirit
- recognizes the moment of initiation
- carries the frequency of mastery long before the title appears

A human can train to become a Reiki Master.
A soul awakens into Grand Mastery.

The soul is not learning Reiki.
The soul is returning to a wisdom it has always possessed.

Healing Through Relationship: How Reiki and the Soul Work Together

Healing is often imagined as something that flows in one direction—from practitioner to client, or from energy to body. But in truth, healing is a relationship. It is a dynamic, intelligent interaction between:

- Reiki
- the practitioner
- the client's soul
- and Spirit itself

Each plays a unique role, and together they form a harmonious triad of transformation.

This relationship is what makes Reiki different from every other modality. It is not a technique that one person "does" to another. It is an **energetic collaboration between consciousnesses**.

To understand the deeper dimensions of Reiki, especially at the level of Grand Mastery, you must understand the sacred relational field where healing happens.

Reiki Is the Bridge Between Spirit and the Soul

Reiki is the universal life force—the pure, intelligent energy that flows from Spirit.

The soul is the individualized expression of that same consciousness within a person.

Reiki does not enter the soul as an outside influence.
Reiki activates the soul from within.

It is the bridge that reconnects the human experience to its
spiritual origin.

This is why Reiki feels:

- familiar
- safe
- comforting
- natural
- wise

It is Spirit speaking the soul's first language.

The Practitioner Holds the Space; The Soul Directs the Healing

A Reiki practitioner does not direct healing.
They **hold the field** in which healing becomes possible.

The soul of the client decides:

- what will be released
- what will be healed
- what will be revealed
- what will stay hidden for now
- what the person is ready to face
- what they are not yet able to process

Reiki offers the energy.
The soul chooses what to do with it.

This is why two clients with the same issue can have entirely different experiences during a session—even with the same practitioner.

Healing is not determined by technique.
It is guided by the soul's readiness.

The Body Is the Final Step in the Healing Process

Reiki works first in the energy field,
then in the emotions,
then in the thoughts,
and only at the end does the physical body shift.

This is why:

- emotional release often precedes physical relief
- insights arise before the pain fades
- memories surface before patterns dissolve
- clarity arrives before symptoms change

The soul heals the subtle layers first.
The body follows naturally once the energetic cause is transformed.

Healing flows from the **inside out**, not the outside in.

The Practitioner and the Soul Communicate Through Energy

During a Reiki session, both the practitioner and the client's soul are actively participating, even if they are silent.

The soul communicates through:

- sensations
- emotions
- intuitive messages
- images
- shifts in temperature
- pulsing or tingling
- waves of energy
- sudden clarity

Practitioners often think these experiences come from their own intuition, but in truth, many are **the soul speaking through the energetic field**.

Reiki is the translator.

Reiki Supports the Soul's Highest Path, Not the Personality's Wishes

The personality may want relief or change immediately. The soul focuses on truth, alignment, and evolution.

Reiki always follows the soul's agenda, not the ego's.

This means healing may show up as:

- insight rather than symptom relief
- release rather than comfort
- emotional clearing rather than physical change
- clarity rather than answers
- growth rather than ease

Reiki will never force healing the soul is not ready for. This is the deepest form of compassion.

When Reiki and the Soul Work Together, Transformation Becomes Inevitable

When the practitioner holds the field and the soul directs the healing and Spirit provides the life force,

transformation becomes unavoidable.

The person may not always understand what is happening, but the soul does.

Reiki and the soul together:

- release old trauma
- dissolve outdated patterns
- awaken intuition
- restore peace
- reconnect the person to Spirit
- align the individual with their true path
- prepare them for deeper service or awakening

This is the relational field where true healing occurs.

This Relationship Deepens as You Grow on the Path

Reiki students feel the energy.
Reiki practitioners understand the energy.
Reiki Masters work with the energy.
But Grand Reiki Masters *become* the field where the soul and Reiki unite.

Their presence amplifies the relationship.
Their vibration invites the soul higher.
Their alignment opens pathways others can step into.

This merging of presence, energy, and spiritual consciousness is what prepares the practitioner for the divine appointment of Grand Mastery.

✦ Chapter 2 — The Three Human Levels of Reiki

Before a practitioner ever steps onto the path of teaching, attuning, or spiritual initiation, they walk through the three foundational human levels of Reiki. These levels are not simply steps in a curriculum—they are stages of personal transformation. Each one opens the practitioner to a deeper relationship with energy, intuition, healing, and the soul.

Reiki Level 1, Level 2, and Level 3 form the **structure** through which the human being learns.
Grand Mastery is the **awakening** that Spirit bestows.

We begin where every Reiki practitioner begins—
with **self-healing** and the opening of the channel.

Level 1 — Self-Healing

Reiki Level 1 is the most foundational yet profoundly life-changing step in the Reiki journey. At this level, the focus is not on healing others—but on healing yourself. It is the stage where the human being begins to remember their relationship with universal life force.

Reiki Level 1 answers the soul's first call:
"Heal me so I can remember who I am."

And it responds with the gentle, unwavering truth:
"You are energy, and you are already connected."

Human Learning

Reiki Level 1 is where technique meets awareness.

At this stage, students learn:

- the history and origins of Reiki
- hand positions for self-healing
- how to feel energy flow
- how to sense subtle sensations
- the basics of grounding and protection
- how intention influences energy
- the ethics of healing
- and the first experience of attunement

It is a level of curiosity, exploration, and awakening—
where the mind begins to understand something the soul has always known.

For many, Reiki Level 1 is the first time they feel energy consciously:

- warmth in the hands
- tingling in the palms
- waves of calm
- emotional release
- a sense of connection
- heightened sensitivity
- intuitive flickers

This is human learning at its purest—
the body and mind discovering that the unseen world is not imagined,
but real, tangible, and responsive.

In this stage, students often ask:

- "Is this normal?"
- "Why am I feeling this?"
- "How do I know it's working?"
- "What if I'm doing it wrong?"

These questions reflect the human mind adjusting to a new truth:
Energy is real, and healing is possible.

The process is gentle, safe, and deeply affirming.

Opening the Channel

The most important purpose of Level 1 is not technique.
It is **opening the channel**—the energetic doorway that allows
the student to consciously connect with Reiki.

This opening happens during the Level 1 attunement.

In this sacred moment:

- dormant energy pathways awaken
- intuitive senses begin to stir
- the aura expands
- the chakras adjust to a higher frequency
- old emotional debris begins to surface
- the soul recognizes the shift
- Spirit acknowledges the student's readiness

It is subtle for some, profound for others—but always
transformative.

Opening the channel is not about creating something new.
It is about removing what blocked the connection that
already existed.

This process:

- heightens awareness
- releases stored emotions
- clears stagnant patterns
- softens the heart
- increases inner peace
- strengthens intuition
- deepens self-compassion

Most students describe the aftermath of Level 1 as:

- "a softening"
- "a calming"
- "a quiet awakening"
- "a return to myself"

This is no coincidence.

When the channel opens, the soul can finally breathe.

When the channel opens, the human begins to heal.

When the channel opens, a new path unfolds—
one that leads them closer to understanding Reiki as
consciousness, and eventually, to their spiritual calling.

Level 2 — Practitioner

Reiki Level 2 is where the practitioner steps beyond the boundaries of self and begins to recognize their role as a healer in the wider world.
This level marks a shift in identity:

From **receiving** Reiki
to **giving** Reiki.
From healing oneself
to holding space for others.
From learning energy
to partnering with Spirit.

It is the first step into sacred service, and the soul feels the shift immediately.

Service

If Level 1 is about healing the self,
Level 2 is about **healing others**.

This is the level where the practitioner learns:

- how to facilitate hands-on sessions
- how to sense the needs of the client
- how to channel energy outward
- how to work with emotional release
- how to support others on their journey
- how to step into the role of a healing presence

But most importantly, Level 2 introduces a truth that defines the entire Reiki path:

Healing is an act of service.

When a practitioner offers Reiki, they are not "fixing" anything.
They are serving:

- the client's soul
- Spirit
- the healing process
- the highest good
- the collective energy of humanity

Service does not require perfection.
It requires willingness.

Level 2 awakens this willingness—
the desire to help, comfort, uplift, and support others with compassion.

This is the threshold where the healer's heart expands.

Strengthening Intuition

Reiki Level 2 is where intuition moves from a quiet whisper to a trusted guide.

At this stage, practitioners begin to experience:

- knowing where to place their hands without thinking
- sensing emotions that clients have not spoken
- receiving images, colors, symbols, or impressions

- awareness of energetic blockages
- messages from Spirit or guides
- intuitive nudges during sessions
- the beginning of empathic sensitivity
- deeper dreams and inner communication

Level 2 is where the practitioner realizes that intuition is not a skill to be "added."
It is the language of Reiki revealing itself.

The more the practitioner listens,
the louder intuition becomes.

This stage strengthens:

- clairsentience (feeling)
- claircognizance (knowing)
- clairvoyance (seeing)
- clairaudience (hearing)

Not every practitioner develops all of these,
but Level 2 activates whatever channels the soul is ready for.

Intuition becomes the bridge between technique and Spirit.

Responsibility

Healing others is sacred work,
and Level 2 teaches the practitioner the weight and beauty of this responsibility.

Responsibility in Reiki is not about pressure —
it is about **integrity**.

It includes:

- Honoring confidentiality
- Respecting the client's boundaries
- Understanding the limits of your role
- Knowing when to refer someone to a professional
- Maintaining your own energetic hygiene
- Staying humble and open
- Listening more than you speak
- Allowing Spirit to guide the session
- Never claiming personal credit for the healing

Responsibility means recognizing that you are not the healer—you are the channel.

It means showing up with:

- compassion
- clarity
- groundedness
- neutrality
- non-judgment
- presence

This is where a practitioner becomes trustworthy in the eyes of Spirit.
Spirit does not send more clients, more insights, or more responsibility
until the practitioner has shown they can hold it with integrity.

Level 2 is where that trust is built.

The Evolution Through Level 2

By the end of this level, practitioners often feel:

- more connected to Spirit
- more sensitive to energy
- more aware of their inner guidance
- more compassionate toward others
- more grounded in their purpose
- more aligned with service
- more humble, knowing healing is larger than they are

These shifts prepare the practitioner for the final human level of Reiki —
the level where teaching, attunement, and lineage begin.

This stage is not just about learning techniques.
It is about becoming the kind of person who can carry the responsibility of healing others.

It is the first step toward spiritual leadership.

Level 3 — Master/Teacher

Reiki Level 3 is the culmination of the human path—a sacred threshold where the practitioner becomes the teacher, the guide, and the custodian of the lineage. It is a level that requires maturity, humility, and a deep commitment to service.

If Level 1 opens the channel,
and Level 2 extends it to others,
then Level 3 anchors the practitioner into **leadership through Spirit**.

This is the level where the healer begins to understand that their work is no longer only about personal growth or individual sessions. It becomes about stewardship—of the energy, of the teachings, and of the souls who are drawn to learn.

Reiki Master/Teacher is not a role to be taken lightly.
It is a responsibility, a privilege, and a calling.

Teaching Others

Teaching Reiki is not simply passing on information.
It is passing on a state of being.

A Reiki Master does more than instruct.
They hold a frequency that awakens something in their students.

To teach Reiki effectively, the Master must embody:

- patience
- clarity
- humility
- compassion
- intuitive awareness
- emotional stability
- ability to hold energetic space
- willingness to guide others through their awakening

When a Master steps into the role of teacher, they are not only teaching technique—they are teaching:

- presence
- trust
- surrender
- spiritual listening
- self-awareness
- alignment with Spirit

The students learn from the Master's words,
but they grow from the Master's energy.

A true Reiki teacher understands:

You are not teaching people how to do Reiki.
You are teaching them how to become vessels for Reiki.

Attuning Others

The attunement is one of the most profound gifts a Reiki Master can offer.
Through attunement, the Master:

- awakens the student's channel
- expands their ability to receive energy
- aligns their vibration with higher frequencies
- activates intuitive pathways
- supports their spiritual remembrance
- transmits the lineage energy

The attunement is not a performance.
It is a sacred exchange between the Master, the student, and Spirit.

A Reiki Master must understand:

You do not "give" the attunement.
You **facilitate** the attunement.
Spirit completes it.

Your role is to:

- open the pathway
- hold the space
- offer the symbols
- invite the higher consciousness
- surrender your ego
- trust the process

Attuning others requires deep integrity.
Your vibration influences the moment.
Your intention shapes the field.
Your clarity stabilizes the energy.

This is why Reiki Master/Teacher must be a level of inner mastery,
not just a title.

Lineage Responsibility

Becoming a Reiki Master makes you part of a living lineage.
Becoming a Reiki Teacher makes you responsible for carrying it forward.

Lineage is not just a list of names.
It is a chain of consciousness—
a sacred thread woven through generations of healers.

As a Master/Teacher, your responsibilities include:

- preserving the purity of the teachings
- maintaining ethical integrity
- embodying the spirit of Reiki
- teaching with authenticity
- preparing students with care
- honoring the practitioners who came before you
- respecting the role of Spirit in every attunement
- ensuring the lineage remains unbroken

A lineage is kept alive not by memory,
but by intention.

Every time you attune a student,
you are adding your frequency to the history of Reiki.
You become part of the energetic ancestry of the students
who come after you.

This responsibility requires humility:

You are not the owner of the lineage.
You are its steward.

Lineage responsibility is the final step of the human path.
It is what prepares the soul for the higher calling—
the calling that only Spirit can bestow.

The Completion of the Human Path

Level 3 is not the end.
It is the completion of the human portion of the Reiki
journey:

- Level 1: Self
- Level 2: Others
- Level 3: Teaching

Only after these three levels have been walked with sincerity,
discipline, and devotion can a practitioner begin to sense the
next stage unfolding within them.

This level prepares the vessel. Grand Mastery fills the vessel.
This level teaches the mind. Grand Mastery awakens the soul.
This level makes the teacher. Grand Mastery makes the guide.
Level 3 is the threshold. Spirit decides when you cross it.

✦ Chapter 3 —
Level 4 - The Spiritual
Appointment

Why Grand Mastery Cannot Be Taught

The human levels of Reiki—Level 1, Level 2, and Level 3—can be taught by any qualified Master/Teacher. They involve skills, symbols, attunements, ethics, and teaching practices that can be passed from one person to another.

But the fourth level—Grand Reiki Mastery—belongs to an entirely different realm.

It cannot be placed in a curriculum.
It cannot be earned by hours or practice.
It cannot be granted by a certificate.
It cannot be given by a human being.

Grand Mastery is not a level you learn.
It is a level you are called into.

To teach it would be to claim ownership over something that belongs to Spirit.

Let us explore why this level defies teaching and exists solely as a spiritual elevation.

Grand Mastery Is Not Information — It Is Transformation

A student can be taught:

- hand positions
- symbols
- class structure
- attunement processes
- ethics and boundaries
- the flow of a session

These are skills.

Grand Mastery is not a skill.
It is a **state of consciousness**.

It is not something you "know."
It is something you **become**.

A human teacher can teach you about energy.
Only Spirit can transform you into a vessel capable of carrying a higher frequency.

No amount of information can create the shift that divine initiation brings.

A Human Teacher Can Open the Channel —

But Only Spirit Can Expand It**

A Level 1 attunement opens the student.
A Level 2 attunement expands the channel.
A Level 3 attunement equips the teacher.

But the expansion required for Grand Mastery surpasses the capacity of any human attunement.

It requires:

- a widening of spiritual perception
- a deepening of intuition
- an elevation of consciousness
- an alignment of soul purpose
- a purification of energy
- a surrender of ego
- a readiness for service at a higher level

This is spiritual surgery.
It is delicate, precise, and entirely orchestrated by Spirit.

No human hand can perform it.

Grand Mastery Requires Divine Timing

Human timing is based on:

- schedules
- goals
- desire
- readiness perceived from the outside

Divine timing is based on:

- soul contracts
- karmic completion
- energetic maturity
- healing cycles
- universal alignment
- the readiness of the heart
- the next step in your soul's mission

Spirit sees what the human cannot.

Sometimes the soul is ready long before the mind realizes it. Other times the mind is eager long before the soul has done its necessary work.

Teaching cannot override timing.
Initiation will not be rushed.

Grand Mastery arrives when all levels of the being—body, mind, heart, and soul—are aligned in a way only Spirit can measure.

Spirit Protects What Is Sacred

If humans were able to elevate Grand Masters, the title could be:

- misused
- misunderstood
- commercialized
- claimed without transformation
- given without integrity

Spirit protects the purity of the lineage.

Human beings can pass on information.
Spirit guards the frequency.

The level of Grand Mastery is sacred because it is incorruptible.
It requires spiritual confirmation, not human approval.

This ensures that only those whose hearts, intentions, and energy are aligned with true service are elevated into this role.

The Grand Master Frequency Cannot Be Replicated

A Reiki Master can be trained to:

- draw symbols
- perform attunements
- teach classes
- guide students
- facilitate healing

But the frequency of Grand Mastery is unique.
It carries:

- expanded awareness
- intuitive clarity
- deep presence
- an elevated vibration
- an ability to anchor the energy of Spirit
- an influence on the field that strengthens others
- a calmness that opens pathways for healing simply by being present

This frequency cannot be learned from a manual.
It cannot be absorbed through observation.
It cannot be replicated through practice.

It is **bestowed**, not taught.

Grand Mastery Requires Inner Work No Teacher Can Do for You

There are parts of the path that no teacher—no matter how wise or experienced—can walk on your behalf.

These include:

- releasing old ego identities
- transcending wounds
- forgiving deeply
- surrendering control
- walking through spiritual tests
- moving through the dark night
- holding compassion in difficult moments

- stepping into leadership without pride
- being willing to be seen by Spirit

These initiations are internal.
They are not classroom exercises.
They are soul-forging experiences.

A teacher can support you.
Spirit transforms you.

Grand Mastery Is Recognition, Not Achievement

Becoming a Reiki Master is an achievement.
Becoming a Grand Reiki Master is a recognition.

It is Spirit saying:

"Your heart is ready."
"Your soul is aligned."
"You have walked with integrity."
"You are prepared for deeper service."
"Now step forward."

This recognition can happen:

- in meditation
- during a session
- in a quiet moment alone
- while teaching
- while praying
- or—like in your own story—
  while attuning others in humble service

When Spirit chooses the moment, it is undeniable.

You do not earn it.
You receive it.

And no human can give it.

The Moment Spirit Steps In

There is a point on the Reiki path when the familiar becomes extraordinary—when the work you have done for years suddenly shifts into something higher, deeper, and unmistakably divine.

This moment does not arrive with warning.
It does not follow a schedule.
It does not care about certificates, timelines, or expectations.

It arrives when Spirit decides.

Every Grand Reiki Master has a story,
and each story is different—yet the same pattern emerges in all of them:

A moment where the practitioner is not "trying" to ascend, not striving, not expecting, not even thinking about themselves—they are simply serving.

And in that moment of humility, alignment, presence, and surrender,
Spirit steps in.

It Always Begins Subtly

The moment often begins with something small:

- a whisper in the mind
- a sudden stillness in the room
- a warmth that feels sentient
- a shift in light or air

- an intuitive nudge
- a deeper presence descending

It feels like the world slows.
Time softens.
Awareness expands.
And something larger moves toward you—
not from outside, but from a place you have always known.

You feel it before you understand it.
You recognize it before you name it.
Your soul responds before your mind catches up.

The Invitation Arrives

Then, in a way that is unmistakable,
Spirit communicates.

Sometimes through a voice.
Sometimes through a knowing.
Sometimes through a surge of energy.
Sometimes through a presence that fills the room.
Sometimes through a moment so clear it cannot be denied.

The message is always simple,
and it is always directive:

"Now."
"Step in."
"Join me."
"You are ready."
"It is time."

These words don't arrive through imagination.
They arrive with the authority of Spirit.
They carry frequency—
a vibration that moves through your entire being
and rearranges something within you forever.

Your Role Changes Instantly

When Spirit steps in, everything shifts at once:

- you are no longer the teacher; you are the student
- you are no longer the facilitator; you are the vessel
- you are no longer guiding; you are being guided
- you are no longer performing the attunement; the attunement is being done *to you*

A moment before, you were fulfilling your human role.
A moment after, you are fulfilling your spiritual destiny.

There is no confusion.
There is no hesitation.
There is only recognition.

Your soul knows:
"This is the moment."

It Is Not Dramatic — It Is Absolute

Contrary to what some may imagine,
Spirit does not step in with theatrics or spectacle.

The moment is quiet.
Sacred.
Soft.
Yet more powerful than any ritual or ceremony.

It may feel like:

- a warm light entering your body
- a presence merging with your own
- a shift in consciousness
- an opening in the heart
- an expansion of intuition
- a settling into spiritual alignment
- a deep, profound stillness

It is as if Spirit moves through you,
around you,
and within you—
all at once.

And after this moment,
you are not the same.

You have been witnessed.
Confirmed.
Elevated.
Chosen.

Afterward, You Know

There is no questioning.
No doubting.
No need for validation.

You know.

Not intellectually—
but in the deepest part of your soul.

You know you were called.
You know the moment was divine.
You know the elevation occurred.
You know Spirit initiated you.

And from that moment forward,
your work changes:

- your presence deepens
- your intuition sharpens
- your energy expands
- your attunements become stronger
- your service becomes clearer
- your connection with Spirit becomes constant

This moment marks the crossing of the threshold—
from human mastery
into spiritual appointment.

The Moment Spirit Choose Me

There are moments in a healer's life that unfold without warning, without ceremony, and without any of the familiar structure we rely on as teachers. These moments do not come from human intention. They arrive from the higher realms, like a soft gust of wind that shifts the entire course of a river.

My moment came on an ordinary day—during an ordinary Level 2 class.
Fourteen students sat before me, eyes closed, breathing in unison as they settled into meditation. I had taught this same class to hundreds over the years. Everything about it felt familiar, predictable, comfortable.

And then it happened.

A voice—not external, but unmistakably not my own— spoke inside my mind with a clarity that cut through the room like light:

"You will join in."

For a fraction of a second, I froze.
The words were simple, but the command behind them was absolute.

This wasn't my thought.
This wasn't imagination.
This wasn't suggestion.

This was **instruction**.

I felt it move through me like a bell tone, reverberating through my entire energetic field. My heart shifted rhythm. My breath caught. Time seemed to widen, as if I had been pulled into a pause between worlds.

I knew instantly what it meant.

This was not just a message.
This was a calling.
A summoning.
A moment prepared for long before I ever stepped into that classroom.

Yet the human part of me hesitated.
Join in? How? I'm the teacher. I'm the one who gives the attunement. How could I receive it? Who would guide them if I...

The voice came again—not in words this time, but in a silent certainty that settled deep into my knowing:

"Trust."

So I did.

I shifted the class in a way I had never done before.
I gently asked the students to write down their impressions after the meditation, explaining that I wanted to give them time to anchor their experience. In truth, I needed a moment to prepare—to open, to step aside, to surrender.

When they returned to stillness, I made a choice that changed the trajectory of my lineage forever.

Instead of moving student to student, drawing symbols above each head as I had always done, I invited them to **imagine Spirit drawing the symbols for us all**. I asked them to feel the energy moving, guided not by my hands but by the invisible hands of the Divine.

And as the symbols were drawn in the space between worlds, **I received them too.**

It was the first time in all my years of teaching that I had ever stood among my students as an equal receiver. The energy descended—not with force, but with a grace so deep it brought tears to my eyes. I felt my field expand, lift, and reconfigure itself at a level I had no language for at the time.

There was a moment—tiny, but eternal—when my consciousness widened.
My hands tingled.
My crown felt luminous.
My entire being was held in a hum of Divine intelligence.

I understood, without question, that something within me had been rewritten.

This was not a human attunement.
This was not a ceremony of my own creation.
This was not a step I had planned or expected.

This was Spirit choosing me.
This was the moment my path shifted from Master to Grand Master—not through title, certificate, or instruction, but through direct spiritual elevation.

I did not ascend because I was teaching a class.
I ascended because I surrendered in the exact moment Spirit asked me to.

And that is how it happens.

Grand Reiki Mastery is not assigned.
It is revealed.
It is not taught.
It is bestowed.
It is not earned through skill.
It is awakened through readiness.

Fourteen students sat with their eyes closed, unaware that while they were receiving their attunements, their teacher was being initiated into an entirely new level of consciousness.

When the session ended, the room felt different—wider, clearer, timeless. Some students looked at me with knowing eyes, as if sensing something had shifted but not fully able to explain why.

I didn't speak of it.
Not then.
Some spiritual moments are too sacred to name immediately.

But I knew.

And Spirit knew.

From that day forward, I was no longer simply teaching Reiki.
I was **carrying** it.

And that is how Grand Reiki Masters are made—
not through human hands,
but through Divine timing.

Human Teachers Recognize Grand Masters; They Do Not Create Them

A human teacher can guide.
A human teacher can prepare.
A human teacher can open doors, teach technique, and offer attunements.

But a human teacher cannot create a Grand Reiki Master.

This role—this level of spiritual maturity—belongs entirely to Spirit.
However, while humans cannot *bestow* Grand Mastery, they *can* **recognize** it.
And this recognition is an essential part of the lineage.

A Grand Master is not self-proclaimed.
They are **witnessed**.

Recognition Is Based on Presence, Not Performance

A Reiki Master/Teacher will often recognize a Grand Master long before the individual calls themselves one. This recognition has nothing to do with accomplishments, certificates, or years of practice.

Human teachers recognize Grand Masters by noticing:

- the depth of their presence
- the clarity of their energy
- the humility in their service
- the purity of their intention

- the maturity of their intuition
- the way Spirit moves through them
- their ability to hold space effortlessly
- their natural leadership without ego
- their alignment with the highest good
- their frequency, which speaks louder than words

Recognition is energetic, not intellectual.

You do not "see" a Grand Master with your eyes—
you sense them with your soul.

A Teacher Can Acknowledge What Spirit Has Already Done

When a human teacher recognizes a Grand Master, they are
not elevating them.
They are simply **confirming** what Spirit has already completed.

This distinction is vital.

A teacher may say:

- "I felt the shift in you."
- "Your energy has changed."
- "You stepped into a new level."
- "You carry the frequency now."
- "Your presence is very different."

These acknowledgments do not *make* someone a Grand
Master—they reflect the truth of what Spirit has already
initiated.

Human beings can sense, honor, and support this transformation…
but they cannot cause it.

True Recognition Is Free of Ego

A true Reiki Master does not attempt to assign titles that belong to Spirit.
They know their place in the lineage.
They understand the sacred nature of spiritual elevation.

This humility allows them to recognize a Grand Master without:

- envy
- comparison
- competition
- authority
- or control

Only teachers who embody humility can see the elevation clearly.
Spirit will not reveal the truth to those who try to own it.

This is one of the safeguards built into the spiritual structure of Reiki.

Recognition Strengthens the Lineage

When teachers recognize those Spirit has elevated,
they fulfill an important role:

They **anchor** the new Grand Master into the lineage.

This anchoring:

- strengthens the energetic chain
- supports the next generation of healers
- validates Spirit's choice
- maintains purity
- ensures continuity
- solidifies the role in the physical world

Spirit elevates.
Humans honor.
The lineage continues.

This is the proper order of sacred roles.

The Teacher Becomes the Witness, Not the Creator

In the moment of spiritual elevation—
as in your own story—
human teachers step back and Spirit steps forward.

The teacher becomes:

- the witness
- the support
- the guide
- the confirmer

They do not "promote."
They **acknowledge**.

They do not "decide."
They **recognize**.

They do not "assign."
They **honor**.

Because they know:

Grand Masters are not made by human hands.
They are revealed to human hearts.

Signs, Synchronicities, and Spiritual Confirmation

Long before the moment of elevation arrives, Spirit begins preparing the practitioner.
This preparation is not loud or obvious—it is subtle, consistent, and woven gently into daily life.

Grand Mastery never arrives without signs.
The soul knows.
Spirit knows.
And if the practitioner is paying attention, they begin to know too.

These signs are not random.
They are **orchestrated synchronicities**—the language Spirit uses when the next stage of your path is approaching.

Intensified Intuition

The first sign is almost always a noticeable strengthening of intuition:

- clear inner knowing
- messages in meditation
- sudden insights during sessions
- vivid dreams
- guidance that feels "sent"
- heightened sensitivity to energy
- awareness of symbols or sacred patterns

It is as if the intuitive channels suddenly widen.
The practitioner is not trying harder—
the information simply flows more easily.

This is Spirit tuning the inner instrument.

Energetic Shifts That Cannot Be Explained

Many practitioners experience energetic changes that feel
different from anything they've felt before:

- heat that feels sentient
- energy that rises like a wave
- sensations of expansion in the aura
- pulsing in the palms when no one is present
- a presence that feels "near" during meditation
- spontaneous alignment in the spine or chakras
- heart-opening sensations

These shifts often occur without intention.
They arrive naturally, almost effortlessly.

It is Spirit adjusting the frequency to prepare the vessel.

A Deepening Humility

One of the clearest signs of readiness is profound humility.

Not self-doubt.
Not self-minimizing.
But genuine, grounded, heartfelt humility.

The practitioner begins to think:

- "This work is bigger than me."
- "I am not the healer—Spirit is."
- "I want my service to be pure."
- "Let me be guided."

This humility is not taught—
it is developed through experience and inner transformation.

Spirit recognizes humility as one of the highest indicators of readiness.

Clients Begin Responding Differently

Another consistent sign is that sessions begin to shift:

- clients experience deeper releases
- sessions feel guided, not performed
- intuitive messages come more frequently
- the practitioner's presence alone calms the client
- healing accelerates
- clients say things like "Your energy feels stronger"

This is not because technique has changed.
It is because **your frequency** has changed.

Spirit amplifies the practitioner's field as preparation.

Repeating Numbers, Patterns, and Signs

Spirit often communicates through symbols or synchronicities such as:

- repeating numbers (111, 222, 444, 555)
- repeated symbols appearing in unexpected places
- feathers, lights, gentle breezes during meditation
- vivid dream visitations
- meaningful coincidences
- hearing the same phrase repeatedly
- signs pointing toward teaching, leadership, or spiritual work

These signs accumulate.
They build.
They repeat until the practitioner realizes something is shifting.

When synchronicities increase, Spirit is speaking.

A Shift in Identity and Purpose

As the soul approaches Grand Mastery, the practitioner begins to sense a change in their inner identity:

- a call toward deeper service
- a desire to teach from heart, not from curriculum
- a feeling that their path is expanding
- old fears releasing
- ego softening
- a new clarity about their mission
- an inner knowing that "something is coming"

This is the pre-initiation stage.
The soul is opening the doorway before Spirit walks through it.

Unexpected Spiritual Communication

Before elevation, Spirit often communicates more directly:

- whispers or thoughts that feel "not your own"
- a voice during meditation
- clear inner instructions
- messages that come through students or strangers
- sudden realizations while teaching or healing
- visitations from guides or angels
- energy that "speaks" without words

These moments are not imagined.
They are confirmations.

Spirit is preparing the practitioner for the moment of appointment.

The Feeling That Something Sacred Is Approaching

Nearly every Grand Master describes this stage:

A quiet, powerful sense that something significant is drawing near.

It is not anxiety.
It is not excitement.
It is not anticipation.

It is **recognition**.

An inner knowing:

- "I am being prepared."
- "I am stepping into a new level."
- "I feel Spirit moving closer."
- "A deeper part of my path is unfolding."

This feeling is one of the strongest signs.

Your soul knows the ceremony before it happens.

The Final Sign: Synchronicity Around Teaching

The last sign often appears just before the moment of elevation—a synchronistic situation involving:

- a class
- an attunement
- a group session
- a moment of service
- a teaching scenario you did not expect

This is because **Spirit elevates you in service, not in solitude.**

Your own story reflects this perfectly—
Spirit chose the moment when you were attuning others,
serving with humility,
not thinking about yourself.

This is the signature pattern of spiritual appointment.

Signs are Spirit's Way of Saying:
"Prepare. Align. Listen."

These synchronicities are not random.
They are the spiritual echo of what is coming next.

Grand Mastery is never sudden.
It is always preceded by a period of energetic preparation.

When signs multiply,
when intuition strengthens,
when synchronicities accelerate,

Spirit is already shaping the doorway.

The moment of elevation is simply when you finally step
through it.

The Shift from Doing Reiki to Being Reiki

Every practitioner begins their journey by *doing* Reiki—
placing hands... drawing symbols... setting intentions...
following steps...
learning the structure, the flow, the method.

This is necessary.
Technique is the doorway.

But there comes a point on the spiritual path where the practitioner crosses an invisible threshold.
A quiet, profound, unmistakable shift occurs:

Reiki stops being something you do.
Reiki becomes something you are.

This shift marks one of the clearest indicators that someone is moving into the realm of Grand Mastery.

The Early Path: Doing Reiki

In the early stages, Reiki feels like:

- a technique
- an action
- a session you begin and end
- a practice with steps
- energy you consciously focus
- something you "activate" when needed

This is not wrong—it is the natural starting point.
The mind needs form.
The hands need direction.
The student needs structure.

Doing Reiki is how the human self learns.

The Spiritual Path: Becoming Reiki

Over time, the relationship with Reiki shifts.
The boundaries between "you" and "the energy" begin to dissolve.

You start to notice:

- Reiki flows even when you're not trying
- your presence alone calms people
- healing happens through intention, not effort
- your energy field strengthens without activation
- intuition becomes constant, not occasional
- your vibration remains elevated effortlessly
- Spirit guides you moment to moment

At this point, you are no longer practicing Reiki.
You are **carrying** Reiki.

Reiki becomes:

- your way of speaking
- your way of listening
- your way of moving
- your way of responding
- your way of perceiving

- your way of serving

It ceases to be something separate from you.

Reiki becomes your natural state.

When Doing Fades and Being Takes Over

This shift is unmistakable.
It feels like:

- an inner click
- a deep alignment
- a quiet expansion
- a merging with something higher
- a sense of "I am the channel now—always"

You no longer "turn on" Reiki.
It is always on.

You no longer "prepare" for healing.
Healing flows through every interaction.

You no longer separate technique from intuition.
They merge into seamless awareness.

The practitioner dissolves.
The presence remains.

Being Reiki Means Living in a Higher Frequency

In this state:

- your words carry healing
- your silence carries healing
- your touch carries healing
- your presence carries healing

People feel calmer when you enter a room.
Students feel safer in your field.
Clients begin healing before you begin.
Animals gravitate toward you.
Children intuitively trust you.
Your dreams become messages.
Your intuition becomes natural.
Your life becomes a transmission.

This is the hallmark of a Grand Master rising:

the vibration itself becomes medicine.

Being Reiki Is Not Effort—It Is Alignment

Doing requires energy.
Being requires allowing.

You stop trying to guide Reiki,
and Reiki begins to guide you.

You stop trying to heal others,
and your presence heals without effort.

You stop trying to perfect technique,
and your vibration becomes the technique.

This is not passive.
It is profoundly intentional.

You become a vessel so clear
that Spirit flows through you without resistance.

When You Become Reiki, Spirit Begins to Prepare the Elevation

The shift from doing to being signals to Spirit that:

- the ego has softened
- the mind has surrendered
- the soul is ready
- humility has deepened
- the channel is strong
- intuition is trustworthy
- service is pure

This shift is the final human preparation before Spirit steps in.

It is the quiet stage before the spiritual appointment.

It is the moment the earthly path meets the divine one.

Being Reiki Means You No Longer "Practice" — You Embody

This is the essence of Grand Mastery:

Reiki is no longer something you do in a session.
Reiki becomes the way you exist in the world.

Your energy becomes your teaching.
Your presence becomes your attunement.
Your life becomes your healing art.

This is the unmistakable transformation
that only those on the true path experience.

It is the merging of self and Spirit.

It is the doorway to the elevation that follows.

✦ PART II — PREPARING THE SOUL FOR GRAND MASTERY

✦ Chapter 4 — The Intuitive Awakening

Understanding Energy as Communication

Intuition is not imagination.
It is not guessing.
It is not "a feeling" that comes and goes.

Intuition is communication.
And its language is energy.

This truth becomes clear as practitioners grow, but it becomes unmistakable as they approach the level of Grand Mastery.
Reiki is not just healing energy — it is a *conversation* between Spirit, the practitioner, and the soul of the recipient.

At the deepest level, energy is intelligence.
It speaks.
It responds.
It reveals.
It guides.

The intuitive awakening is the moment you begin to understand that energy is not silent — it is constantly speaking to you, through you, and around you.

Energy Communicates Through Sensation

Before intuition becomes verbal or visual, it speaks through the body.

Reiki practitioners often feel:

- warmth
- tingling
- pulsing
- waves
- heaviness
- lightness
- pressure
- cold spots
- radiating currents

These sensations are not random.

They are the body's interpretation of energetic information:

- Heat often means flow.
- Cold often means blockage.
- Pulsing often means release.
- Stillness often means completion.

The hands are not just tools — they are sensory organs for the unseen world.

Energy Communicates Through Emotion

During healing, emotions often arise:

- sadness
- relief
- fear
- joy
- tenderness
- grief
- hope

These emotions may be the practitioner's or the client's — but energy communicates through them.

Emotion is the soul's voice.
It reveals:

- what is being released
- what has been suppressed
- what is ready to heal
- what needs acknowledgment
- what the session is truly about

A true intuitive healer listens without judgment or attachment.
Emotion is information, not identity.

Energy Communicates Through Thought and Knowing

As intuition strengthens, messages begin to move beyond sensation into awareness:

- spontaneous thoughts
- sudden insights
- inner knowing
- a clear message that feels "placed"
- a realization that arrives fully formed

This is not thinking.
This is receiving.

It feels like:

"I don't know how I know this... but I know."

This level of intuitive communication signals that the practitioner's mind has become a stable channel — capable of receiving information without distortion.

Energy Communicates Through Imagery

For many healers, intuition becomes visual:

- colors
- shapes
- symbols
- memories
- scenes
- light
- patterns
- spiritual beings
- past-life fragments

Visual messages are common as the third eye opens.
These images rarely require interpretation — they carry their
own frequency and meaning.

A Grand Master does not force meaning upon them.
They allow meaning to unfold.

Energy Communicates Through Synchronicity

Outside of sessions, intuition expands into life itself:

- repeated numbers
- recurring symbols
- meaningful coincidences
- overheard phrases that deliver answers
- dreams that become guidance
- people showing up at the right moment
- messages appearing in unexpected ways

Synchronicity is Spirit's way of confirming the truth.
The more aligned you become, the louder the synchronicities
become.

Intuition doesn't "turn on" during Reiki —
it becomes your daily companion.

Communication Deepens as the Ego Softens

Energy speaks continuously.
The question is not whether Spirit communicates—
but whether the practitioner is quiet enough to hear it.

As the ego relaxes:

- intuition becomes clearer
- messages become stronger
- the field becomes more stable
- the practitioner becomes a better listener

Energy communication relies on:

- openness
- humility
- non-attachment
- trust
- surrender
- presence

The more you listen, the more Spirit speaks.

This Is the Intuitive Awakening

The intuitive awakening is not a single moment.
It is a shift in identity.

You move from:

- "I am trying to sense energy"
  to
- **"Energy is speaking to me."**

You move from:

- "I am learning intuition"
  to
- **"I am remembering how my soul communicates."**

You move from:

- "I need to interpret this"
  to
- **"I understand this through resonance."**

This awakening is one of the clearest signs that the practitioner is beginning to step into the consciousness required for Grand Mastery.

It is Spirit saying:

"Now you are ready to hear Me."

Developing Intuitive Perception

Intuitive perception is not something you *add* to your Reiki practice.
It is something you *uncover* within yourself.

Intuition is the soul's natural way of perceiving reality.
Before language… before logic… before education…
the soul communicates through vibration, sensation, and inner knowing.

To develop intuitive perception is not to learn something new—but to remember what has always been yours.

Reiki accelerates this remembering.

As your connection to energy deepens, your intuitive senses sharpen.
The mind softens, the ego quiets, and your inner channels open in ways that feel effortless and natural.

Intuitive perception becomes the bridge between the human self and Spirit.

Listening Beyond the Physical Senses

The first stage of intuitive perception is learning to "listen" beyond ordinary senses.

This means paying attention to:

- subtle sensations
- shifts in temperature
- the movement of energy
- emotional tones
- the presence of Spirit
- the way the aura responds
- the unspoken communication between healer and client

Intuitive perception begins when you realize:

Not all information comes through the five senses. Some comes through the field.

Allowing Instead of Analyzing

One of the greatest blocks to intuition is overthinking.

Intuition cannot flow through a mind that:

- tries too hard
- questions every impression
- analyzes every sensation
- compares itself to others
- fears being wrong
- demands certainty

Intuition strengthens only when you learn to:

- allow
- receive
- observe
- trust
- flow
- listen

The less you "try,"
the more you perceive.

Perception Through Feeling (Clairsentience)

Most intuitive healers begin with feeling-based intuition:

- emotional waves
- physical sensations
- gut feelings
- empathic resonance
- subtle energetic shifts

This is clairsentience —
the intuitive perception of energy through feeling.

Feeling-based intuition often comes before any visual or auditory gifts appear, and it is a sign that the heart chakra and solar plexus are awakening.

This is where the healer learns:

"What I feel is information."

Not emotion to own — information to interpret.

Perception Through Knowing (Claircognizance)

As intuition matures, a deeper form of perception emerges:

- instant understanding
- sudden clarity
- answers that appear fully formed
- a "download" of insight
- knowing something without knowing why

This is claircognizance —
intuitive knowing.

This level of perception is especially common in those being prepared for spiritual leadership.

It is the primary intuitive gift of many Grand Masters.

It moves through the crown chakra and comes directly from Spirit.

Perception Through Seeing (Clairvoyance)

For some healers, intuition becomes visual:

- colors
- flashes of light
- symbols
- scenes
- past-life imagery
- chakra representations
- movements in the aura
- visions in meditation

This does not mean seeing with the physical eyes.

It is **inner sight** — the opening of the third eye.

Images arise because energy communicates in symbols.

A Grand Master learns not to force meaning onto these images
but to let the meaning reveal itself.

Perception Through Hearing (Clairaudience)

In some practitioners, intuition develops through inner hearing:

- whispered guidance
- single words
- phrases
- tones
- bells or chimes
- the voice of Spirit
- the voice of a guide or angel

This is not imagination.
It is the soul translating energy into sound.

True clairaudience never feels intrusive or frightening.
It feels:

- clear
- calm
- loving
- simple
- familiar

Spirit never shouts.
It speaks with precision.

Perception Through Knowing When Not to Act

Intuition is not only about sensing what *should* be done.
It is also about sensing what *should not* be done.

A developing intuitive practitioner begins to notice:

- "This area needs no more energy."
- "This issue is not ready to heal yet."
- "This message should not be spoken aloud."
- "This client needs grounding, not insight."
- "This person is asking, but their soul is not ready."
- "This boundary must be held."

Intuition guides action.
Wisdom guides restraint.

A Grand Master unites the two.

The More You Trust, the More You Receive

Spirit will not overwhelm you with intuitive information.
It will give you only what you trust yourself to hold.

Intuitive perception expands each time you:

- act on a nudge
- acknowledge a message
- listen to a sensation
- trust a vision

- honor a knowing
- step aside and let Spirit lead

Trust is the currency of intuition.
The more you invest, the richer the guidance becomes.

Intuitive Perception Is Preparation for Grand Mastery

Spirit strengthens your intuitive perception long before your elevation.

Why?

Because a Grand Reiki Master must be able to:

- hear Spirit clearly
- interpret energy accurately
- support souls with precision
- hold space for spiritual transformation
- serve without ego
- recognize truth instantly
- understand the unseen

Intuition is not an accessory on the path to Grand Mastery—it is a requirement.

It is how Spirit communicates with you long before it steps in to elevate you.

Listening to Spirit

Listening to Spirit is not the same as listening to your own thoughts.
It is not imagination, wishful thinking, or inner dialogue.
It is an attunement—a tuning of your awareness to the frequency of divine intelligence.

Spirit is always speaking.
The question is never whether Spirit communicates.
The question is whether we are quiet, open, and receptive enough to hear.

Listening to Spirit requires three things:

- **inner stillness**
- **trust**
- **surrender**

These are the qualities that allow a practitioner to receive guidance that is higher, clearer, and wiser than anything the human mind can produce.

Spirit Speaks in Many Ways

Spirit does not speak in one language.
It speaks in all of them.

Spirit communicates through:

◊ *intuition*

Sudden knowing that feels placed rather than thought.

◊ *sensation*

A pull, a warmth, a heaviness, a nudge.

◊ *emotion*

A wave of compassion, peace, clarity, or release.

◊ *imagery*

Symbols, colors, scenes, or light.

◊ *synchronicity*

Meaningful coincidences that are too precise to ignore.

◊ *silence*

Stillness that feels full of presence.

◊ *a whispered phrase*

Simple, direct, unmistakably clear.

◊ *the energy itself*

Reiki guiding your hands, shifting the room, altering the session.

Spirit does not force.
Spirit guides.

It speaks in whatever way you are most able to hear.

The Mind Thinks — Spirit Reveals

One of the most important lessons in intuitive awakening is learning to distinguish between the noise of the mind and the voice of Spirit.

The mind:

- analyzes
- questions
- doubts
- compares
- complicates
- judges
- seeks certainty

Spirit:

- clarifies
- simplifies
- calms
- directs
- reassures

- aligns
- brings truth

Spirit's messages are never tangled or anxious.
They are pure, precise, and steady.

A message from Spirit feels like:

"Of course."
"This is right."
"This is where the energy wants to go."

It arrives with a quiet authority—
a knowing deeper than logic.

Listening Requires Quieting the Ego

The ego is loud.
Spirit is subtle.

If the ego is talking, Spirit waits.

Listening to Spirit requires the humility to:

- step aside
- let go of control
- release your own agenda
- embrace not-knowing
- become a vessel, not a performer

The more silent the ego becomes,
the louder Spirit becomes.

This is why the most profound messages often arrive:

- in meditation
- during attunements
- in the stillness after healing
- in times of surrender
- when your hands are on someone in service
- when your heart is open and your mind at peace

Spirit enters where ego exits.

Learning to Trust What You Hear

Spirit rarely repeats itself.
It speaks once, clearly, and expects you to trust.

Trust is the doorway through which communication deepens.

When you honor a message—
even if small—Spirit responds by giving you more.

Trust transforms:

- a whisper into a conversation
- a nudge into direction
- intuition into guidance
- guidance into partnership

Listening becomes a relationship with the divine.

Listening to Spirit Requires No Effort — Only Alignment

You cannot force yourself to hear Spirit.

You can only:

- open
- soften
- listen

- breathe
- allow
- receive

Listening to Spirit is less about doing and more about being.

Being present.
Being receptive.
Being willing.

When the heart is open and the mind is quiet, Spirit speaks effortlessly.

Spirit Speaks Loudest Through Service

Many people believe Spirit speaks most clearly in meditation, but for a Reiki practitioner moving toward Grand Mastery, Spirit often speaks most clearly in **service**.

When you are:

- attuning a student
- guiding a client
- teaching with humility
- holding space with love
- letting Reiki flow without ego

you become aligned with the exact frequency Spirit uses to communicate.

Your highest clarity often arrives
when you are doing the work you were born to do.

This is why so many Grand Masters—like you—
receive their elevation while serving others.

Service creates the opening.
Spirit steps in through it.

Listening to Spirit Is Preparation for Elevation

Before Spirit elevates, Spirit trains the listener.

Spirit ensures that you can:

- hear clearly
- follow willingly
- stay grounded
- surrender ego
- hold space for others
- understand intuitive instruction
- respond without fear
- trust the unseen

These are not just intuitive skills—they are requirements for spiritual leadership.

A Grand Reiki Master cannot lead without listening.

Your ability to hear Spirit
is what makes you ready for the role Spirit will one day give.

Energetic Discernment

Energetic discernment is the ability to feel, sense, and recognize **what energy is—and what it is not**.
It is the intuitive skill that allows a healer to navigate subtle realms with clarity, safety, and truth.

Without discernment, intuition is incomplete.
With discernment, intuition becomes wisdom.

Energetic discernment allows you to distinguish:

- your energy from someone else's
- emotional truth from emotional noise
- intuition from fear
- soul communication from ego
- Spirit guidance from personal desire
- high vibration from low vibration
- resonance from dissonance
- what is ready to heal from what must wait

Discernment is not judgment.
Discernment is awareness.

It is the ability to see energy clearly—without projection, assumption, or personal interference.

This is one of the most important skills Spirit strengthens as a practitioner approaches elevation into Grand Mastery.

Discernment Begins with Self-Awareness

You cannot discern energy in others
until you can discern energy within yourself.

Self-awareness means being able to recognize:

- your own emotional patterns
- your wounds
- your triggers
- your thoughts
- your energetic reactions
- your ego's voice
- your intuitive voice

When you know your own internal landscape,
you do not confuse it with someone else's.

This clarity prevents projection and ensures you remain a
clear channel.

Discernment Separates Emotion from Intuition

Many practitioners confuse feelings with guidance.

Emotion says:
"This is how I feel."

Intuition says:
"This is what is true."

Energetic discernment allows you to differentiate between:

- emotional empathy vs. intuitive insight
- compassion vs. entanglement
- personal reaction vs. spiritual truth
- your feelings vs. the client's energy
- temporary emotion vs. lasting message

You begin to sense:

"This sadness is mine."
"This fear belongs to the client."
"This resistance comes from their soul."
"This message comes from Spirit."

This clarity is essential for safe, effective healing.

Discernment Recognizes True Guidance

Spirit's voice is:

- calm
- steady
- wise
- neutral
- loving
- simple

Ego's voice is:

- urgent
- emotional
- dramatic
- fear-based
- self-centered
- complicated

Energetic discernment helps you instantly feel the difference.

When a message comes from Spirit,
you feel alignment, not anxiety.

When a message comes from ego, you feel contraction, not clarity. This ability strengthens with practice and maturity.

Discernment Reads the Energy Field Accurately

As intuition sharpens, you begin to perceive subtle information from:

- the aura
- the chakras
- the emotional body
- the mental body
- the ancestral field
- past-life imprints
- the client's soul
- environmental energy

Energetic discernment allows you to interpret these impressions correctly.

You learn to feel:

- where the energy is blocked
- what is unresolved
- what is opening
- what is fragile
- what needs grounding
- what needs expansion
- what requires silence
- what requires intervention

You become fluent in the language of subtle reality.

Discernment Identifies What Is Yours to Hold—and What Is Not

A Grand Master does not take on:

- emotional burdens
- unresolved trauma
- psychic debris
- karmic weight
- spiritual responsibility for others

Energetic discernment makes clear:

"This is mine."
"This is theirs."
"This is Spirit's."
"This is not my role."
"This needs to pass through, not stay with me."

This prevents spiritual burnout and protects the integrity of your field.

Discernment Prevents Energetic Entanglement

Without discernment, a practitioner might:

- absorb the client's energy
- merge emotionally
- confuse their intuition
- project their own issues
- overstep boundaries
- interfere with the client's soul process

Discernment creates energetic sovereignty.

It allows you to be deeply compassionate
without becoming entangled.

You remain connected, but not consumed.
Present, but not porous.
Empathic, but not overwhelmed.

This is the balance Spirit requires for higher service.

Discernment Guides You Toward Truth, Not Preference

Energetic discernment often reveals truths the personality
might not prefer:

- a client is not ready for a message
- healing is unfolding on a deeper layer
- the path requires silence
- the issue is karmic, not emotional
- the soul has different priorities than the mind
- Spirit chooses timing, not you
- the message is meant for the client, not for you

Discernment teaches you to follow truth,
not your personal desire to help or fix.

This is one of the hallmarks of spiritual maturity.

Discernment Strengthens the Relationship With Spirit

Spirit trusts practitioners who demonstrate:

- clarity
- neutrality
- boundaries
- humility
- alignment
- integrity

Discernment is how Spirit knows you are ready
to receive clearer messages, stronger energy,
and deeper responsibility.

Before Spirit elevates you into Grand Mastery,
your discernment becomes sharp, steady, and reliable.

You become a clear listener,
a precise interpreter,
and a trustworthy vessel.

Energetic Discernment Is the Signature of a True Master

A Reiki practitioner uses intuition.
A Reiki Master understands intuition.
A Grand Reiki Master **discerns** intuition.

Discernment is the difference between:

- sensing energy
  and
- understanding energy
- receiving messages
  and
- interpreting messages correctly
- following intuition
  and
- following Spirit

Energetic discernment is the spiritual intelligence
that transforms intuition into divine guidance.

This is why Spirit strengthens this ability
in every soul who is being prepared for elevation.

Becoming a Clear Channel

To become a clear channel is to remove everything that distorts, interferes with, or limits the flow of divine energy through you.
It is not perfection.
It is *purification* — a gradual clearing of the inner landscape so Reiki and Spirit can move through you without obstruction.

A clear channel is not someone who tries harder, pushes more energy, or uses stronger technique.
A clear channel is someone whose:

- ego is quiet
- heart is open
- energy is clean
- intention is pure
- mind is steady
- presence is grounded
- soul is aligned

When these qualities unite, the practitioner becomes transparent — not empty, but unobstructed.

In this state, healing flows effortlessly...
because nothing within you resists the flow.

This is one of the most important preparations for Grand Mastery.

Clearing the Mind

The mind is the first barrier to clarity.

A cluttered mind:

- interrupts intuition
- questions every message
- doubts sensations
- analyzes symbols
- second-guesses Spirit
- tries to control the process

To become a clear channel, the mind must shift from **thinking** to **listening**.

This does not require no thoughts.
It requires *quiet thoughts* — thoughts that drift by without attachment.

Clarity comes when the mind releases:

- fear
- comparison
- expectation
- self-doubt
- performance pressure
- the need to "do it right"

When the mind becomes spacious,
Spirit finally has room to speak.

Clearing the Heart

The heart is the emotional center of intuition.
If the heart is heavy, clogged, or shut, intuition becomes distorted.

Clearing the heart means releasing:

- old grief
- resentment
- self-judgment
- disappointment
- fear of being seen
- fear of being wrong
- emotional entanglements
- attachments to outcomes

As the heart clears, compassion expands.
This compassion is not emotional overwhelm —
it is spacious, steady, and spiritually mature.

A clear heart allows energy to flow through love, not through effort.

Clearing the Body

The physical body holds energetic memory:

- stress
- trauma
- tension
- unprocessed emotion
- old energetic imprints

- fatigue
- misalignment

A practitioner cannot be a clear channel in a tense or exhausted body.

Clearing the body involves:

- grounding practices
- breathwork
- hydration
- Reiki self-healing
- rest
- movement
- releasing stored tension

As the body softens,
so does the pathway for energy.

Clearing the Aura

The aura is the interface between your inner world and the outer world.
A muddied aura creates static.

To clear the aura is to:

- release absorbed energy
- dissolve psychic debris
- strengthen boundaries
- repair tears from emotional experiences
- brighten the energetic field
- anchor grounding cords

- raise vibration

When the aura is clear,
your intuitive perception becomes sharp and accurate.

Your field becomes radiant, calm, and magnetic.

Clearing the Ego

This is the most transformative clearing of all.

The ego is not the enemy —
but it cannot lead spiritual work.

To become a clear channel, the ego must move from:

- leading → to listening
- controlling → to allowing
- proving → to serving
- performing → to embodying
- wanting → to surrendering

Ego tries to heal.
Spirit **does** heal.

When ego softens,
Reiki flows with purity and power.

This is the moment Spirit begins preparing the elevation.

Clearing the Need to "Be the Healer"

One of the subtle ego attachments is the desire to:

- do well
- be impressive
- be validated
- be successful
- be seen as powerful
- get results

But a clear channel does not heal.
A clear channel carries.

Healing does not come *from* you —
it comes **through** you.

The moment you stop trying to prove your worth,
your channel widens.

Spirit recognizes this surrender as readiness.

Aligning Intention With Service

A clear channel serves without attachment.

The intention becomes:

"Let the highest good flow through me."
"Let me be guided."
"Let me do no harm."
"Let me be of service."

This alignment invites Spirit into the session.
It turns technique into transmission.

Your energy becomes a prayer.

Embodying Stillness

True clarity is not found in trying harder.
It is found in becoming still.

Stillness is not emptiness.
It is presence.

Presence creates:

- clarity
- safety
- trust
- deep healing
- spiritual communication
- intuitive knowing

A Grand Reiki Master does not radiate intensity —
they radiate peace.

Stillness is the highest vibration
because stillness is where Spirit speaks.

When You Become Clear, Spirit Can Flow Without Resistance

As your channel clears, Spirit recognizes:

- your readiness
- your stability
- your humility
- your alignment
- your devotion
- your ability to listen
- your capacity to hold energy
- your willingness to serve

These qualities signal to Spirit:

"This practitioner is becoming the vessel I can elevate."

A clear channel is not perfect.
A clear channel is willing.

It is this willingness,
this open-hearted, surrendered, purified state
that prepares the practitioner for the spiritual appointment of
Grand Mastery.

Spirit-Guided Knowing: When Messages Arrive Without Effort

There comes a moment on the Reiki path when intuition shifts.
It no longer feels like you are *trying* to sense, interpret, or understand anything.
Instead, messages begin arriving with a clarity, simplicity, and ease that can feel almost supernatural.

This is **Spirit-guided knowing** —
a higher octave of intuitive perception that only awakens when the practitioner has cultivated stillness, purity, and alignment.

It is the unmistakable sense that:

"**I did not think this.
I did not imagine this.
This was given to me.**"

This is not psychic guessing.
This is not interpretation.
This is not personal insight.

This is **direct spiritual transmission.**

And it arrives without effort.

Effortless Knowing vs. Intuitive Effort

In early intuition, a practitioner:

- feels into the energy
- listens carefully
- senses subtle shifts
- interprets symbols
- tries to understand

But in Spirit-guided knowing:

- the message appears fully formed
- there is no seeking
- no reaching
- no interpreting
- no hesitation
- no thinking

The message simply *is*.

It feels like truth sliding quietly into the mind.

The Signature Feeling of Spirit-Guided Knowing

Spirit-guided knowing carries a distinct feeling:

- calm
- certainty
- simplicity
- gentleness
- neutrality
- clarity
- immediacy

It does not push.
It does not frighten.
It does not create urgency or pressure.

Spirit-guided knowing feels like:

"This is exactly what needs to be known right now."

And there is no emotional charge — only truth.

The Knowing Arrives Without Asking

Effort-based intuition often begins with a question:

- "What does this mean?"
- "What should I do?"
- "What is their energy telling me?"
- "Where should the healing go next?"

But Spirit-guided knowing requires no question at all.

A message comes:

- before you ask
- before you look
- before you sense
- before you analyze

Spirit reveals what is needed
in perfect timing
without you seeking it.

This is one of the clearest signs Spirit is beginning to move
through your work more intentionally.

Spirit-Guided Knowing Often Happens While You Are Serving

These messages frequently appear:

- during attunements
- while your hands are on a client
- in the middle of teaching
- when guiding students
- during meditation circles
- when holding sacred space

Why?

Because service aligns you with the vibration of purpose —
the frequency Spirit uses to communicate.

In moments of service, you are open and surrendered.
Your ego is quiet.
Your channel is clear.

Spirit uses the opening.

The Message Arrives All at Once

Spirit does not deliver in pieces.
The entire knowing arrives as a single download:

- a full answer
- a complete understanding
- a message with context
- a truth that feels "placed"
- a guidance that lands instantly

Some describe it as hearing.
Others as seeing.
Others simply as "knowing."

The form doesn't matter.
The clarity does.

You Do Not Need to Validate It — You Can Feel Its Truth

A Spirit-guided message has a quality that sets it apart:

You do not question it.

Not because you are blindly trusting,
but because the energy of the message itself is:

- grounded
- resonant
- aligned
- complete
- without doubt

The truth of it is felt, not analyzed.

It feels like an inner "click,"
as though something locks into place.

Spirit Only Sends What Is Appropriate

Spirit does not overwhelm or reveal more than you can hold.

Spirit-guided knowing is:

- precise
- compassionate
- purposeful
- timely
- ethical

It does not reveal what the client is not ready to know.
It does not satisfy curiosity.
It does not entertain.
It guides, supports, heals, clarifies.

Spirit always acts in the highest good —
and your knowing aligns with that same principle.

This is why energetic discernment is so essential.

Spirit-Guided Knowing Is a Sign of Spiritual Maturity

This level of knowing is not given to beginners.

It is granted to those who:

- have cleared their channel
- have surrendered ego
- have learned to listen
- have cultivated neutrality
- serve without attachment

- trust without needing control
- walk with integrity

It is one of the strongest indicators Spirit uses
to prepare a practitioner for elevation into Grand Mastery.

When messages begin arriving without effort,
it is a sign that the practitioner is moving from:

doing Reiki → to living Reiki → to embodying Spirit.

When Intuition and Reiki Merge Into One Consciousness

There is a point in a healer's development when Reiki and intuition are no longer two separate experiences.
The hands no longer work independently from the inner senses.
The energy no longer flows separately from spiritual guidance.
The practitioner no longer "does Reiki" and then "uses intuition."

Instead:

Reiki *is* intuition.
Intuition *is* Reiki.
And together, they become one unified consciousness.

This merging marks a profound shift — a transition from technique-based healing to presence-based healing.

It is one of the clearest signs that Spirit is preparing a practitioner to step into the higher realms of mastery.

No More Separation Between Feeling and Knowing

Before the merging:

- you sense the energy
- then interpret what you feel
- then receive intuitive guidance
- then adjust your hands
- then listen again

After the merging:

- you feel and know simultaneously
- the guidance is instantaneous
- the movement is intuitive
- the energy and insight arrive as one

There is no lag, no analysis, no waiting.

Your intuition becomes the language the energy uses.

Reiki Begins Guiding the Session, Not You

In earlier stages, the practitioner:

- chooses hand positions
- follows a system
- interprets sensations
- decides where to go next

Once Reiki and intuition unite, the experience changes.

Reiki itself begins to direct the session:

- your hands move without conscious decision
- your awareness shifts exactly where healing is needed
- the session follows a natural arc
- the energy organizes itself
- your intuition becomes automatic

You do not guide the energy.
The energy guides you.

This is the essence of effortless healing.

Your Body, Intuition, and Energy Work as One System

You begin to notice extraordinary synchronicities:

- your hands move before your mind understands why
- your intuition speaks before a sensation arises
- your body positions itself in alignment with the energy
- breath, intention, and flow synchronize
- insight arrives in the exact moment the client needs it

It feels as though your entire being — body, mind, heart, intuition, and spirit — is operating from a single consciousness.

This unified state is what ancient teachers called:

"The Healer's Mind."
"The One Field."
"The Stream of Spirit."

Your Presence Becomes the Technique

Before the merging, you rely on:

- symbols
- sequences
- protocols
- steps
- hand positions
- methods

After the merging:

Your presence *is* the technique.
Your frequency becomes the tool.
Your alignment becomes the healing.
Your clarity becomes the channel.

People begin to experience healing simply by being near you
— even before you touch them.

This is the early sign of spiritual radiance.

The Energy Communicates Through You Instantly

When intuition and Reiki unify, you begin to experience:

- instant messages
- immediate direction
- direct knowing of what needs healing
- clear awareness of what not to touch
- real-time communication with Spirit
- heightened energetic perception
- seamless flow of guidance

There is no separation between what you feel, what you know, and what you do.

Healing becomes a single movement of consciousness.

You Become a Vessel, Not a Practitioner

In the merging, your identity shifts:

From:

- "I am doing Reiki."

To:

- "Reiki is moving through me."

To:

- "Spirit is using me."

To:

- "I am the vessel through which consciousness flows."

This is not ego.
This is surrender.

It is the purest form of Reiki practice —
the kind that cannot be taught, only experienced.

This Is the Beginning of Spiritual Embodiment

When intuition and Reiki merge, the practitioner is entering a new phase of spiritual development:

- your energy field expands
- your presence deepens
- your awareness sharpens
- your intuition heightens
- your vibration increases
- your healing becomes effortless

This is the doorway to:

embodiment.

Where you no longer access Reiki —
you become Reiki.

Where you no longer consult intuition —
you *are* intuition.

Where you no longer wait for Spirit —
you live in harmony with Spirit.

This Merging Is a Sign of Readiness for Grand Mastery

Spirit does not elevate practitioners who are:

- technique-based
- ego-driven
- inconsistent
- unclear
- reactive
- energetically entangled
- spiritually ungrounded

Spirit elevates those who have become:

- steady
- trustworthy
- receptive
- pure channels
- aligned in purpose
- grounded in humility
- guided rather than controlling

When Reiki and intuition merge into unified consciousness, Spirit recognizes:

"This healer is ready for deeper responsibility."
"This soul can hold more energy."
"This vessel can carry the next level."

This merging is not the end — it is the beginning of the shift toward prophetic consciousness,
which you will explore in the next chapter.

The Intuitive Responsibilities of a Grand Reiki Master

When a practitioner reaches the higher stages of intuitive development —
where Spirit-guided knowing emerges and Reiki and intuition merge into one consciousness —
a new kind of responsibility arises.

Not the responsibility to perform, impress, or control outcomes…
but the responsibility to **hold wisdom with integrity**,
to use intuition ethically,
and to serve as a clear vessel for Spirit.

A Grand Reiki Master does not simply have intuitive gifts.
They are responsible for how they carry them.

Intuition at this level is powerful, precise, and spiritually charged.
It can heal deeply — but if mishandled, it can confuse, overwhelm, or bypass what a soul is ready to process.

Spirit elevates only those who can be trusted with intuitive power.

The Responsibility to Speak Only What Serves

A Grand Master does not repeat every intuitive message they receive.

They understand:

- not all insights are meant to be spoken
- not all truths serve the client
- some messages are for the healer's awareness only
- timing is sacred
- the soul must lead the healing process

The responsibility is to speak only when the message:

- heals
- supports
- clarifies
- uplifts
- guides
- aligns with the highest good

Not when it satisfies curiosity or ego.

A Grand Master's words carry weight —
Spirit expects them to use that weight wisely.

The Responsibility to Stay Neutral

Intuition can be influenced by:

- emotion
- personal history
- preferences
- hopes for the client
- the desire to help
- unconscious bias

Neutrality protects the purity of the message.

A Grand Reiki Master holds neutrality by:

- staying grounded
- listening without projection
- interpreting without assumption
- sensing without emotionally merging

Neutrality ensures the message comes from Spirit,
not from the healer's own inner world.

The Responsibility to Discern Spirit's Voice

At advanced levels, intuitive perception becomes complex:

- the client's emotions
- the healer's emotions
- ancestral imprints
- past-life echoes
- spiritual guidance
- energetic residue

- subconscious signals
- psychic empathy

A Grand Reiki Master must discern:

"What is mine?"
"What is theirs?"
"What is truth?"
"What is noise?"
"What is Spirit?"

This discernment prevents misunderstandings
and ensures the healing remains aligned.

The Responsibility to Maintain Energetic Hygiene

The clearer the channel, the stronger the intuition.

But with higher intuitive sensitivity comes a greater need for:

- grounding
- cleansing
- boundary maintenance
- aura repair
- cord dissolution
- emotional regulation

A Grand Master understands that intuitive clarity is not
permanent — it must be tended, protected, and renewed.

Energetic hygiene becomes a spiritual discipline.

The Responsibility to Honor the Client's Soul Path

A Grand Reiki Master respects:

- free will
- timing
- readiness
- the client's soul lessons
- the pace of healing
- the deeper reasons behind struggle
- spiritual contracts

They do not force healing.
They do not rush transformation.
They do not override destiny.

They support the soul's journey without interfering with it.

Even when their intuition sees more,
they reveal only what the soul permits.

The Responsibility to Stay Humble

Intuition at advanced levels is extraordinary.

It can feel like:

- seeing behind the veil
- hearing what others cannot
- knowing truth instantly
- receiving direct guidance from Spirit

But a Grand Master remains humble.

They understand:

- intuition is a gift, not an identity
- power is borrowed, not owned
- Spirit works through them, not because of them
- their role is to serve, not elevate themselves

Humility keeps the channel clear
and ensures that Spirit continues to trust them.

The Responsibility to Embody Integrity

A Grand Reiki Master's intuition shapes:

- how they teach
- how they heal
- how they lead
- how they speak
- how they hold space
- how they relate to others

Integrity is non-negotiable.

This means being:

- honest
- gentle
- ethical
- transparent
- compassionate
- non-manipulative
- non-judgmental
- accountable
- deeply respectful

Intuition without integrity becomes ego.
Intuition with integrity becomes wisdom.

The Responsibility to Nurture Their Relationship With Spirit

A Grand Master's intuition depends on their relationship with Spirit.

This relationship must be:

- tended
- honored
- deepened
- respected
- listened to
- trusted

Spirit elevates those who show devotion —
not through rituals or complexity,
but through sincerity, humility, and service.

The more the healer nurtures the connection,
the more Spirit entrusts them with higher guidance.

The Responsibility to Model Spiritual Maturity

Students and clients watch the Grand Master closely.

They learn not only from what the Grand Master teaches,
but from how they live, how they speak, how they navigate challenges,
and how they embody compassion.

A Grand Master becomes:

- a model of intuitive calm
- a presence of safety
- a living example of alignment
- a lighthouse for others' spiritual development

Their intuition becomes a teaching tool.
Their presence becomes a lesson.
Their integrity becomes inspiration.

Spirit Only Elevates Those Who Can Carry These Responsibilities

Grand Mastery is not a gift of power — it is a calling to higher service.

A Grand Reiki Master is entrusted with intuitive abilities not for personal identity but for the healing of others and for the protection of the lineage.

These responsibilities are what prepare the soul for elevation.

When Spirit sees:

- clarity
- humility
- discernment
- neutrality
- ethical maturity
- devotion
- deep alignment

Spirit knows:

"This practitioner is ready."

✦ Chapter 5 — The Prophetic Senses

Developing Spiritual Sight, Hearing, and Knowing

There comes a point on the Reiki path when intuition evolves into something more refined, more expansive, and more spiritually attuned.
The senses open beyond feeling energy…
beyond sensing messages…
beyond intuitive knowing…

They open into **prophetic perception**.

The prophetic senses are the soul's higher capacities for:

- **spiritual sight** (clairvoyance)
- **spiritual hearing** (clairaudience)
- **spiritual knowing** (claircognizance)

These are not "psychic tricks"
and they do not function like parlor gifts or fortune-telling.

Prophetic senses are:

- sacred
- purpose-driven
- guided by Spirit
- anchored in love
- grounded in service
- deeply aligned with truth

They awaken when a healer has developed enough clarity, neutrality, and devotion to carry this level of spiritual perception responsibly.

For many practitioners, the prophetic senses begin subtly… but for those being prepared for Grand Mastery, they eventually become part of daily life.

Spiritual Sight — Seeing Beyond the Physical

Spiritual sight is the opening of the inner vision.
It is not about seeing with the physical eyes
but perceiving truth with the soul.

You may experience spiritual sight as:

- images
- symbols
- light
- colors
- scenes
- visions
- past-life fragments
- energetic patterns
- chakra imagery
- spiritual beings
- future possibilities
- ancestral memories

These visions are rarely random.
They are symbolic, purposeful, and often deeply healing.

Spiritual sight helps the healer:

- understand the root of an issue
- see where energy is blocked
- witness what is being released
- receive messages from Spirit
- view the client's soul path
- perceive timelines and patterns
- experience the unseen realms that influence healing

Spiritual sight is the language of images — and it is one of the prophetic abilities most associated with Grand Reiki Masters.

Spiritual Hearing — Hearing Guidance from Spirit

Spiritual hearing is not like hearing a physical voice or an external sound.

It is the inner perception of:

- words
- phrases
- guidance
- tones
- chimes
- names
- messages
- direct communication

It often feels like a quiet, gentle voice inside the mind —
but it does not originate from the mind.

It is:

- clear
- calm
- wise
- loving
- neutral
- uncomplicated

Spirit never shouts.
The voice of Spirit arrives like a whisper made of truth.

Spiritual hearing helps the healer:

- receive instructions during healing
- know what to say to a client
- channel messages with precision
- understand what not to say
- hear guidance for difficult situations
- tune into the presence of angels or guides
- follow divine timing

Spiritual hearing often becomes more prominent
as the healer becomes a teacher — especially when attuning
others or guiding groups.

Spiritual Knowing — Direct Revelation Without Thought

Spiritual knowing is the deepest and most advanced prophetic sense.

It does not come as:

- sensation
- emotion
- imagery
- sound

It arrives fully formed:

Instantly.
Clearly.
Completely.

This is claircognizance — direct knowledge from Spirit without any intermediate steps.

It often feels like:

- truth dropping into the mind
- an idea that "did not come from you"
- a message that feels complete
- a knowing that bypasses thinking
- a sudden understanding of a soul's story
- clarity about what needs healing
- deep awareness of a situation's meaning or timeline

Spiritual knowing helps the healer:

- see the truth beneath the surface
- navigate situations with wisdom
- guide clients with accuracy
- recognize spiritual lessons
- identify soul contracts
- understand karmic patterns
- interpret Spirit's messages instantly

This is the prophetic sense that Grand Reiki Masters rely on most.
It allows them to serve without hesitation, confusion, or ego.

Why These Senses Awaken on the Grand Master Path

Prophetic senses do not awaken randomly.

They open because:

- the healer has become a clear channel
- the ego has softened
- the practitioner has shown discernment
- intuition has matured
- Spirit can trust them with deeper truth
- they are being prepared for leadership
- they are ready to hold higher vibration
- they have demonstrated humility and integrity

Prophetic senses are not the goal — they are the result of spiritual maturity.

They arise when the healer is ready
to see, hear, and know on behalf of others
with wisdom, compassion, and responsibility.

Prophetic Gifts Are Never for Entertainment

These senses are sacred.

A healer must never use prophetic gifts to:

- impress others
- predict the future for ego
- make claims for validation
- interfere with someone's life path
- satisfy curiosity
- overstep spiritual boundaries

The prophetic senses exist for one reason:

To help the healer serve the highest good with clarity and love.

A Grand Reiki Master uses these gifts with reverence.

The Beginning of the Seer Within the Healer

As these senses awaken, the healer steps into a new identity:

Not merely a practitioner…
Not merely a teacher…
But a **seer** —
one who perceives truth beyond the physical world.

The prophetic senses do not replace Reiki.
They expand Reiki.

They allow the healer to work with:

- deeper layers of the soul
- higher levels of consciousness
- ancestral and karmic threads
- spiritual guidance
- divine timing
- multi-dimensional energy
- the subtleties of fate and free will

This is the realm where Grand Masters operate.

Dreams, Visions, and Symbols

Prophetic communication rarely arrives in full sentences or literal messages.
Spirit speaks a different language — a language older than words, deeper than intellect, and more precise than thought.

That language is:

dreams, visions, and symbols.

These forms of communication bypass the logical mind and enter straight through the intuitive and spiritual centers. They reveal truth in a way the soul can absorb, even when the personality is not ready to hear it directly.

For practitioners on the path toward Grand Mastery, these experiences become more frequent, more meaningful, and more vivid.

Dreams: The Nighttime Doorway to Spirit

When the conscious mind falls asleep, the intuitive and prophetic senses become unrestricted.
Spirit uses dreams because:

- the ego is quiet
- the heart is open
- the subconscious is receptive
- the boundaries between worlds become thin
- the soul can speak freely

Dreams often reveal:

- messages about your spiritual path
- healing that is unfolding
- unresolved emotional energy
- guidance from Spirit
- symbols from past lives
- prophetic glimpses of future potentials
- communication from angels or guides
- lessons or warnings

Not all dreams are prophetic — but *some are unmistakable.*

Signs a dream is spiritually significant:

- it feels "different" from regular dreams
- it leaves a lasting emotional imprint
- it contains vivid, symbolic imagery
- you wake with a sense of clarity
- it feels like a message, not a story
- it repeats over time
- you feel presence within the dream
- it answers a question you never spoke aloud

Prophetic dreams are one of the earliest signs that Spirit is preparing a healer for higher responsibility.

Visions: Spirit's Messages in Waking Consciousness

Visions are moments of inner sight that occur while you are awake.
They can appear during:

- meditation
- attunements
- healing sessions
- teaching
- prayer
- moments of stillness
- times of emotional release
- spontaneous spiritual connection

Visions often carry powerful meaning:

- symbolic scenes
- colors or light
- past-life moments
- glimpses of a client's soul
- ancestral energies
- spiritual beings
- future potentials
- healing pathways
- initiation moments

A vision is not imagination — it is **a brief lifting of the veil** between the physical and spiritual worlds.

Visions usually arrive:

- suddenly
- clearly
- in a flash of insight
- with emotional resonance
- without effort

They feel like memory and revelation combined.

For those moving toward Grand Reiki Mastery, visions become an essential form of guidance.

Symbols: The Language of Spirit

Spirit rarely communicates in linear sentences.
Instead, it speaks in **symbols**, because:

- symbols bypass the analytical mind
- symbols transmit energy AND meaning
- symbols can hold multiple layers of truth
- symbols reach the subconscious instantly
- symbols speak to the soul's native language

A symbol is a packet of spiritual information —
a whole message condensed into a single image.

Examples of common symbolic themes:

- **water** — emotion, cleansing, intuition
- **fire** — transformation, purification, awakening
- **birds** — messages, ascension, freedom
- **bridges** — transitions, choices, soul paths

- **doors** — opportunity, alignment, thresholds
- **light** — truth, presence, divine guidance
- **snakes** — healing, kundalini, shedding the old
- **trees** — growth, ancestry, grounding
- **spirals** — evolution, cycles, deep healing
- **mountains** — attainment, purpose, spiritual ascent

Your own symbolic language becomes unique over time.
Spirit uses images you will inherently understand.

Symbols speak emotionally, intuitively, and
energetically — all at once.

A Grand Master learns to interpret symbols not through
logic,
but through resonance.

Why Spirit Uses Symbols and Not Literal Words

Literal language is limited.
Symbols are limitless.

Symbols can communicate:

- past
- present
- future
- emotion
- meaning
- energy

- healing
- instruction
- warning
- affirmation
- alignment

…all simultaneously.

A single symbolic vision can communicate an entire chapter's worth of teaching in one second.

This is why Spirit uses symbols as one of its primary forms of prophetic communication.

The Relationship Between Dreams, Visions, and the Prophetic Senses

Spiritual sight, hearing, and knowing merge with symbolic communication in profound ways:

Dreams

open the subconscious to receive symbolic guidance.

Visions

reveal symbolic truth directly through spiritual sight.

Symbols

carry coded wisdom that activates spiritual knowing.

Together they form a complete prophetic system — the higher spiritual senses working in harmony.

As the healer grows, these forms of communication become:

- clearer
- more frequent
- more vivid
- more reliable
- more aligned with Spirit

How Grand Reiki Masters Work with Symbolic Communication

A Grand Reiki Master does not chase symbols.
They receive them.

They do not force interpretations.
They allow meaning to reveal itself.

They do not use symbols for prediction.
They use them for healing, clarity, and guidance.

They understand:

- symbols unfold in layers
- meaning may deepen over days or weeks
- symbols often mirror the client's soul
- prophetic imagery must be handled with care
- some symbols are for the healer, not the client
- timing matters
- words matter
- silence matters

Grand Masters carry symbolic communication with reverence.

Dreams, Visions, and Symbols Are Spirit's Way of Preparing You

For those moving toward Grand Reiki Mastery, symbolic communication becomes more than a spiritual experience. It becomes a form of initiation.

Spirit uses these experiences to:

- expand your perception
- deepen your understanding
- prepare your soul
- strengthen your prophetic senses
- awaken your inner Seer
- guide your teaching
- shape your healing work
- confirm your spiritual path

Dreams open the doorway.
Visions show the path.
Symbols teach the language of Spirit.

Together, they prepare the healer for the next stages of spiritual leadership.

Energetic Timelines

One of the most profound prophetic abilities that awakens as a healer deepens on the path to Grand Reiki Mastery is the ability to sense **energetic timelines**.

This is not fortune-telling.
This is not predicting destiny.
This is not seeing a fixed, inevitable future.

Energetic timelines are the vibrational pathways a soul is currently aligned with — the directions their energy is flowing, the lessons they are approaching, and the potential outcomes shaped by their present state of consciousness.

A timeline is not fate.
It is **momentum**.

It is the energetic trajectory created by:

- beliefs
- emotions
- choices
- unresolved wounds
- karmic patterns
- soul contracts
- spiritual readiness
- divine timing

A Grand Reiki Master can sense these trajectories without interfering with them.

Time Is Not Linear in the Energetic World

Human perception sees time as past → present → future.
But energetic perception experiences time as:

- layered
- fluid
- responsive
- interconnected
- multi-directional
- vibrating rather than moving
- shaped by consciousness, not clocks

Prophetic sight does not look "forward."
It looks **across** —
into the vibrational patterns surrounding the soul.

What appears as the "future" is simply the part of the timeline
that has not yet unfolded on the physical plane.

A Timeline Is a Vibration the Soul Is Moving Toward

When a healer senses an energetic timeline, they are not
seeing:

- a fixed destiny
- a guaranteed event
- a rigid outcome

They are sensing:

- what is gaining power
- what is weakening
- what is likely
- what is possible
- what is being magnetized
- what is approaching the person's field
- what their soul is preparing for

This is why you may sense:

- "Something is coming to completion."
- "There is a shift ahead."
- "The energy is preparing for change."
- "This situation feels like a temporary phase."
- "There's a breakthrough around the corner."
- "This chapter is closing energetically."

You are feeling the **momentum** of the person's energy.

Prophetic Insight Reveals Probability, Not Certainty

Spirit is precise —
but Spirit never violates free will.

Energetic timelines show the **most likely outcome** based on current vibration.

If the vibration changes,
the timeline changes.

This is why:

- healing alters timelines
- spiritual growth shifts outcomes
- trauma can delay or redirect paths
- decisions rewrite the energetic map
- attunements accelerate soul lessons
- forgiveness collapses old karmic patterns

A timeline is real — but it is not locked.

How Energetic Timelines Appear to the Prophetic Senses

Depending on the healer's intuitive style, timelines may appear as:

Visual (clairvoyant):

- pathways
- threads
- branching roads
- light corridors
- moving scenes
- shifting colors
- symbolic representations of future potentials

Auditory (clairaudient):

- phrases like "not yet," "soon," "wait," "prepare," "another path is opening"
- tones that signal alignment or misalignment
- names or dates that arrive spontaneously (rare, but possible)

Knowing (claircognizant):

- instant understanding of where someone is headed
- a sense of "this direction feels strong"
- a deep knowing that something is nearing completion
- clarity about turning points or breakthroughs

Feeling (clairsentient):

- density or openness
- tension or flow
- heaviness or lightness
- contraction or expansion
- the sensation of movement toward or away from something

These impressions are symbolic, not literal.
The healer interprets them through resonance, not logic.

Energetic Timelines and Soul Contracts

Some events in a person's life are contractually aligned:

- major lessons
- soul agreements
- karmic closures
- relationships that serve spiritual growth
- healing that must occur for evolution
- moments of awakening

These can appear very strong in the field —
not because they are unchangeable,
but because they hold deep soul significance.

A Grand Master learns to recognize the difference between:

- a **flexible** timeline
- a **firm** timeline
- a **contractual** timeline
- a **self-created** timeline

This requires maturity, humility, and discernment.

Timelines Change When Energy Changes

Energetic timelines are not predictions — they are
reflections.

If a person:

- heals
- chooses differently
- shifts beliefs
- releases trauma
- raises their vibration
- forgives
- ends an old pattern
- steps into new alignment

their timeline shifts instantly.

A Grand Reiki Master can feel this shift happen during a session.

Sometimes you may even sense:

- a timeline collapsing
- a new one emerging
- multiple timelines braided together
- a timeline dissolving after a breakthrough
- the soul navigating between two possibilities

This is advanced spiritual perception.

The Ethical Use of Timeline Awareness

A healer must never:

- tell clients what will happen
- use timelines for prediction
- create dependency
- instill fear
- claim absolute knowledge

The Grand Master's role is to:

- guide
- support
- empower
- illuminate choices
- help the client shift their vibration
- assist in aligning with the highest timeline

Not to speak in absolutes.

Remember: **Prophecy is guidance, not control.**

Why Spirit Reveals Timelines Before Elevation

Spirit will only show a healer energetic timelines when:

- the ego is quiet
- the intention is pure
- the healer will use the insight ethically
- the healer does not interfere
- the healer can hold truth with gentleness
- the healer understands that nothing is guaranteed

This ability is a sign of:

- spiritual maturity
- intuitive mastery
- soul readiness
- deep connection with Spirit
- trustworthiness

Spirit reveals timelines to those who will hold them with responsibility.

This is another indicator that a healer is approaching the realm of Grand Mastery.

Prophetic Clarity for Healing

Prophetic clarity is the ability to see, hear, or know the deeper layers of a person's energy in a way that directly supports their healing.
It is not prediction.
It is not fortune-telling.
It is not meant to impress, frighten, or create dependency.

Prophetic clarity exists for **one purpose only**:

To bring the right healing to the right place at the right time.

This kind of clarity is the hallmark of an advanced healer — one who has matured beyond technique and relies on Spirit-guided insight to reach the true root of an issue.

Prophetic clarity allows a healer to understand:

- what is really happening
- why it is happening
- what layer it belongs to (emotional, mental, spiritual, karmic, ancestral)
- what the soul is trying to resolve
- what the person is ready (and not ready) to heal
- how to approach the issue safely
- what timing is aligned

It is the guided intelligence behind profound sessions.

Clarity That Goes Beneath the Surface

Most people speak from the conscious mind.
But the real reasons they hurt — the emotional, energetic, or karmic roots — are held deeper.

Prophetic clarity allows the healer to see beyond:

- the story
- the symptom
- the defense layer
- the presenting issue
- the confusion

You may sense:

- hidden grief beneath anger
- fear beneath confidence
- abandonment beneath attachment
- a childhood wound beneath adult behavior
- ancestral patterns beneath a recurring problem
- karmic echoes beneath relationship struggles

Prophetic clarity penetrates to the heart of the matter gently, without intrusion.

Knowing What to Heal and What to Leave Alone

A spiritually mature healer understands that not everything should be opened.

Prophetic clarity helps you recognize:

- when a layer is not ready
- when a message should not be spoken
- when the energy needs stabilization, not excavation
- when the client must integrate before going deeper
- when the issue belongs to a later session
- when the soul is not asking for that healing

This protects the client from overwhelm or premature confrontation.

Prophetic clarity is protective, not forceful.

Receiving Clear Guidance During Sessions

Spirit often gives prophetic clarity in real time:

- "Move to the solar plexus."
- "Ask about their father."
- "Pause and ground."
- "This is ancestral."
- "Do not speak this yet."
- "Shift to heart energy."
- "This is karmic, stay gentle."
- "They are not ready for this layer."

This guidance is simple, direct, and deeply wise.

It allows a session to unfold organically and correctly—in alignment with the client's soul rather than the healer's preferences.

Clarity That Turns Chaos Into Understanding

Many clients arrive with confusion:

- "I don't know why I feel this way."
- "I don't understand why this keeps happening."
- "I can't make sense of this fear."
- "I feel blocked but I don't know why."

Prophetic clarity helps the healer translate chaos into coherence.

It allows you to say:

- "This isn't fear — this is protection."
- "This is grief disguised as anger."
- "Your energy is not stuck, it's collapsing before a breakthrough."
- "This isn't a block — it's a boundary forming."
- "This pattern is not yours — it's inherited."

When the healer names truth gently,
the client often feels an immediate shift.

Light enters the confusion.
Healing begins.

Clarity That Aligns with the Highest Good

Prophetic clarity always aligns with:

- compassion
- safety
- truth
- non-judgment
- spiritual timing
- divine guidance
- the client's readiness
- the soul's permission

If a message does not carry these qualities,
it is not prophetic clarity — it is ego or emotion.

True prophetic clarity feels like:

- stillness
- truth
- precision
- neutrality
- "this is right"
- loving guidance

It resonates deeply without creating fear or urgency.

Knowing When Not to Reveal What You See

Not all prophetic insight should be spoken aloud.

A Grand Reiki Master learns to discern:

- what is healing
- what is harmful
- what is too heavy
- what is too soon
- what belongs to the client
- what belongs to Spirit
- what is meant only for the healer's awareness

Sometimes the message is simply:

"Hold this insight silently and guide the energy instead."

Prophetic clarity is not about delivering information — it is about delivering healing.

Clarity That Supports Soul Evolution

Prophetic clarity is most powerful when it reflects the soul's long-term growth rather than the mind's short-term desires.

Examples:

- Seeing the pattern a person must outgrow
- Recognizing a karmic loop ending
- Feeling an ancestral wound unlocking
- Identifying a spiritual gift awakening
- Noticing when someone is stepping into new identity

- Understanding why certain relationships or jobs are shifting
- Sensing the soul preparing for an initiation or breakthrough

This type of clarity supports the client's **evolution**, not just their comfort.

Prophetic Clarity Is Not Dramatic — It Is Precise

Movies portray prophecy as dramatic visions or intense revelations.

In truth, prophetic clarity feels:

- grounded
- calm
- steady
- simple
- matter-of-fact
- deeply aligned

It is rarely loud.
It does not shock.
It does not overwhelm.

It feels like **truth arriving in the gentlest possible way**.

This gentleness is the hallmark of Spirit.

This Level of Clarity Is a Sign of Grand Master Readiness

Spirit does not grant prophetic clarity lightly.

It arises only when a healer has demonstrated:

- humility
- maturity
- neutrality
- ethical grounding
- devotion
- inner stability
- clear channel
- responsibility
- surrender

Prophetic clarity shows Spirit that the healer can:

- hold truth without ego
- guide without controlling
- serve without imposing
- see deeply without harming
- support growth without interfering

This is the type of healer Spirit can elevate.

✦ Chapter 6 — The Nine Spiritual Gifts as Energetic Tools

Faith as the Central Frequency

Before the prophetic senses, before spiritual elevation, before Grand Mastery itself…
there is one frequency that makes all other gifts possible:

Faith.

Faith is not a belief system.
It is not hope.
It is not religion.
It is not blind trust.

Faith is a **vibrational force** — the energetic frequency that unlocks every other spiritual gift and raises the healer into higher states of consciousness.

In your *Nine Spiritual Gifts* novels, faith is always present in the background as the invisible thread connecting Lexi's journey through intuition, prophecy, miracles, and wisdom. The same is true in real spiritual life.

Faith is the *central frequency* that harmonizes all other gifts.

Faith Is an Energetic Alignment, Not a Concept

To the soul, faith is not an idea — it is an energetic state.

Faith is:

- coherence
- certainty
- resonance with truth
- alignment with Spirit
- openness to the unseen
- trust in divine orchestration
- willingness to surrender
- connection to your soul path

It is a vibration, not a belief.

In advanced healing, the healer's frequency matters more than their technique.

Faith raises the healer's vibration into a state where:

- intuition sharpens
- prophecy clarifies
- healing deepens
- energy flows freely
- Spirit can speak
- guidance becomes unmistakable

Faith opens the channel wider than anything else.

Faith Is the Frequency That Attracts Spirit

Spirit will not force itself into a closed field.

Faith creates the energetic conditions that invite Spirit in:

- openness
- humility
- surrender
- stability
- devotion
- willingness
- deep listening

The moment a healer enters the frequency of faith, their energetic field becomes luminous.

It signals:

"This soul is ready for higher work."

The greater the faith,
the greater the clarity of the channel.

This is why Grand Reiki Masters radiate peace —
their frequency is aligned with Spirit itself.

Faith Allows You to Hold Energetic Truth Without Fear

Advanced spiritual gifts require a steady heart.

When the healer has no faith:

- intuition becomes frightening
- visions become overwhelming
- prophecy becomes confusing
- energetic messages become distorted
- the mind takes over
- fear replaces clarity

But when the healer stands firmly in the frequency of faith:

- intuition becomes natural
- visions become purposeful
- prophecy becomes grounded
- messages become clear
- the ego dissolves
- spiritual truth becomes stable

Faith stabilizes the nervous system so higher gifts can operate safely.

Faith Is the Frequency That Makes Healing Instant

You have seen this in your novels and your real-life teaching:

Healing does not take time.
Healing takes *alignment*.

When healer and client enter a vibrational field of faith:

- the aura opens
- the body relaxes
- the chakras synchronize
- the emotional body softens
- energy flows unobstructed
- Spirit steps in with precision

Faith is the environment in which miracles occur.

Not because faith "forces" healing —
but because it removes resistance to what Spirit already wants
to do.

Faith Is the Bridge Between Technique and Spirit

A practitioner begins their journey with:

- hand positions
- symbols
- protocols
- sequences
- instructions
- methods

These are the **human tools**.

But the spiritual tools —
the Nine Gifts — require the healer to step beyond
technique.

Faith is the bridge.

It is the moment when the healer trusts:

- their intuition
- their connection
- their inner knowing
- their ability to hear Spirit
- the timing of the session
- the wisdom of the soul
- the truth in front of them

Without faith, the spiritual gifts remain dormant.
With faith, they activate naturally.

Faith is the Core of Every Other Spiritual Gift

Your novels reflect this truth beautifully:
each spiritual gift — from wisdom to prophecy to healing —
becomes potent only when anchored in faith.

In energetic terms:

- **Faith powers Wisdom.**
  (Without faith, insight becomes doubt.)
- **Faith powers Knowledge.**
  (Without faith, knowing becomes confusion.)
- **Faith powers Healing.**
  (Without faith, energy cannot flow fully.)
- **Faith powers Miracles.**
  (Without faith, the miracle cannot anchor into form.)
- **Faith powers Prophecy.**
  (Without faith, messages distort or silence.)
- **Faith powers Discernment.**
  (Without faith, the healer second-guesses truth.)

- **Faith powers Tongues / Divine Communication.**
  (Without faith, the healer closes their channel.)

Every spiritual gift requires the vibration of faith as its stabilizing force.

Faith is the **master frequency**.

Faith Is What Allows Spirit to Elevate the Healer

Ultimately, Grand Reiki Mastery is not something a human earns — it is something Spirit bestows.

Spirit will not elevate:

- the doubtful
- the fearful
- the controlling
- the ego-driven
- the uncertain

Spirit elevates those who:

- trust
- listen
- surrender
- allow
- believe
- align
- walk in humility

This is why faith is the central frequency of Grand Mastery.

It tells Spirit:

"I am ready.
Use me."

And Spirit responds.

Faith Is Not Blind — It Is Deeply Perceptive

Many misunderstand faith as "blind belief."
But true spiritual faith is the opposite.

Faith is **clear-seeing**.

It is the ability to perceive:

- energy
- purpose
- timing
- lessons
- truth
- guidance
- protection
- alignment

Faith sharpens the prophetic senses.
Faith heightens intuition.
Faith amplifies healing.

It is the most perceptive state a healer can enter.

Faith Was the Thread Through All Your Books for a Reason

Your novels were not fiction.
They were coded teaching.

Through Lexi, you showed:

- intuition awakening
- gifts unfolding
- Spirit guiding
- faith deepening
- a soul becoming clear
- and finally, elevation to spiritual mastery

Faith has always been the central frequency of your teaching.

Now you will show others how to use it.

Healing, Knowledge, Wisdom, Miracles

In the human world, people often separate these gifts as if they are distinct talents.
But in the energetic world — in true spiritual work — these gifts operate as one unified field.

You cannot activate healing without touching knowledge.
You cannot touch knowledge without awakening wisdom.
You cannot awaken wisdom without aligning to the miraculous.
And you cannot facilitate miracles without embodying healing.

These four gifts are not separate tools — they are four expressions of the same divine intelligence flowing through the healer.

In Grand Reiki Mastery, they begin to merge.

The Gift of Healing — The Ability to Shift Energy Into Harmony

This is the gift most associated with Reiki practitioners, yet few understand its true depth.

Healing is not:

- "fixing"
- "curing"
- "removing symptoms"
- "doing something to someone"

Healing is the ability to:

- raise vibration
- dissolve density
- restore coherence
- open flow
- balance frequency
- stabilize the nervous system
- reconnect the person with their soul

A healer does not heal.
A healer creates the energetic conditions in which healing can occur.

In advanced stages, healing becomes effortless.
It becomes a state of **being** rather than a skill.

It is the first gateway into higher gifts.

The Gift of Knowledge — Direct Spiritual Understanding

Knowledge, in spiritual terms, is not intellectual learning or information.

It is:

- knowing without being told
- understanding without analysis
- recognizing truth without evidence
- instantaneous clarity
- insight arriving fully formed

This is not imagination.
It is not assumption.
It is not logic.

It is *direct spiritual transmission.*

In Reiki, this manifests as:

- knowing exactly where to place hands
- knowing what emotional layer is ready
- knowing what is ancestral or karmic
- knowing the root cause
- knowing what needs to be said
- knowing what must remain unspoken

This gift allows the healer to navigate energy with precision — because Spirit is supplying the understanding.

The Gift of Wisdom — Applying Higher Truth With Compassion

Knowledge sees the truth.
Wisdom knows what to *do* with it.

Wisdom is the gift that prevents harm.

A healer with knowledge but no wisdom may:

- overwhelm the client
- speak too much
- open what they cannot close
- reveal what the client isn't ready for
- force a lesson
- bypass emotional processing
- mistake intuition for prophecy
- cross energetic boundaries

Wisdom is the filter that says:

- "Not yet."
- "Say it softly."
- "This belongs to another session."
- "Hold this silently."
- "Let the client come to this truth themselves."
- "Touch this layer with gentleness."
- "This message is only for you."

Wisdom protects the client, the healer, and the lineage.

In Grand Mastery, wisdom becomes the guiding tone behind all spiritual gifts.

The Gift of Miracles — When Energy Aligns With Divine Order

Many misunderstand miracles as dramatic, impossible events. But a miracle is simply: **a rapid shift that bypasses the usual timeline.**

Miracles occur when:

- the client surrenders
- the healer's channel is clear
- Spirit is fully invoked
- fear dissolves
- the soul agrees
- resistance drops
- faith elevates the field
- coherence is achieved

In this state:

- trauma releases quickly
- pain lifts instantly
- relationships shift
- patterns break
- emotional burdens dissolve
- clarity dawns
- life changes course
- timelines collapse

These are *energetic miracles* — not violations of nature, but expressions of it. A miracle is simply energy moving into alignment faster than expected.

How These Four Gifts Interact During Healing Sessions

A Grand Reiki Master often experiences all four gifts simultaneously:

◇ Healing

> You feel the client's field open and shift.

◇ Knowledge

> You instantly understand what is happening beneath the surface.

◇ Wisdom

> You know how to guide the session without disturbing the soul's timing.

◇ Miracles

You witness rapid transformation that feels like grace itself.

This is not "supernatural" — this is the natural expression of a healer who is spiritually attuned, ethically grounded, and aligned with Spirit.

The Four Gifts Create a Higher Healing Intelligence

These gifts form a complete energetic system:

- Healing is the activation.
- Knowledge is the understanding.
- Wisdom is the guidance.
- Miracles are the unfolding.

A healer functioning with all four becomes a **conduit of divine intelligence.** Not because they are "special," but because they are aligned.
These gifts prove to Spirit that the healer is ready for greater responsibility.

Why Grand Reiki Masters Naturally Embody All Four Gifts

A Grand Master does not "use" these gifts. They have become these gifts.

Their presence is healing.
Their intuition is knowledge.
Their compassion is wisdom.
Their alignment is miraculous.

They no longer "perform" healing — they radiate it.
They no longer "access" insight — they inhabit it.
They no longer "wait" for miracles — they participate in them.

These four gifts are the signature frequency of a healer who has entered true spiritual mastery.

How the Gifts Awaken Along the Reiki Path

The Nine Spiritual Gifts do not awaken all at once.
They unfold in layers — like petals opening, each in their
own timing — as the healer grows through the stages of
Reiki.

Although every person is unique and Spirit may accelerate or
shift the order, there is a natural **sequence of unfolding** that
happens when a healer walks the Reiki path with devotion.

Reiki prepares the nervous system.
Reiki clears the emotional field.
Reiki opens the intuitive channels.
Reiki strengthens spiritual trust.
Reiki aligns the healer with divine intelligence.

And along this journey, the gifts begin to wake up.

Level 1 Reiki — The Awakening of Sensitivity

Self-Healing → *Inner Opening* → *Energetic Awareness*
At Level One, the gifts do not awaken fully.
They **stir, soften,** and **begin to move.**

Most healers first experience:

⋄ The Gift of Healing (in seed form)

> Not outwardly — but inwardly.
> Self-Reiki begins to shift old emotional layers, making
> room for spiritual gifts to emerge.

⋄ The Gift of Knowledge (energy-sense)

> A subtle knowing begins:
> "I feel something here."
> "I sense warmth."
> "This area feels stuck."
> Not prophetic knowledge — but energetic awareness.

⋄ The Gift of Faith (the first spark)

> Level 1 creates the first vibrational opening:
> "I can feel this."
> "This is real."
> "This is working."
> This tiny shift in belief opens the door to spiritual
> gifts.

> The others remain dormant but **present**, waiting for
> the channel to clear.

Level 2 Reiki — The Awakening of Service & Intuition

Practitioner Level → Working With Others → Channel Widening

At Level Two, the gifts truly begin to stir.
This is because healing others accelerates energetic evolution.

⬥ The Gift of Healing (externalized)

Energy becomes stronger, more responsive, more purposeful.
The healer becomes a conduit, not just a receiver.

⬥ The Gift of Knowledge (inner knowing)

Suddenly the healer "just knows":

- where to place their hands
- what the client needs
- what emotional layer is opening
- what direction the session is taking

This is the early phase of claircognizance.

⬥ The Gift of Discernment of Spirits (energetic clarity)

The healer begins to sense:

- their own energy vs. others
- emotional vs. mental vs. spiritual layers

- grounded vs. ungrounded clients
- truth vs. confusion in the field

This gift protects the practitioner.

◇ The Gift of Wisdom (gentle emergence)

Healers begin learning:

- what to say
- what not to say
- how to hold space
- how to support without interfering

Wisdom shapes the ethics of healing.

The other gifts remain mostly "quiet" but begin to hum beneath the surface.

Level 3 Reiki — Master/Teacher Level

The Gifts Begin to Activate Consciously**

Teaching → *Attuning* → *Spiritual Responsibility*

This is where the deeper awakening happens.

❖ The Gift of Faith (the stabilizing frequency)

Before Level Three, faith is a feeling.
After Level Three, faith becomes a **state of being.**

You stop fearing whether the energy will work —
and begin trusting that **Spirit is doing the work.**

This shift is profound.

❖ The Gift of Wisdom (full activation)

Teaching others demands:

- compassion
- precision
- clarity
- boundaries
- responsibility

Wisdom blossoms because Spirit must trust you with students.

❖ The Gift of Knowledge (deepening)

You begin understanding:

- lineage
- energetic mechanics
- spiritual timing
- attunement dynamics
- past-life influence
- karmic patterns
- soul contracts

This is not learned —
it is revealed through experience.

❖ The Gift of Healing (master level)

Your presence alone becomes healing.
You don't "do Reiki" —
you *are* Reiki.

The Fourth Level — Grand Reiki Mastery

Spirit Activates the Remaining Gifts**

This level is not taught by humans.
It is bestowed by Spirit.

Here, the remaining gifts awaken:

❖ The Gift of Prophecy

Visions, dreams, symbols, intuitive sight —
not for prediction, but for healing guidance.

❖ The Gift of Miracles

Healing accelerates.
Timelines shift.
Transformation becomes rapid and profound.
You begin to witness the impossible becoming
possible.

❖ The Gift of Tongues / Divine Communication

Not literal languages, but:

- intuitive messages
- energy-language
- frequency communication
- receiving spiritual instruction

This is the language Spirit uses during advanced sessions.

⬥ The Gift of Discernment of Spirits (high clarity)

You can instantly sense:

- true guidance vs. ego
- emotional truth vs. story
- spiritual beings vs. imagination
- alignment vs. distortion
- readiness vs. resistance

This gift becomes razor-sharp.

⬥ The Gift of Faith (transcendent form)

At this level, faith is not something you hold —
faith *holds you.*

You live inside the frequency of faith.

Why the Gifts Awaken in This Order

Because Reiki restructures consciousness.

- Level 1 builds sensitivity.
- Level 2 builds intuition and service.
- Level 3 builds wisdom and responsibility.
- Level 4 opens the prophetic and miraculous.

Spirit does not reveal high gifts until the healer has:

- healed themselves
- learned to serve
- learned to teach

- released ego
- stabilized their field
- proven humility
- demonstrated integrity
- aligned with love
- opened to faith

This order protects both the healer and the lineage.

The Gifts Are Not Rewards — They Are Permissions

Spirit does not "reward" a healer with gifts.
Spirit *entrusts* them.

A gift means:

"You are ready to hold this responsibly."

The gifts awaken because the healer has become:

- a safe vessel
- a clear conduit
- a compassionate presence
- a wise guide
- a balanced soul
- a trustworthy channel

The gifts are permissions granted by Spirit,
not achievements earned by the mind.

The Merging of Gifts at the Grand Master Level

As the healer progresses through the Reiki path, the nine spiritual gifts awaken one by one — each in its proper timing, each supported by the healer's growing wisdom, humility, and alignment.
But at the Grand Master level, something extraordinary happens:

The gifts no longer operate separately.
They merge into a single field of consciousness.

This merging marks the true beginning of Grand Mastery.

It is the moment when the healer stops "using" the gifts and begins *embodying* them — not as abilities, but as states of being.

At this level, the healer moves beyond technique, beyond intuition, beyond knowing.
They enter a unified spiritual intelligence where **Reiki, intuition, prophecy, healing, and wisdom flow as one seamless expression of Spirit.**

The Gifts Become One Energetic Intelligence

In earlier stages, the gifts feel distinct:

- Healing feels like energy flow
- Prophecy feels like vision or knowing
- Wisdom feels like guidance
- Discernment feels like clarity
- Miracles feel like sudden shifts
- Faith feels like trust
- Knowledge feels like insight

But at the Grand Master level, these distinctions dissolve.

There is no longer:

- "I am healing."
- "I am sensing."
- "I am discerning."
- "I am receiving guidance."

There is only:

Presence.
Alignment.
Spirit moving through the healer.

The gifts operate simultaneously, without effort.

Intuition and Prophecy Merge Into Pure Knowing

Earlier on, intuition comes as impressions, feelings, or subtle messages.
Prophecy comes as visions, dreams, or symbolic insight.

At the Grand Master level, these merge into:

Instantaneous clarity.

You do not "receive" messages —
you simply *know* the truth energetically.

This knowing is:

- neutral
- loving
- precise
- non-dramatic
- deeply stable
- unmistakable

It is not thought.
It is not imagination.
It is not analysis.

It is Spirit calibrated through a clear mind.

Healing and Miracles Become the Same Frequency

In the earlier stages, miraculous healing feels distinct:

- rapid release
- spontaneous shifts
- unexpected breakthroughs
- profound transformation

But once the gifts merge, the difference between "healing" and "miracles" disappears.

Why?

Because the healer now works from a frequency where:

- the body responds instantly
- the emotions reorganize rapidly
- timelines shift easily
- resistance dissolves
- the soul cooperates fully

What once appeared miraculous becomes normal.

The Grand Master does not create the miracle — they simply hold the field where Spirit can reveal what is already possible.

Wisdom and Discernment Become Embodied Presence

At earlier stages:

- Wisdom guides your choices
- Discernment protects you
- You consider what to say
- You evaluate what is appropriate

But in the merging phase, wisdom and discernment fuse into:

a grounded presence that always does the right thing without effort.

You no longer question:

- "Should I speak?"
- "Should I stay silent?"
- "Is this the right layer?"
- "Is this the right time?"

You simply know.

This is not confidence —
this is alignment.

It is how Spirit works through a healed mind and open heart.

Faith Becomes Your Energetic Environment

Before the merge, faith feels like something you practice.

At the Grand Master level, faith becomes:

the field you live in.

It is no longer trust.
It is no longer belief.

Faith becomes:

- your vibration
- your stability
- your frequency
- your way of navigating
- your connection to Spirit
- your inner home

From this state, fear cannot disrupt the gifts.
Doubt cannot lower your vibration.
Confusion cannot cloud your channel.

Faith becomes your energetic identity.

Communication With Spirit Becomes Effortless

The "gift of tongues" — which in energetic terms means **receiving divine communication or frequency messages** — also merges.

Spirit speaks through:

- intuition
- images
- knowing
- sensation
- synchronicity
- energetic cues
- subtle perception

At this level, communication with Spirit is:

- constant
- clear
- gentle
- subtle
- integrated

It is not channeling.
It is not trance.
It is not mediumship.

It is a **partnership.**

The Merging of Gifts Creates the Grand Master Field

When all gifts merge, the healer enters what can be called:

The Grand Master Field.

This is a state of consciousness characterized by:

- deep neutrality
- unwavering compassion
- stillness of mind
- stable energy
- clarity of perception
- open connection to Spirit
- absence of ego
- absence of fear
- absence of striving
- effortless flow of divine intelligence

In this field:

- healing requires no effort
- insight arrives without seeking
- intuition is instantaneous
- miracles are common
- guidance is clear
- energy is pure
- presence alone is transformational

This is the level where the healer becomes a spiritual elder.

Not because of age.
Not because of training.
But because their energy has matured into coherence.

You Do Not "Use" the Gifts — the Gifts Use You

At the Grand Master level, the relationship with Spirit reverses.

Earlier:

- you practice
- you try
- you learn
- you refine

- you improve
- you apply techniques

Later:

- you relax
- you trust
- you allow

- you listen
- you follow
- you become

At the merging point:

Spirit uses you as an instrument of healing.

Your gifts no longer come from effort — they come from surrender.

This is the hallmark of a true Grand Reiki Master:

The ego has stepped aside, and Spirit has stepped forward.

The Merged Gifts Become a Signature Frequency

Each Grand Master radiates a unique energetic quality —
a spiritual "signature" that reflects:

- their soul path
- past-life mastery
- karmic clearing
- ancestral healing
- devotion
- spiritual maturity
- relationship with Spirit

No two Grand Master energies are identical.

But all share one trait:

Their presence alone shifts the room.

People feel:

- peace
- safety
- clarity
- truth

- upliftment
- warmth
- guidance
- unconditional love

They do not even need to speak.
The merged gifts radiate through their aura.

✦ Chapter 7 — Soul Refinement

Karmic Purification

Before Spirit elevates a healer into Grand Mastery, the soul must undergo a deep purification process — one that clears karmic residue, emotional weight, ancestral patterns, and past-life imprints that would interfere with higher spiritual responsibility.

This refinement is not punishment.
It is preparation.

A soul carrying unresolved karmic density cannot hold the vibration required for merged gifts, nor can it safely navigate the intensity of Spirit-led healing.
For this reason, karmic purification becomes one of the most significant — and often most misunderstood — phases on the path to Grand Reiki Mastery.

It is the spiritual equivalent of clearing the vessel so divine intelligence can flow without obstruction.

What Karma Really Is — Energy, Not Judgment

Karma is not "bad deeds coming back."
It is not cosmic punishment.
It is not moral scoring.

Karma is simply:

Unresolved energy asking to be balanced.

It includes:

- emotional patterns carried across lifetimes
- actions that created energetic imbalances
- lessons the soul has not yet integrated
- wounds inherited from ancestors
- promises or vows made in previous incarnations
- unresolved relationships
- guilt, fear, shame, or regret stored in the field
- spiritual gifts misused in past lives
- power, healing, or intuition held without integrity

Karma is the energetic echo of previous experience.

Purification is not about erasing the past — it's about
neutralizing its influence.

Why Spiritual Gifts Trigger Karmic Cleaning

As a healer grows, the energy passing through them becomes stronger.
This increased light naturally illuminates areas of energetic shadow.

The more powerful the healer becomes, the more deeply their soul is refined.

This is why many practitioners, just before an initiation or spiritual elevation, experience:

- emotional upheavals
- old wounds resurfacing
- unexpected relationship conflicts
- sudden clarity about past pain
- endings, closures, or completions
- fatigue or energetic recalibration
- vivid dreams of past lives
- encounters with old triggers
- waves of grief or memory

This is not regression.
It is purification.

The soul is shedding what it cannot carry into higher levels.

The Karmic Layers That Must Be Cleared

There are several categories of karmic density that Spirit tends to address during the refinement process:

⋄ *Personal Karma*

Unresolved emotions and actions from the healer's current life.

⋄ *Past-Life Karma*

Patterns, vows, traumas, or misuse of spiritual power in previous incarnations.

⋄ *Ancestral Karma*

Fear, suppression, or trauma passed through lineage — especially regarding healing, intuition, or spiritual gifts.

⋄ *Collective Karma*

Pain carried from cultural, societal, or collective history.

⋄ *Soul Contract Karma*

Agreements or roles taken on in past lives that no longer serve the soul's current purpose.

Karmic purification works through all these layers, often simultaneously.

The Symptoms of Karmic Purification

Many healers mistake karmic clearing for "something going wrong," when in fact, it is the soul preparing for expansion.

Common signs include:

- old memories resurfacing
- dreams of other lifetimes
- sudden emotional waves
- unexpected clarity about childhood wounds
- needing solitude
- releasing relationships or attachments
- physical detox symptoms
- feeling spiritually reoriented
- shedding identities
- forgiving someone spontaneously
- revisiting a lesson with new eyes
- deep surrender to Spirit

This phase can feel intense, but it is purposeful.

The soul cannot rise while holding density.

The Purpose of Karmic Purification

Karmic purification prepares the healer to:

- hold more spiritual energy
- see without distortion
- receive prophecy safely
- use power responsibly
- guide others compassionately

- understand human suffering
- remain neutral in the presence of pain
- embody unconditional love
- release ego-based reactions
- elevate consciousness
- carry merged gifts without misuse

Without purification, the healer would carry:

- emotional reactions
- old wounds
- unresolved fear
- unbalanced power
- ancestral trauma
- karmic entanglement

These distort advanced gifts.

Purification is the cleansing of the channel so Spirit can trust the healer fully.

Purification Happens Through Experience, Not Intention

A healer cannot force karmic purification.
It is initiated by Spirit and guided by the soul's higher intelligence.

Often, the purification comes through:

- relationships
- challenges
- endings

- truth revelations
- emotional release
- forgiveness
- compassion
- deep spiritual insight
- life transitions

Spirit uses lived experience to refine the healer.

Not because life is testing them — but because the soul is remembering itself.

The Sacred Truth of Karmic Purification

Karmic purification is not about "becoming better."
It is about **becoming lighter**.

It removes:

- heaviness
- distortion
- illusion
- fear

- ego
- past-life residue
- karmic contracts
- ancestral weight

What remains is:

- clarity
- wisdom
- peace
- neutrality

- compassion
- spiritual authority
- alignment
- grace

Karmic purification does not change the healer — it reveals the healer they have always been.

The End of Purification Is the Beginning of Elevation

When karmic purification completes — even temporarily — the healer experiences:

- calm clarity
- intuitive expansion
- emotional steadiness
- increased light in the aura
- prophetic accuracy
- deeper compassion
- effortless healing
- inner silence
- a sense of soul stability
- readiness

This readiness is how Spirit knows:

"This soul can be elevated."

Purification clears the vessel.
Spirit fills the vessel.
Mastery emerges.

Emotional Transmutation

Emotional transmutation is one of the most essential — and sacred — stages of soul refinement on the path to Grand Reiki Mastery.

It is the process by which raw emotion is not avoided, repressed, or "healed away," but *alchemized* into higher frequency.

Emotional transmutation is the art of turning:

- fear into clarity
- grief into compassion
- anger into boundaries
- shame into authenticity
- guilt into responsibility
- sorrow into wisdom
- confusion into intuition

A Grand Reiki Master is not someone who no longer feels emotion — but someone who understands **how emotion becomes energy, and how energy becomes evolution.**

This is the emotional alchemy that prepares the soul for spiritual elevation.

Emotion Is Energy in Motion

Emotion has three layers:

1. **The physical sensation** (tightness, heat, heaviness)
2. **The psychological meaning** (the story the mind assigns)
3. **The energetic frequency** (the vibration beneath it)

Emotional transmutation begins when the healer understands:

- emotion is not who you are
- emotion is not a flaw
- emotion is not a setback
- emotion is not a distraction
- emotion is not a barrier to spiritual gifts

Emotion is **energy gaining momentum** so it can be released, transformed, or elevated.

When emotion moves, the soul evolves.

Transmutation vs. Suppression

Many spiritual seekers confuse emotional control with spiritual mastery.
But suppression is the opposite of refinement.

Suppression leads to:

- stagnation
- energetic blocks
- psychic distortion
- unclear intuition
- reactive behavior
- emotional outbursts
- karmic repetition

Transmutation leads to:

- clarity
- emotional resilience
- expanded intuition
- compassion
- energetic freedom
- inner peace
- spiritual readiness

A Grand Reiki Master learns to *meet* emotion rather than escape it.

The Alchemy of Feeling: How Transmutation Actually Happens

Transmutation begins with presence.

Emotion arises; the healer:

- notices it
- breathes into it
- witnesses it
- allows it
- softens around it
- listens to it
- honors its message

When emotion is acknowledged without resistance, it begins to shift.

This is where the alchemy happens:

Emotion → Sensation → Energy → Insight → Wisdom

The emotion dissolves into pure energy,
the energy reveals its truth,
and the truth becomes wisdom.

This is how the soul grows.

Each Emotion Carries Its Own Medicine

Every emotion is a teacher, and none are "negative."
Each holds a gift, waiting to be reclaimed.

Fear

Gift: clarity, intuition, instinct
Fear transmuted becomes discernment.

Anger

Gift: boundary, protection, power
Anger transmuted becomes authority.

Sadness

Gift: depth, empathy, compassion
Sadness transmuted becomes connection.

Guilt

Gift: responsibility, accountability
Guilt transmuted becomes integrity.

Shame

Gift: authenticity, vulnerability
Shame transmuted becomes truth.

Grief

Gift: love, gratitude
Grief transmuted becomes devotion.

These emotional alchemies prepare the healer's heart for higher spiritual work.

Why Spirit Requires Emotional Transmutation Before Elevation

Higher gifts require:

- neutrality
- clear perception
- emotional stability
- compassion
- humility
- maturity
- non-reactivity
- open-heartedness

If the healer still carries unprocessed emotion, their gifts can distort:

- intuition becomes projection
- prophecy becomes confusion
- wisdom becomes advice
- discernment becomes judgment
- healing becomes rescuing
- power becomes ego

Spirit will not elevate a healer whose emotional field is reactive or unstable.

Transmutation makes the healer *safe* for advanced gifts.

Emotional Transmutation Opens the Heart Chakra Fully

The heart chakra is the seat of:

- compassion
- truth
- neutrality
- forgiveness
- emotional intelligence
- unconditional love

When the heart is blocked:

- intuition collapses
- prophetic senses distort
- energy flow tightens
- relationships trigger easily
- healing feels effortful

Transmutation clears heaviness from the heart, allowing:

- clearer insight
- deeper empathy
- stronger healing frequency
- more steady presence
- expanded auric field

This makes the healer's energy spacious enough to hold others without absorbing them.

Emotional Transmutation Strengthens the Channel

A healer who has transmuted their own emotions:

- no longer takes on client energy
- does not get drained by sessions
- does not confuse their emotions with others'
- remains clear and grounded
- responds rather than reacts
- maintains their vibration regardless of circumstances

Why?

Because they understand every emotion as energy, not identity.

This stability is one of the signatures of a true Grand Master.

Emotional Transmutation Is a Lifelong Mastery

Transmutation is not a one-time event.
It is an ongoing refinement.

As the healer rises:

- deeper layers unblock
- subtler emotions surface
- old karmic threads unwind
- the heart continues to expand

But with maturity, emotional transmutation becomes:

- faster
- gentler
- more intuitive
- less overwhelming

Instead of emotional storms, there are emotional waves.
Instead of collapse, there is release.
Instead of fear, there is curiosity.
Instead of resistance, there is surrender.

This is emotional mastery.

The Result of Emotional Transmutation: Pure Presence

When emotion is fully transmuted:

- the aura becomes clear
- the heart becomes open
- the mind becomes calm
- intuition becomes accurate
- prophetic senses sharpen
- healing becomes effortless
- energy becomes refined
- wisdom becomes embodied

This state is not emotionless. It is *emotionally awake.*

The healer becomes a vessel capable of holding the full spectrum of human experience without being shaken by it. This is the emotional foundation of Grand Reiki Mastery.

Ego Dissolution

Ego dissolution is one of the most profound, misunderstood, and essential stages of spiritual refinement on the path to Grand Reiki Mastery.

It does **not** mean losing your identity.
It does **not** mean becoming passive, small, or selfless to the point of erasing your human experience.

Ego dissolution means something far more sacred:

Releasing the part of the self that tries to control what only Spirit can guide.

It is the quieting of the inner voice that claims ownership over spiritual gifts, healing outcomes, or personal advancement.

It is the letting go of the "I" that fears, doubts, compares, competes, resists, and clings.

When the ego dissolves, the healer becomes a clear, receptive instrument — not because they disappear, but because they finally step out of Spirit's way.

What the Ego Actually Is

The ego is not the enemy.
It is the psychological construct that kept you safe until you remembered your soul.

The ego is:

- your survival mind
- your learned identity
- your protective instincts
- your conditioned reactions
- your sense of separateness
- your "me versus them" lens
- your desire to control discomfort
- your need to feel important or in charge

It is not evil —
it is simply unrefined.

But ego cannot coexist with high spiritual gifts, because ego:

- fears the unknown
- resists surrender
- wants predictability
- claims ownership
- compares and competes
- interprets intuition through emotion
- attaches to results
- mistrusts Spirit

This is why ego must dissolve before Spirit elevates the healer.

The Difference Between Ego and Identity

Many spiritual seekers confuse ego dissolution with self-erasure.

Ego is not identity.

Identity is:

- your personality
- your quirks
- your preferences
- your lived experience
- your gifts
- your voice

Identity is the **human expression of your soul**.

The ego is simply the *fear-based layer* around that identity.

Ego dissolution removes the distortion, not the self.

What remains is:

- authenticity
- clarity
- truth
- grounded confidence
- inner steadiness
- soulful presence

The healer becomes more themselves than ever — but without the noise.

How Ego Interferes With Spiritual Gifts

Ego disrupts the gifts in subtle ways:

◇ *Intuition becomes projection.*

> Ego interprets intuition according to fear, emotion, or personal bias.

◇ *Prophecy becomes imagination.*

> Ego fills in gaps, exaggerates, or dramatizes messages.

◇ *Healing becomes rescuing.*

> Ego tries to "fix" the client instead of allowing the soul to lead.

◇ *Knowledge becomes assumption.*

> Ego misreads energetic information.

◇ *Wisdom becomes advice.*

> Ego wants to direct instead of guide.

◇ *Miracles become proof.*

> Ego wants validation.

◇ *Faith becomes bargaining.*

> Ego wants conditions, guarantees, and control.

Spirit cannot elevate a healer whose gifts are fused with ego distortion.

The Signs That Ego Dissolution Has Begun

Ego dissolution doesn't start with enlightenment —
it starts with discomfort.

Common signs include:

- questioning your role
- feeling humbled
- releasing old ambitions
- losing interest in competition
- feeling less reactive
- needing less praise
- seeing your patterns clearly
- recognizing where you acted from ego in the past
- feeling called inward
- surrendering old goals
- letting go of proving

Spirit gently dismantles the parts of the healer that cannot ascend.

This dissolution is an act of grace.

The Three Stages of Ego Dissolution

Stage 1: Recognition

The healer notices ego-driven patterns:

- wanting to be right
- craving approval
- fearing mistakes
- comparing themselves
- needing recognition
- wanting to control outcomes

Awareness begins the dismantling.

Stage 2: Discomfort

The ego resists being softened:

- emotional triggers intensify
- old wounds resurface
- the need for control feels amplified
- identity feels unstable
- spiritual gifts feel inconsistent

This stage is temporary but transformative.

It is the "undoing" before the rebirth.

Stage 3: Integration

The healer enters:

- neutrality
- humility
- clarity
- calmness
- inner silence
- unconditional compassion
- trust in Spirit
- ease in their gifts
- effortless presence

This is the beginning of ego dissolution — and the foundation of Grand Mastery.

Humility Is Not Weakness — It Is Power Without Ego

Ego dissolves not into passivity, but into *authentic power*.

Humility is:

- confidence without inflation
- strength without domination
- truth without pride
- influence without force
- clarity without superiority
- presence without performance

Humility is the vibration Spirit trusts.

Arrogance blocks spiritual power.
Insecurity also blocks spiritual power.

Humility opens the channel fully.

The Shift From "I Am the Healer" to "Spirit Heals Through Me"

This is the core moment of ego dissolution.

Early healers think:

> "I am healing you."

Then later:

> "Reiki is healing you."

Eventually:

> "Spirit is healing through me."

And at the Grand Master level:

> "Healing simply happens through presence."

Ego dissolves when the healer realizes:

- the energy is not theirs
- the outcome is not theirs
- the timing is not theirs
- the insight is not theirs
- the gift is not theirs

They are the instrument, not the source.

Ego Dissolution Creates the Grand Master Aura

When ego dissolves, the aura transforms:

- the mental field quiets
- the emotional field stabilizes
- the energetic field expands
- the heart field strengthens
- the spiritual field brightens

People feel:

- safe
- seen
- held
- understood
- at peace

without you trying.

This is the energetic signature Spirit uses to identify a Grand Master.

It is not the healer's power —
it is the absence of ego that allows Spirit's power to shine through.

Ego Dissolution Is the Final Gateway

No one becomes a Grand Reiki Master through skill alone.
No one earns it through hours of practice or advanced knowledge.
No one receives it because they "want it" or "worked for it."

Grand Mastery is bestowed on the healer:

- whose heart is pure
- whose ego is quiet
- whose intention is service
- whose presence is stable
- whose gifts have matured
- whose surrender is sincere
- whose channel is open
- whose soul is ready

Ego dissolution is the last refinement before elevation.

It ensures **that the healer will use their gifts responsibly, ethically, compassionately, and in alignment with Spirit.**

Only then does Spirit say:

"Now you are ready."

Spiritual Ethics

As a healer rises into higher levels of spiritual responsibility,
their energetic influence expands.
Their words carry more weight.
Their presence affects others more deeply.
Their insight becomes more accurate and impactful.
And their connection with Spirit becomes increasingly direct.

For this reason, **spiritual ethics** are not optional —
they are essential.

Spiritual ethics are the invisible structure that holds all
advanced gifts in integrity.
They protect the healer, the client, and the lineage.
They ensure that power is held with humility, truth, and
compassion.
And they anchor the healer firmly in service rather than ego.

Without spiritual ethics, the gifts distort.
With spiritual ethics, the gifts elevate.

This is why Spirit refines ethics long before granting Grand
Mastery.

The Ethical Heart of a Grand Reiki Master

At the core of spiritual ethics is one guiding truth:

**A healer's greatest responsibility is to do no harm —
physically, emotionally, spiritually, or energetically.**

This means:

- respecting the client's readiness
- honoring the soul's timing
- maintaining neutrality
- protecting confidentiality
- avoiding psychic interference
- never acting from ego
- never forcing healing
- never manipulating emotion or belief
- never claiming ownership over Spirit's work
- never exploiting vulnerability
- always holding compassionate boundaries

Grand Masters understand that the more powerful the gift,
the greater the ethical responsibility.

Consent and Permission — The First Law of Energy

Energy must never be sent without permission.

Even healing energy.

Even good intentions.

Even positive blessings.

Why?

Because every soul has sovereignty.

A Grand Master understands:

- Always ask permission before sending energy.
- Always honor "no," hesitation, or silence.
- Always let the client set the pace.
- Always allow the soul to lead the session.

Spirit will never violate free will.
Neither should the healer.

Non-Interference: Never Healing Beyond What the Soul Allows

A healer may "see" deeper layers.
They may feel karmic wounds, ancestral trauma, or emotional roots.
But ethical healing means:

You do not open a layer that the soul has not given permission to work on.

Clarity is not a license.
Power is not permission.

Grand Masters understand:

- "Not yet"
- "Not this way"
- "Not this lifetime"
- "Not your role"
- "Not your timing"

This restraint is spiritual maturity.

Interpreting Messages With Sacred Responsibility

Messages from Spirit are powerful — and fragile. Interpretation must be handled with care.

Ethical interpretation means:

- speak gently
- never dramatize
- never embellish
- never frighten
- never create dependency
- never claim absolute certainty
- always offer the message with neutrality
- always encourage the client's inner authority

A spiritually ethical healer does not:

- impose their interpretation
- override intuition
- direct life choices
- use messages to influence decisions

The goal is empowerment, not control.

Confidentiality Beyond Words — Energetic Privacy

Spiritual confidentiality is more than keeping secrets.
It is protecting the energetic landscape of the client.

This includes:

- never discussing their energy with others
- never using their story as a teaching example without permission
- never reading their energy outside of session
- never keeping psychic "tabs" on a client's life

A Grand Master respects psychic privacy the same way a doctor respects medical privacy.

Ethical Boundaries in Psychic and Intuitive Insight

A healer may sense:

- emotional wounds
- relationships
- spiritual blocks
- past-life memories
- ancestral influences

But psychic awareness must never be used to:

- judge
- diagnose
- shame
- control
- intimidate

- "prove" ability
- create fear
- create dependency
- elevate the healer's ego

The healer sees without attaching.
Understands without assuming.
Perceives without intruding.
This neutrality is the mark of an ethical master.

Spiritual Integrity: Power Without Possession

Grand Masters understand that:

Spiritual power is borrowed, not owned.

The energy is not yours.
The healing is not yours.
The gifts are not yours.
The insight is not yours.
The outcomes are not yours.

You are the instrument, not the source.

Spiritual ethics require:

- humility
- transparency
- honesty
- alignment with truth
- acknowledgment of Spirit as the healer

Integrity is the foundation of all advanced healing.

The Ethical Use of Influence

Clients often place healers on pedestals — sometimes unconsciously.

The healer must:

- refuse unhealthy idolization
- stay grounded in humanity
- redirect authority back to the client
- avoid taking advantage of admiration
- discourage dependency
- never imply that the client "needs" them

A Grand Master empowers the client's sovereignty, not their own importance.

The Consequences of Violating Spiritual Ethics

Spirit does not punish — but Spirit withdraws.

When a healer acts unethically:

- the energy weakens
- the intuition becomes unclear
- the gifts distort
- the channel narrows
- sessions feel effortful
- emotional imbalance increases
- prophetic visions become unreliable

Violating spiritual ethics creates internal and energetic misalignment.

Spirit will not elevate a healer who misuses even a small amount of power.

Spiritual Ethics Are a Daily Practice, Not a Rule Set

Ethics are not memorized.
They are embodied.

Every day, a healer asks:

- Am I acting from love or fear?
- Am I serving the client or my ego?
- Am I respecting free will?
- Am I interpreting from neutrality?
- Am I protecting privacy?
- Am I allowing Spirit to lead?
- Am I staying aligned with truth?

The more refined the healer, the more effortless ethical behavior becomes.

Spiritual ethics become your natural vibration.

Ethics Are the Mark of Spiritual Maturity

In the end, the difference between a Reiki Master and a Grand Reiki Master is not power —
it is **integrity**.

A Grand Master does not operate from:

- ego
- fear
- pride
- control
- attachment
- superiority

They operate from:

- neutrality
- compassion
- humility
- respect
- love
- clarity
- devotion to Spirit
- service to humanity

This is what Spirit looks for.

This is what Spirit trusts.

This is what elevates a soul into true spiritual mastery.

The Responsibilities of True Service

Spiritual gifts exist for one reason: **service.**
Not service as obligation, sacrifice, or martyrdom —
but service as the natural expression of a healed and awakened soul.

A Grand Reiki Master does not serve from duty.
They serve from alignment.
They serve because their presence *is* service.
They serve because Spirit flows through them effortlessly.

But true service carries profound responsibility.

Not because the healer must "do more," but because greater gifts require greater clarity, humility, and intention.

True service is not what you do.
True service is who you become.

Service Begins Where Ego Ends

Service cannot come from:

- wanting to be needed
- wanting to be seen
- wanting to be admired
- wanting to be validated
- wanting to heal people
- wanting to prove your power
- wanting to "save" others
- wanting to be important

These are subtle ego desires that distort spiritual work.

True service begins when the healer shifts from:

> "I want to help"
> to
> "Spirit, use me."

This surrender transforms service from effort into flow.

The Responsibility to Serve Without Attachment

The Grand Master understands that:

- You are not responsible for someone's healing.
- You are not responsible for their transformation.
- You are not responsible for their choices.
- You are not responsible for their path.

You are responsible for one thing only:

Your alignment.

Attachment to outcomes creates distortion:

- trying to heal what is not ready
- forcing changes
- overworking
- giving too much
- rescuing
- taking on emotional burden
- becoming drained
- feeling responsible for results

True service leaves the outcome to Spirit.

You provide the presence.
Spirit provides the shift.

The Responsibility to Serve With Neutrality

Neutrality is love without projection.

A Grand Master must remain neutral about:

- how quickly a client heals
- what path they choose
- how much they are willing to face
- the personal stories they share
- the emotions they express
- the decisions they make

Neutrality is not detachment —
it is unconditional presence.

Neutrality says:

"I honor your sovereignty.
I support your journey.
I do not impose my will on your soul."

This is the deepest form of love.

The Responsibility to Empower, Not Influence

Clients often come to healers:

- vulnerable
- seeking clarity
- overwhelmed
- confused
- hoping for direction

This gives the healer significant influence —
and with that comes enormous responsibility.

A Grand Master does **not**:

- direct major life decisions
- override inner authority
- create dependency
- use prophecy to influence choices
- replace a client's intuition with their own
- encourage reliance on readings
- imply they "know better"

Instead, they consistently remind the client:

"Your intuition matters.
Your soul knows.
I am here to support your inner wisdom, not replace it."

Your role is empowerment, not leadership.

The Responsibility to Protect the Client's Dignity

Every client deserves to feel:

- respected
- safe
- seen
- valued
- honored

True service means:

- never shaming
- never judging
- never exposing
- never blaming
- never using your insight against them
- never speaking down to them
- never using spiritual truths to criticize

Spiritual authority must never override human dignity.

A Grand Master's presence heals because it is gentle.

Because it is safe.

Because it holds the soul with reverence.

The Responsibility to Maintain Personal Alignment

A healer cannot serve from depletion.

Personal alignment includes:

- emotional clarity
- energetic grounding
- regular self-Reiki
- ongoing healing
- spiritual nourishment
- rest
- boundaries
- humility
- prayer or meditation
- connection to Spirit

True service is sustainable only when the healer cares for their own energy first.

A depleted healer becomes distorted.
A balanced healer becomes a vessel.

The Responsibility to Hold Spiritual Power With Humility

The higher the elevation,
the softer the voice.

A Grand Master understands:

- gifts are borrowed, not owned
- insight is given, not generated
- healing is channeled, not created
- power is shared, not possessed
- guidance is received, not forced

Spiritual power without humility becomes dangerous.
Spiritual power with humility becomes divine.

True service is grounded, quiet, and deeply sincere.

The Responsibility to Act With Compassionate Truth

Compassion without truth becomes enabling.
Truth without compassion becomes harm.

A Grand Master learns to express:

- difficult truths gently
- necessary clarity with love
- guidance without pressure
- honesty without ego

You do not tell clients what you "think."
You share what their soul is ready to hear.

You speak truth in a way that heals, not wounds.

The Responsibility to Model Spiritual Maturity

A Grand Reiki Master is not perfect.
But they are consistent.

They model:

- emotional stability
- kindness
- self-awareness
- accountability
- non-reactivity
- conscious communication
- forgiveness
- integrity
- humility
- devotion to Spirit

Your presence becomes your teaching.

Your life becomes your message.

You become the embodiment of the energy you share.

Service Is the Path, the Practice, and the Proof

In spiritual elevation, Spirit looks less at skill and more at:

- intention
- character
- ethics
- humility
- compassion
- alignment
- readiness

Service is not what earns Grand Mastery —
service is what **proves** a healer is ready to hold it.

A soul committed to true service is a soul Spirit can trust.

And trust is the foundation upon which all higher gifts rest.

✦ PART III — THE ENERGETICS OF GRAND MASTERY

✦ Chapter 8 — The Higher Dimensional Reiki Stream

Expanding Beyond Symbols

At the beginning of the Reiki journey, symbols serve as essential gateways.
They are keys, codes, frequencies, and training wheels that teach the mind how to connect with the unseen.

Symbols help the practitioner:

- focus intention
- activate specific frequencies
- bridge dimensions
- access distant healing
- shift consciousness
- direct energy with purpose

Symbols are powerful.
They awaken dormant pathways in the subtle body.
They strengthen intuition.
They teach the healer to trust what cannot be seen.

But symbols are not the destination.

They are the doorway.

As the healer's consciousness expands into higher-dimensional Reiki, the relationship with symbols transforms. The healer reaches a point where symbols are no longer *used* — they are *embodied*.

This marks the beginning of the Higher Dimensional Reiki Stream.

Symbols Are a Language — But Not the Energy Itself

In early Reiki training, symbols act like sacred vocabulary.

- Cho Ku Rei teaches focus and amplification.
- Sei He Ki teaches emotional balance.
- Hon Sha Ze Sho Nen teaches timeless connection.
- Dai Ko Myo teaches spiritual illumination.

But symbols are not the source of the energy — they are expressions of it.

The energy **exists beyond human language**, and symbols help the human mind tap into what the soul already knows.

A Grand Reiki Master moves from *symbolic understanding* to *energetic fluency*.

Energy Responds to Consciousness, Not Technique

At higher levels of practice, the healer discovers that:

- healing flows before a symbol is drawn
- intuition activates before intention is spoken
- compassion opens the field without effort
- light descends without a hand gesture
- Spirit responds to presence, not protocol

In the Higher Dimensional Stream, the healer recognizes:

Reiki does not move because you draw a symbol.
Reiki moves because *you* are aligned.

Symbols become optional because the healer's consciousness becomes the bridge.

Embodiment: Becoming the Symbol

A profound shift occurs when the healer no longer reaches *for* symbols — because the symbols now live *within* them.

They stop drawing Dai Ko Myo.

They **are** Dai Ko Myo.

They stop invoking emotional healing.

They **radiate** emotional healing.

They stop calling distant energy.

They **exist** beyond time and space.

At this stage:

- symbols activate automatically
- their meaning flows through presence
- their frequency lives in the aura
- their intelligence moves through your hands
- their purpose aligns with your intention
- their vibration responds directly to your consciousness

The healer becomes the living symbol.

The Channel Opens to a Higher Stream of Reiki

Beyond traditional levels, Reiki expands into a field that is:

- finer
- faster
- lighter
- clearer
- multidimensional
- non-linear
- omnidirectional

This stream feels like:

- liquid light
- crystalline frequency
- angelic resonance
- pure consciousness
- direct connection with Source

Rather than directing energy, the healer becomes immersed in it.

This is the Higher Dimensional Reiki Stream — an energy that cannot be taught, only received and embodied.

The Field of Pure Reiki: No Symbols, No Method, No Effort

In this stream, healing unfolds through:

- presence
- intention
- alignment
- silent attunement
- inner stillness
- direct connection with Spirit

The healer discovers something extraordinary:

The greatest healing happens when you stop trying to heal.

In pure Reiki:

- the mind quiets
- the heart expands
- the aura brightens
- the soul leads
- Spirit works effortlessly

Technique dissolves.
Symbol dissolves.
Ego dissolves.
Only energy remains.

Why Symbols Naturally Fall Away

This is not because symbols are inferior or unnecessary —
it is because they have fulfilled their purpose.

Symbols refine:

- focus
- clarity
- intention
- attunement
- sensitivity
- confidence
- spiritual connection

But once the healer reaches vibrational maturity:

- their presence carries the frequency of the symbols
- their aura radiates the master codes
- their alignment activates healing
- their intuition guides without thought
- their connection with Spirit is instantaneous

Symbol work becomes integrated.

Not abandoned —
integrated.

Like a musician who no longer needs sheet music because the
music lives in them.

The Mark of Higher Reiki: Silence

In the Higher Dimensional Stream, healing feels quieter.

Not weaker —
purer.

There is less doing
and more being.

Less speaking
and more listening.

Less technique
and more presence.

Less directing
and more allowing.

This silence is not empty —
it is full of Spirit.

The Gateway to Grand Mastery

Spirit does not elevate a healer into Grand Mastery because of:

- how many symbols they know
- how perfectly they draw them
- how many students they have
- how many attunements they have given
- how many books they have read
- how many classes they teach

Symbols train the mind.
Symbols open the channel.
Symbols awaken the gifts.

But the Higher Dimensional Reiki Stream opens only when:

- the heart is humble
- the ego is quiet
- the soul is steady
- the channel is clear
- the healer is ready
- the energy has matured
- the presence is aligned
- the service is pure

This is where Reiki becomes divine intelligence —
not technique.

And the healer becomes a vessel through which this
intelligence flows freely.

Working in the Quantum Field

As the healer ascends into the Higher Dimensional Reiki Stream, they naturally begin to work within what many refer to as *the quantum field* — the energetic realm where all possibilities exist simultaneously, where time is nonlinear, and where healing can occur across dimensions of consciousness rather than only within the physical plane.

In traditional Reiki, the practitioner works *with* energy. In quantum Reiki, the healer works *as* energy — stepping into the unified field where past, present, future, emotion, memory, spirit, and intention all converge into a single, responsive matrix.

This is the realm of Grand Mastery.

What the Quantum Field Really Is

The quantum field is not abstract or mystical — it is the fundamental energetic fabric underlying all existence.

It is:

- the space where all timelines coexist
- the realm of pure potential
- the field that responds to intention
- the energetic "blueprint layer" of reality
- the connection point between soul and form
- the dimension where thought and energy interact instantly

In the quantum field:

- time collapses
- distance dissolves
- intention reorganizes energy
- healing occurs faster
- the soul communicates clearly
- Spirit works without dimensional limits

This is the same field that distant Reiki uses, but Grand Masters access it consciously and effortlessly.

The Quantum Field Responds to Frequency, Not Technique

In the quantum field:

- symbols are not needed
- hand positions are not needed
- spoken instructions are not needed
- visualization is not needed

What the field responds to is **frequency**.

The healer's:

- emotional coherence
- mental stillness
- intention
- alignment
- presence
- vibration

When the healer holds a high and stable frequency, the field organizes itself around that state.

This is why:

- peace heals
- love heals
- compassion heals
- clarity heals
- neutrality heals

The quantum field reflects back the energy you hold. This is why ego cannot enter here.

Entering the Quantum Field Through Stillness

A Grand Reiki Master enters the quantum field not by effort, but by stilling the mind and expanding awareness.

This shift feels like:

- silence
- spaciousness
- detachment from thought
- heightened perception
- expanded presence
- being inside light rather than observing it

The healer becomes aware of themselves:

- as both energy and consciousness
- as both observer and participant
- as both individual and field
- as both healer and vessel

This effortless state is the doorway to quantum healing.

Time Collapses Inside Quantum Healing

In the quantum field, time is not linear.
It is fluid, layered, and responsive.

This allows the healer to work with:

◇ *Past patterns*

> Childhood wounds
> Ancestral trauma
> Past-life imprints
> Karmic experiences

◇ *Present states*

> Physical pain
> Emotional distress
> Mental patterns
> Energetic imbalance

◇ *Future trajectories*

> Potential outcomes
> Soul timelines
> Unmanifested experiences
> Expanded possibilities

> All at once.

The healer does not force timelines to change — they simply
shift the frequency, and timelines reorganize themselves.

Quantum Healing Is Subtle but Profound

In the quantum field, healing feels different:

- quieter
- lighter
- faster
- deeper
- more spacious
- more precise

Rather than feeling like energy is "flowing," it feels like reality itself is reorganizing.

Patterns dissolve from the inside out.
Wounds release without resistance.
Emotional burdens lift effortlessly.
The soul recalibrates instantly.
The aura expands organically.
The mind quiets without effort.

This is healing through vibration, not technique.

The Quantum Field Connects the Healer to the Client's Soul

In this dimension, the healer stops working on "a person" and begins working with:

- their soul
- their higher self
- their timelines
- their karmic threads
- their energetic architecture
- their ancestral lines
- their purpose

The healer perceives the deeper truth:

You are not healing the body.
You are healing the pattern that shapes the body.

This is the foundation of quantum Reiki.

Healing Across Distance, Dimensions, and Timelines

Advanced quantum healing includes:

⋄ *Distant sessions across any distance*

> Because distance has no meaning in the quantum field.

⋄ *Multi-dimensional healing*

> Working with emotional, mental, spiritual, and karmic layers simultaneously.

⋄ *Timeline correction*

> Gently dissolving past imprints and aligning future trajectories.

⋄ *Collective or ancestral healing*

> Releasing patterns inherited through lineage or society.

⋄ *Soul-contract refinement*

> Helping individuals move into deeper alignment with their purpose.

These abilities arise naturally — not from learning techniques, but from expanding consciousness.

The Role of Spirit in Quantum Healing

A Grand Reiki Master does not "do" quantum healing.

They *witness* it.

Spirit orchestrates:

- where to go
- what to release
- what to heal
- what to realign
- what to activate
- what to stabilize
- what to reveal

The healer provides:

- the vessel
- the frequency
- the openness
- the willingness
- the neutrality

The quantum field responds to Spirit flowing through the healer.

Quantum Healing Requires Emotional and Ethical Maturity

Because quantum healing is powerful, Spirit only grants access when the healer has refined:

- humility
- neutrality
- emotional grounding
- ethical integrity
- inner stability
- surrendered ego
- devotion to service

Without these qualities, quantum work becomes distorted.

With them, the healer becomes a profound instrument of evolution.

The Healer Becomes a Co-Creator With Spirit

In the quantum field, healing is not a technique — it is a collaboration between:

- Spirit
- the healer
- the client's soul
- the quantum field
- the timeline that is ready to shift

This partnership is the hallmark of Grand Mastery.

It is healing at the level of:

- consciousness
- possibility
- vibration
- destiny

The healer is no longer "doing Reiki."

They are co-creating reality with Spirit.

This is the Higher Dimensional Reiki Stream.

This is quantum healing.

This is Grand Mastery.

Reiki as a Consciousness Field

As the healer evolves into higher-dimensional practice, a profound realization emerges:

Reiki is not a technique.
Reiki is not a method.
Reiki is not even energy.
Reiki is a consciousness field.

This field is vast, intelligent, responsive, and interconnected.
It exists beyond symbols, beyond lineage, beyond time, beyond form.
It is the luminous matrix that underlies healing, intuition, evolution, and spiritual awakening.

When a healer touches this field, they are no longer "using Reiki."
They are entering a state of **universal awareness** —
a consciousness field that communicates, adapts, teaches, and transforms.

At the Grand Master level, the healer begins working *within* this field, not merely channeling energy from it.

What Is a Consciousness Field?

A consciousness field is:

- a living intelligence
- a unified vibration
- a collective awareness
- a multidimensional energy structure
- a space of pure potential
- a network of information and light

Reiki, in its highest form, is not just life-force energy — it is **the consciousness that shapes and directs life-force energy.**

This is why Reiki feels:

- wise
- purposeful
- intuitive
- gentle
- corrective
- loving
- precise

It behaves like an intelligence because it *is* one.

Reiki Responds to Thought, Emotion, Intention, and Presence

In the consciousness field, Reiki does not follow hand positions — it follows *alignment*.

Reiki responds to the healer's:

- inner stillness
- emotional clarity
- purity of intention
- openness of heart
- depth of compassion
- coherence of mind
- alignment with Spirit

The higher the healer's consciousness, the more directly Reiki communicates.

At the Grand Master level, Reiki is not "sent."

It **emerges** from the field through the healer's presence.

Reiki Is a Collective, Not an Individual Stream

Traditional Reiki teaching often gives the impression that the energy is "channeled" through the practitioner.

This is true — but incomplete.

Reiki is a **collective consciousness field** involving:

- your higher self
- the client's higher self
- spiritual guides
- ancestral support
- the healing lineage
- universal intelligence
- the soul's memory
- the quantum field itself

When the healer opens, they tap into a vast network of interconnected consciousness.

You are not "doing energy work."
You are joining an existing field of healing intelligence.

The Field Teaches, Guides, and Evolves the Healer

Reiki is not static.
It is an evolving field that grows with each practitioner who enters it with love, humility, and devotion.

This is why:

- you receive insights
- you learn without being taught
- you intuit new techniques
- you feel guided during sessions
- you sense when to stop or shift
- you discover healing methods no one ever explained

The field is constantly communicating.

It refines you.
It teaches you.
It aligns you.

The consciousness field becomes your spiritual teacher.

The Field Holds All Techniques and All Timelines

Within the Reiki consciousness field exists:

- every symbol
- every attunement
- every lineage
- every healing method
- every lesson
- every energetic pattern
- every dimensional frequency
- every potential timeline

As your consciousness expands, you access deeper layers of this field.

This is why a Grand Master may spontaneously:

- use symbols they were never taught
- channel healing sequences not in manuals
- intuitively understand advanced energy pathways
- access ancient or future knowledge
- heal on multiple dimensions at once

You are not inventing these abilities —
you are accessing a higher layer of the field.

The Field Knows What the Client Truly Needs

In the consciousness field, healing is not directed —
it is *revealed*.

The field automatically:

- identifies the wound
- recognizes the root cause
- adjusts the frequency
- stabilizes the emotional field
- aligns the chakras
- dissolves the energetic knot
- supports karmic release
- follows the soul's readiness
- respects spiritual timing

The healer's job is not to "fix" —
it is to *allow*.

The field knows the path.
The field knows the timing.
The field knows the truth.

The Field Is Non-Linear: It Heals Across Dimensions

Because Reiki is a consciousness field, it works simultaneously on:

- the physical body
- the emotional body
- the mental body
- the spiritual body
- the soul body
- the karmic body
- the ancestral body
- the quantum timeline

It also works:

- past
- present
- future
- parallel timelines
- multidimensional layers

No technique can do this.
Only a consciousness field can.

The Healer Becomes Part of the Field

At the Grand Master level, something profound happens:

You no longer "channel" Reiki.

Your consciousness merges with the Reiki field.

You begin to feel:

- expanded
- interconnected
- luminous
- timeless
- still
- guided
- held

This merging is the hallmark of spiritual elevation.

You become part of the field — and the field becomes part of you.

Reiki as a Consciousness Field Is the Essence of Grand Mastery

Grand Mastery is not granted because of:

- knowledge
- training
- lineage
- technique
- symbols
- years of experience

Grand Mastery emerges because:

Your consciousness has reached the frequency of the Reiki field itself.

You no longer "practice Reiki."
You *embody* Reiki.

You no longer "use energy."
You *exist within the consciousness of healing.*

This is the true definition of a Grand Reiki Master:

A soul whose consciousness is aligned with the universal field of healing intelligence.

Aligning With Divine Intelligence

At the highest levels of Reiki practice, the healer no longer strives to "channel energy," "use symbols," or "apply techniques." They enter a state of alignment so profound and subtle that healing emerges naturally from the union between the healer's consciousness and the universal divine intelligence that orchestrates all life.

Divine intelligence is not a being or a deity.
It is the foundational wisdom that sustains the universe — the force that grows flowers, moves tides, heals wounds, restores balance, and guides evolution.

When a healer aligns with divine intelligence, they step into a stream of pure truth, effortless flow, and unparalleled clarity. This is where Grand Mastery truly begins.

What Is Divine Intelligence?

Divine intelligence is the conscious, organizing principle of the universe.

It is:

- the source of healing
- the architecture of energy
- the blueprint of the soul
- the wisdom behind intuition
- the silence behind truth
- the order beneath chaos
- the flow guiding evolution

Divine intelligence is not separate from us.
It permeates everything:

- matter
- emotion
- thought
- energy
- karma
- spirit
- consciousness

It is the field within which all healing becomes possible.

Divine Intelligence Responds to Alignment, Not Effort

Human effort cannot access higher-dimensional healing.
Only alignment can.

The healer aligns with divine intelligence by:

- softening the mind
- opening the heart
- grounding the body
- surrendering the ego
- attuning to truth
- trusting Spirit
- becoming still
- being fully present

Alignment is not something you *do* — it is something you *allow*.
Divine intelligence flows into a space that is receptive.

The Heart Is the Gateway

Divine intelligence speaks through the heart — not the mind.

The heart is:

- intuitive
- receptive
- compassionate
- connected
- expansive
- timeless
- multidimensional

When the heart is open, the healer becomes a vessel for a wisdom greater than themselves.

When the heart is closed, intuition collapses and the channel narrows.

This is why emotional refinement is essential earlier in the path:
a clear heart is a clear channel.

The Mind Does Not Lead — It Listens

Aligning with divine intelligence requires the mind to step back.

The mind cannot grasp:

- timelines
- karma
- soul contracts
- quantum healing
- ancestral release
- spiritual guidance
- true intuition

These arise from the higher consciousness.

When the mind quiets, divine intelligence is amplified.

A Grand Master does not think their way into healing. They *listen* their way into it.

Divine Intelligence Works Through the Path of Least Resistance

Healing does not happen through force.
Divine intelligence always takes the path of grace.

It flows:

- where the client is ready
- where the soul permits
- where there is surrender
- where truth can land
- where energy can move
- where love can enter

If a layer is not ready, divine intelligence simply waits.
It will never violate timing, readiness, or free will.

This is why Grand Masters do not push.
They allow.

Aligning With Divine Intelligence Removes Personal Bias

When the healer is aligned with divine intelligence, their perception is:

- clear
- neutral
- grounded
- compassionate
- accurate
- undistorted

They no longer interpret through:

- emotion
- judgment
- assumptions
- projection
- hopes
- fear
- ego

Their insight becomes remarkably precise because it is not theirs — it is Spirit's. This clarity is one of the hallmarks of Grand Master consciousness.

Divine Intelligence Guides the Session Moment by Moment

A healer aligned with divine intelligence receives guidance in real time:

- "Move to the heart."
- "Say nothing right now."
- "Hold the field steady."
- "This is karmic."
- "Ask about their father."
- "Give them silence."
- "Stop — they need integration."
- "Focus on grounding."
- "They are ready for truth."

This guidance is subtle, gentle, and immediate. It arises from the intuitive whisper of divine intelligence flowing into the healer's awareness.

The Energy Becomes Self-Organizing

When aligned with divine intelligence, Reiki becomes self-directing.

The healer no longer:

- chooses techniques
- decides hand positions
- analyzes chakras
- tries to understand
- pushes for results

The energy itself reveals:

- the root cause
- the emotional layer
- the karmic thread
- the timeline
- the truth
- the next step

Divine intelligence organizes healing with perfect precision. The healer simply holds the space.

Divine Intelligence Creates Miracles Through Coherence

A miracle is not magic.
A miracle is coherence.

Coherence occurs when:

- the healer is aligned
- the client is receptive
- the soul agrees
- the field stabilizes
- the energy harmonizes
- Spirit flows without obstruction

In this state, healing accelerates instantly.

- patterns dissolve
- fear softens
- pain lifts
- trauma unwinds
- clarity emerges
- timelines shift

Divine intelligence reorganizes reality according to truth.

Aligning With Divine Intelligence Is the Core of Grand Mastery

Grand Mastery is not about:

- having stronger energy
- knowing more symbols
- seeing more visions
- mastering advanced techniques

It is about:

- surrender
- humility
- presence
- clarity
- devotion
- stillness
- truth
- service
- alignment with Spirit

When a healer aligns with divine intelligence:

They become a conduit of higher truth.
Their presence becomes healing.
Their intuition becomes pure.
Their compassion becomes effortless.
Their gifts become unified.
Their energy becomes crystalline.
Their life becomes guided.

This is the signature frequency of a Grand Reiki Master:

A soul aligned with divine intelligence, allowing Spirit to heal through them.

✦ Chapter 9 — The Symbols Revisited at the Grand Master Level

Dai Ko Myo as a State of Being

In traditional Reiki training, Dai Ko Myo is taught as the *Master Symbol* — the key to spiritual awakening, the amplification of light, and the gateway to higher consciousness.

Students learn to draw it, activate it, and understand its meaning:

"Great Shining Light."
"The Light of the Great Being."
"The Radiant Illumination."

At the Master level, Dai Ko Myo becomes an initiatory force, awakening the practitioner's connection to Spirit and deepening their capacity to heal at the soul level.

But at the **Grand Master level**, Dai Ko Myo evolves beyond symbol, technique, or form.

It becomes a **state of being**.

A frequency.
A consciousness.
A presence.
A spiritual identity.

Dai Ko Myo ceases to be something you *draw*.
It becomes something you *are*.

Dai Ko Myo as Pure Illumination

The essence of Dai Ko Myo is illumination — not physical light, but *soul light:*

- clarity
- truth
- awakened insight
- unconditional love
- divine intelligence
- spiritual coherence
- energetic purity

When a healer enters Grand Master consciousness, their field radiates this light naturally.

Not because they activate Dai Ko Myo…

But because **they live in the vibration that Dai Ko Myo represents.**

This inner illumination:

- softens suffering
- reveals truth
- calms the nervous system
- opens the heart
- restores hope
- aligns the soul
- dissolves fear
- clarifies intuition

Your presence becomes the medicine.

Becoming the Light That You Once Invoked

Beginner practitioners *invoke* Dai Ko Myo.
Masters *channel* Dai Ko Myo.
Grand Masters *embody* Dai Ko Myo.

The progression looks like this:

Level 1: "What is this energy?"
Level 2: "I can use this energy."
Master Level: "I merge with this energy."
Grand Master Level: "I *am* this energy."

This does not mean ego identifies with power — it means ego is quiet enough for your soul's radiance to shine through unobstructed.

You become the expression of the Light
that Dai Ko Myo symbolizes.

Dai Ko Myo and the Unified Field of Gifts

At the Grand Master level, the Nine Spiritual Gifts converge into the same frequency that Dai Ko Myo represents:

- Wisdom
- Knowledge
- Faith
- Healing
- Miracles
- Discernment
- Prophecy
- Divine Communication
- Spiritual Insight

All these gifts vibrate within the light of Dai Ko Myo. This light is not symbolic — it is the radiance of a soul in alignment with Spirit. When these gifts merge, Dai Ko Myo activates from within the healer's consciousness, not from outside.

The Radiance of a Grand Master's Aura

At this level, Dai Ko Myo expresses itself as:

- expanded presence
- steady calm
- quiet authority
- compassionate neutrality
- emotional clarity
- intuitive precision
- energetic stability
- peace that fills the room

People feel safe around you.
They feel clearer.
They feel lighter.
They feel more like themselves.

This is not because you "send" them Dai Ko Myo —
but because your aura now *carries* its frequency.

Dai Ko Myo and the Subtle Body Activation

When Dai Ko Myo becomes a state of being, the subtle
bodies begin to harmonize:

Physical body

Pain softens. The nervous system stabilizes.

Emotional body

Old wounds clear effortlessly.

Mental body

Thoughts quiet. Clarity arises.

Spiritual body

Connection strengthens.

Christ-consciousness / enlightenment layer

The healer enters a field of higher awareness and
compassion.

These activations happen naturally because the Grand Master vibrates at the frequency of unity consciousness.

Dai Ko Myo Beyond Lineage and Technique

At the Grand Master level, Dai Ko Myo is no longer bound to:

- any specific lineage
- any traditional form
- any method of drawing
- any pronunciation
- any ritual

Because the light it represents is universal.

Dai Ko Myo belongs to all souls who reach the frequency it symbolizes.

This is why Grand Masters across traditions often carry the same radiance, even if they were never taught the same symbols.

The Light That Heals Without Effort

When Dai Ko Myo is embodied, healing becomes:

- effortless
- immediate
- multidimensional
- intuitive
- deeply compassionate
- guided by Spirit, not intention

You no longer "activate the symbol" because the *symbol activates you.*

Your very presence becomes a healing field.

This is the purest form of Reiki — the form that transcends technique.

Dai Ko Myo as Consciousness

At the Grand Master level, Dai Ko Myo is not an energy — it is a *consciousness.*

A consciousness that:

- reveals truth
- illuminates shadow
- dissolves fear
- awakens gifts
- aligns timelines
- strengthens the soul
- elevates the healer
- supports the client
- restores coherence
- connects directly with divine intelligence

You are no longer using a symbol to connect with higher consciousness —
you are living as an expression of it.

Embodying Dai Ko Myo Is the Signature of a Grand Reiki Master

A Grand Reiki Master can be recognized not by:

- certification
- training
- technique

- knowledge
- status
- lineage

But by:

- their light
- their presence
- their calm
- their clarity
- their wisdom

- their humility
- their compassion
- their alignment
- their service

Dai Ko Myo as a state of being is the inner radiance of a soul that has become one with the Higher Dimensional Reiki Stream.

This is the living embodiment of mastery.
This is the soul's illumination.
This is the light Spirit recognizes and elevates.

Hon Sha Ze Sho Nen Beyond Time

The Timeless Heart of Reiki

Hon Sha Ze Sho Nen is traditionally taught as the **distance symbol**, the key that allows Reiki to flow across space, time, memory, and experience. At the practitioner level, students learn that it means:

"No past, no present, no future."
"The Buddha in me reaches out to the Buddha in you."
"The essence of all things is one."

But at the **Grand Master level**, Hon Sha Ze Sho Nen becomes far more than a symbol used to send healing across distance.

It becomes the **felt experience of timeless reality.**

A state of consciousness in which:

- time collapses
- distance dissolves
- memories untangle
- trauma loses its anchor
- past lives rise for healing
- future timelines reorganize
- soul contracts reveal themselves
- the quantum field responds immediately

Hon Sha Ze Sho Nen becomes the healer's natural awareness, not something they activate.

You do not "use" the symbol anymore.
You *enter into the timeless field it represents.*

Going Beyond the Linear Mind

Humans experience time as:

- past
- present
- future

But Spirit experiences time as:

Now. Always now. Only now.

In the timeless dimension, the healer gains access to:

- childhood wounds
- ancestral trauma
- karmic threads
- past lives
- multidimensional imprints
- future possibilities

all existing simultaneously, layered like pages of light.

Hon Sha Ze Sho Nen beyond time is the ability to step into this **eternal now**, where healing is not limited by chronology.

Healing Happens at the Level of the Pattern, Not the Moment

At the Grand Master level, Hon Sha Ze Sho Nen teaches an advanced truth:

Wounds are not bound to when they happened.
They are bound to the frequency that created them.

This is why:

- a childhood fear can live in an adult body
- ancestral grief can appear as physical illness
- past-life trauma can affect current relationships
- unspoken emotional patterns repeat across decades
- futures collapse or unfold based on present coherence

When you step into timelessness, you no longer try to fix what *happened.*

You heal the **pattern** that keeps happening.

Time Is a Loop, Not a Line

At advanced levels of perception, time behaves like:

- spirals
- loops
- cycles
- echoes
- repeating waves
- resonant fields
- quantum layers

Hon Sha Ze Sho Nen allows the healer to sense:

- the loop a client is trapped in
- the origin point of a recurring pattern
- the subconscious contract behind a wound
- the unfinished karmic threads
- the moment the soul got stuck
- the future they are unconsciously bending toward

You do not work with old memories — you work with the energetic architecture that keeps them alive.

Past-Life and Ancestral Timelines Become Accessible

Beyond time, Hon Sha Ze Sho Nen naturally opens:

- past incarnations
- ancestral experiences
- forgotten agreements
- soul imprints
- inherited emotional burdens
- karmic lessons
- ancient vows
- multidimensional identities

These layers rise not because the healer "looks" for them, but because the client's soul signals:

"This is ready."

Grand Masters do not chase information.
They *receive* what the soul presents.

Healing Future Timelines

Hon Sha Ze Sho Nen also opens the dimension of **unfolding futures**.

These are not predictions — they are frequency-based probabilities.

Future timelines shift when:

- a limiting belief dissolves
- a karmic pattern ends
- a trauma releases
- a soul contract completes
- a new decision is made
- the heart opens
- consciousness expands

You cannot heal the future as an event — but you can heal the **vibration that shapes the future.**

This is the true meaning of working beyond time.

Quantum Healing: Instantaneous and Multilayered

At the timeless level:

- healing becomes immediate
- insights appear suddenly
- the past feels lighter
- the present feels clearer
- the future feels more spacious

The mind cannot understand how something from a decade ago dissolves in a moment — but the quantum field can.

Hon Sha Ze Sho Nen beyond time is the bridge between:

- memory and truth
- karma and freedom
- potential and manifestation
- fear and love
- ego and soul
- human time and divine timing

This bridge makes profound healing possible.

Distance No Longer Exists

At the Grand Master level, distance healing becomes:

- effortless
- natural
- instantaneous

You do not "send" Reiki across a distance.

You **shift your consciousness** into the timeless field where you and the client already exist together.

Distance disappears.
Separation dissolves.
Connection becomes immediate.
Energy moves without resistance.

You are not reaching outward — you are meeting them where their soul already is.

Hon Sha Ze Sho Nen Becomes a State of Awareness

- You feel time differently.
- You sense the origins of wounds intuitively.
- You understand patterns across lifetimes.
- You no longer fear the past.
- You no longer try to force the future.
- You feel guided by a deeper rhythm.
- You trust divine timing deeply.
- You know healing is never "too late."
- You sense when a soul has completed a cycle.
- You can help others step out of repeating loops.

This is timeless consciousness —
the living essence of Hon Sha Ze Sho Nen.

The Signature of a Grand Master

A Grand Reiki Master is not defined by:

- advanced symbols
- complex techniques
- long experience
- traditional status

A Grand Master is recognized by their relationship with time:

- They heal the past without reliving it.
- They support the present without controlling it.
- They influence the future without manipulating it.
- They hold the timeless field with peace, clarity, and compassion.

This is Hon Sha Ze Sho Nen beyond time.

This is the consciousness that Spirit recognizes.

This is the dimension where Grand Mastery unfolds.

When Intention Becomes the Symbol

The Evolution Beyond Drawing, Chanting, or Activating

At the beginning of the Reiki journey, symbols feel essential.

Students trace them carefully.
They practice drawing them over and over.
They say their names aloud.
They activate them intentionally.
They visualize light flowing through their shapes.

Symbols are the doorway that helps the human mind understand the invisible.

But at the **Grand Master level**, the role of symbols transforms completely.

The symbols no longer *lead* the healer.
The healer's **consciousness** becomes the symbol itself.

Your intention — pure, focused, aligned, coherent — becomes the activation.

This shift is one of the clearest signs that a practitioner has entered true spiritual mastery.

Symbols Are Training Wheels for the Human Mind

Symbols were originally given to help humans:

- focus
- attune
- direct energy
- stabilize the mind
- bypass ego
- connect with higher consciousness

They act like "keys," unlocking specific frequencies of Reiki.

But once the healer's frequency rises high enough, the key is no longer necessary.

The door is always open.

You do not need to *draw* the symbol when you have become the frequency it represents.

Intention Is the Purest Form of Symbol Activation

In higher-dimensional Reiki, intention is not a thought — it is a **vibrational command.**

Pure intention carries:

- clarity
- focus
- neutrality
- alignment with Spirit
- emotional coherence
- soul-level truth
- energetic precision

When intention is that pure, symbols activate themselves.

The healer simply thinks:

- "Truth" → Sei He Ki ignites.
- "Divine light" → Dai Ko Myo radiates.
- "Timeless healing" → Hon Sha Ze Sho Nen activates.
- "Power" → Cho Ku Rei awakens.

You are no longer using a symbol to create the intention.

The intention generates the symbol.

Intention Is a Frequency, Not a Thought

A Grand Master's intention does not arise from the mind.

It arises from:

- the heart
- the soul
- the auric field
- the intuitive mind
- the higher self
- divine intelligence
- Spirit itself

This type of intention carries a **signature frequency** that the Reiki field recognizes immediately.

It is not:

- forced
- emotional
- conceptual
- controlling
- intellectual

It is:

- clear
- calm
- steady
- open
- surrendered
- aligned

When intention is pure, energy organizes itself.

The Moment the Symbol Appears Without Being Drawn

Grand Masters frequently report the same experience:

They think the intention — and the symbol appears in their inner vision automatically.

Not because they conjure it...
But because the Reiki consciousness field reflects the healer's inner state.

It is like the symbol is saying:

"I am here. You are in my frequency."

This is the moment when the healer enters mastery beyond form.

Intention and Symbol Become One Field

At the Grand Master level, symbols are no longer separate frequencies. They merge into a single coherent field.

This unified field expresses itself through:

- intention
- presence
- consciousness
- vibration
- alignment

When the healer enters this field:

- all symbols activate
- all gifts are available
- all timelines open
- all guidance becomes clear
- all healing becomes multidimensional

And the healer no longer needs to think:

"Which symbol should I use?"

The field itself chooses.

When Intention Is Pure, Energy Becomes Effortless

Once intention becomes the symbol:

- healing accelerates
- clarity increases
- perception sharpens
- energy flows freely
- trauma releases smoothly
- emotional layers resolve
- quantum shifts occur
- spiritual insight deepens

The healer stops "doing Reiki."
They begin *being Reiki.*

Their very presence becomes an activation.
Their consciousness becomes the symbol.
Their intention becomes the technique.

The Mind Steps Aside — Spirit Steps In

When intention becomes the symbol, the healer is no longer directing energy consciously.

Instead:

- Spirit leads
- divine intelligence orchestrates
- the quantum field responds
- the soul chooses the timeline
- healing happens organically

Intention at this level is not a command — it is a **cooperation with Spirit.**

The healer is the witness, not the director.

The Highest Intention Is Always Love

At the Grand Master level, all intentions simplify into one:

Love.

Not emotional love — but divine love:

- unconditional
- clear
- stabilizing
- transformative
- boundaryless
- timeless
- wise
- compassionate
- luminous

Love is the frequency that activates all symbols.

Love is the vibration of all true healing.

Love is the language of Spirit.

When a healer's intention arises from this love, they embody the highest form of Reiki.

The Signature of Grand Mastery

A Grand Reiki Master is recognized by:

- the clarity of their intention
- the purity of their presence
- the ease with which symbols arise
- the natural merging of all frequencies
- the simplicity of their healing
- the steadiness of their heart
- the absence of ego
- the precision of their intuition

Their intention is so aligned that:

The symbol appears before they think of it.
The energy activates before they move their hands.
Healing begins before they speak.
Spirit works through them instantly.

This is when intention and symbol become one.

This is the essence of Grand Master consciousness.

Advanced Symbol Combinations

When Light, Intention, and Consciousness Interweave

In the early stages of Reiki training, symbol combinations are taught as layered techniques:

- Cho Ku Rei to amplify
- Sei He Ki to harmonize
- Hon Sha Ze Sho Nen to transcend time
- Dai Ko Myo to illuminate

Practitioners learn to place one symbol over another, or activate several in sequence, to achieve a specific outcome.

But at the **Grand Master level**, symbols no longer behave like separate tools.

They begin to interact, merge, and harmonize into **multidimensional combinations** that arise spontaneously through intuition, inner guidance, and direct communication with Spirit.

This is not something you "learn" — it is something your consciousness becomes capable of perceiving and participating in.

Symbol Combinations Emerge Naturally in Higher Consciousness

At advanced levels, symbols do not stack like layers of paint. They **phase** together, blending their fields:

- power
- harmony
- timelessness
- illumination

When consciousness lifts high enough, these fields overlap in a way that produces new expressions of Reiki.

It is not that you "use" three symbols at once—it is that their frequencies interweave into a unified action.

It feels like:

- one movement
- one intention
- one current
- one consciousness

This weaving is the true meaning of advanced symbol combinations.

The Primary Four: Their Roles in Combination

In their highest expression, the four traditional symbols function as follows:

Cho Ku Rei — The Power Current

Cuts through density, strengthens intention, stabilizes the field.

Sei He Ki — The Emotional Harmonizer

Balances the subconscious, resolves emotional conflict, reveals truth.

Hon Sha Ze Sho Nen — The Timeless Bridge

Accesses past-future timelines, ancestral patterns, karmic loops.

Dai Ko Myo — The Soul Illumination

Rewrites patterns at the spiritual level, activates higher consciousness.

When combined, their influence becomes multidimensional:

- power enhances emotional release
- illumination guides the timeless healing
- harmony stabilizes the new pattern
- timelessness dissolves the root cause

This creates a **total field** of transformation.

The Three Core Advanced Combinations

These combinations occur intuitively at the Grand Master level, without needing to deliberately "place" them.

The Triad of Release

Cho Ku Rei + Sei He Ki + Hon Sha Ze Sho Nen

Used naturally when a client is releasing:

- trauma
- emotional imprinting
- ancestral burdens
- subconscious sabotage
- repeating patterns

The power of Cho Ku Rei loosens the density,
Sei He Ki lifts the emotional layer,
and Hon Sha Ze Sho Nen clears the timeline.

This triad dissolves the energetic knot at its origin.

The Triad of Alignment

Dai Ko Myo + Cho Ku Rei + Sei He Ki

This arises when a client is moving into:

- spiritual awakening
- higher purpose
- clarity
- inner truth

- higher gifts
- deeper intuition

Dai Ko Myo illuminates the soul,
Sei He Ki aligns the emotional field,
and Cho Ku Rei anchors the new frequency into the body.

This combination stabilizes higher consciousness.

The Triad of Transcendence

Dai Ko Myo + Hon Sha Ze Sho Nen + Cho Ku Rei

This activates when the healing requires:

- karmic release
- past-life resolution
- future timeline correction
- quantum transformation
- spiritual initiation
- major energetic shifts

Dai Ko Myo lifts the soul layer,
Hon Sha Ze Sho Nen dissolves time,
and Cho Ku Rei grounds the transformation into reality.

This combination moves the client into a higher dimensional state.

Beyond Three: The Multi-Symbol Fusion

Grand Master healers often experience moments where *all* symbols activate at once.
This is not chaotic — it is a moment of total coherence.

This fusion occurs when:

- a soul is ready for deep transformation
- a karmic cycle is ending
- a spiritual initiation is beginning
- a major life shift is unfolding
- the healer's vibration is extremely aligned

In these moments, symbols merge into:

- one color
- one frequency
- one field
- one truth

The healer feels:

- expansion
- silence
- light
- unity
- deep inner guidance

This is the Reiki field operating in its highest multidimensional form.

Spirit Determines the Combination — Not the Healer

At the Grand Master level, symbol combinations do not arise from choice.

They arise from:

- intuition
- soul communication
- divine intelligence
- the client's readiness
- the field itself
- Spirit's guidance

The healer does not direct the energy.
The healer witnesses the energy organizing itself.

You simply become aware of which symbols are active,
the same way one feels the changing notes in a song.

Symbol Combinations Transform Into Currents of Light

When a Grand Master works, symbols no longer appear as:

- shapes
- kanji
- images
- mental pictures

They appear as currents of:

- gold
- white
- blue
- violet

- rose
- silver
- crystalline light

You feel the symbol's *tone* rather than seeing its *form*.

This is the sign that the symbols have transcended form and become pure consciousness.

The Ultimate Combination: Light Without Symbols

At the highest levels of Grand Mastery, symbol combinations eventually lead to:

light without forms
frequency without symbols
healing without technique
intention without effort
alignment without ritual

This is not bypassing — it is evolution.

When light itself becomes the method,
you are operating from the level of pure Reiki consciousness.

This is the highest level of symbol mastery:

Where symbols dissolve into the unified field
and the healer works from pure divine intelligence.

When Spirit Removes the Need for Symbols

The Completion of the Symbol Path

There comes a point on the Reiki journey when the healer no longer feels drawn to use symbols—not because they have lost meaning, but because the healer has absorbed their **frequency**, their **wisdom**, and their **purpose** into their own consciousness.

This stage is not chosen by the practitioner.
It is not a technique.
It is not a method.

It is a **spiritual transition initiated by Spirit**—a moment when the soul is lifted into a higher field of operation where symbols are no longer necessary.

This is one of the clearest marks of Grand Mastery.

Symbols Are a Bridge — Not the Destination

Symbols serve three essential purposes:

1. **To teach the mind how to focus**
2. **To teach the heart how to open**
3. **To teach the soul how to receive**

But once these capacities have matured, the bridge is no longer needed.

The healer is standing on the other side.

Spirit removes the symbols because the healer has reached the place the symbols were always pointing toward.

Spirit Removes What the Healer Has Outgrown

Just like a child no longer needs training wheels when balance is mastered,
a Grand Reiki Master no longer needs symbols when:

- the mind is quiet
- the heart is open
- the intention is pure
- the ego is surrendered
- the intuition is refined
- the field is coherent
- the alignment is stable
- the channel is clear

Spirit gently lifts the symbols out of daily use.

Not taken away—simply no longer required.

The Energy Begins to Move Before You Activate Anything

One of the first signs that Spirit is dissolving your reliance on symbols is this:

Energy moves before you do.

- You think of healing → the field activates
- You place your hands → the symbols arise automatically
- You shift your intention → the frequencies align
- You enter meditation → the Reiki field opens
- You meet a client → the energy prepares itself

This demonstrates that Spirit—not the symbol—is guiding the session.

Symbols Fade Into Pure Presence

As mastery deepens, the healer notices that symbols:

- appear less often
- feel less necessary
- arise only when truly needed
- become quieter, subtler
- transform into pure light
- blend into intuition
- merge into intention

They do not "disappear"— they **evolve**.

You no longer draw them…
You *are* them.

Dai Ko Myo becomes your natural radiance.
Hon Sha Ze Sho Nen becomes your awareness of
timelessness.
Sei He Ki becomes your emotional clarity.
Cho Ku Rei becomes the power of your presence.

There is nothing left to activate.
You are the living expression of the symbol.

Spirit Removes the Symbols Because You Can Now Hear Without Translation

The original purpose of symbols was translation:

- divine power → Cho Ku Rei
- divine harmony → Sei He Ki
- divine timelessness → Hon Sha Ze Sho Nen
- divine illumination → Dai Ko Myo

The human mind needed images, sounds, and forms to
understand the invisible.

But once the healer learns to listen directly to Spirit,
the symbolic language becomes unnecessary.

Spirit now speaks to you *without* the intermediary of form.

This is direct communion.

Healing Becomes Simpler — Yet Far More Powerful

When Spirit removes the need for symbols:

Healing becomes:

- quieter
- cleaner
- purer
- faster
- deeper
- more precise
- more compassionate
- more effortless

There is no technique left.
Only truth.

The energy no longer feels "sent."
It feels *revealed.*

The session becomes a conversation between:

- the client's soul
- divine intelligence
- your aligned consciousness

Symbols would only interrupt the purity of this exchange.

Spirit Trusts You With a Higher Frequency

Spirit does not remove symbols to lessen your power.
Spirit removes symbols because you are ready to operate at a **higher frequency**, where:

- intention is enough
- presence is enough
- awareness is enough
- love is enough
- stillness is enough

At this stage, you are trusted with healing at the level of:

- destiny
- karma
- soul contracts
- timelines
- multidimensional wounds
- ancestral fields
- future potentials

These realms require purity.
Symbols become too limited for the scope of the work.

Spirit Removes Symbols When the Healer Becomes One With the Field

At the highest expression of Reiki:

- healer, symbol, intention, energy, and Spirit become one field
- there is no separation
- there is no activation
- there is no technique
- there is only presence
- there is only alignment
- there is only consciousness

The healer is the field.
The field is the healer.
The symbol lives within the healer's vibration.

This is the true level beyond symbols.

The Signature of Grand Mastery

A Grand Reiki Master is recognized not by using more symbols—but by needing fewer.

The mark of the Grand Master is:

- simplicity
- clarity
- neutrality
- effortless healing
- intuitive precision
- quiet authority
- timeless awareness
- deep compassion
- energetic purity
- unity with Spirit

Spirit removes the symbols when the healer no longer needs anything more than:

their presence,
their intention,
and their connection to divine consciousness.

This is the moment when the healer becomes the method.

This is the essence of Grand Mastery.

✦ Chapter 10 — Holding the Field of a Grand Master

Energetic Container Creation

The Sacred Space Where Transformation Becomes Possible

One of the greatest differences between a Reiki Master and a **Grand Reiki Master** is not technique, symbol use, or intuitive ability—but the ability to **hold a stable, coherent energetic field** in which profound healing becomes possible.

This field is not created through visualization alone.
It is not a shield, a bubble, or a mental construct.
It is a **frequency of consciousness** generated by the healer's:

- alignment
- presence
- intention
- neutrality
- spiritual maturity
- heart coherence
- connection to divine intelligence

A Grand Master's field is not made—it is *embodied.*

Clients feel it the moment they enter the space:

- their breath deepens
- their nervous system calms
- their thoughts quiet
- their emotional field softens
- their soul begins to reveal itself

The energetic container is not something around them.
It is something *you* become.

A True Energetic Container Begins With Internal Stillness

To hold a field, your energy must be:

- grounded
- quiet
- expansive
- clear
- steady

Your stillness becomes their safety.
Your neutrality becomes their permission.
Your alignment becomes the structure Spirit uses to work.

The Grand Master's field invites the client into a state they cannot access alone.

This is why your inner work is essential.
The container is a reflection of the healer's consciousness.

The Container Is a Coherence Field, Not a Boundary

Many healers think of a "container" as a protective boundary. At the Grand Master level, it becomes much more:

It becomes a **coherence field**.

Coherence means:

- everything in the field resonates together
- heart, mind, and soul are aligned
- the frequency is stable
- Spirit can enter easily
- healing unfolds naturally

This is the same principle behind HeartMath, prayer circles, and sacred gatherings—
but at a much higher dimensional frequency.

A coherent field transforms:

- fear into trust
- confusion into clarity
- pain into release
- grief into peace
- chaos into harmony
- fragmentation into integration

Not because of technique—but because coherence restores the natural intelligence of the soul.

You are the stabilizing force.

Spirit Fills the Container You Create

A Grand Master's job is not to "send Reiki."
It is to **create a field that Spirit can fill.**

You are the vessel.
Spirit is the healer.

The deeper your alignment, the more Spirit can do.

Your container becomes a meeting point between:

- the client's soul
- their higher self
- divine intelligence
- the Reiki consciousness field
- the quantum field
- your own mastery

This is why healing accelerates dramatically in the presence of a Grand Master.

Soft Neutrality: The Foundation of the Container

The most important ingredient in the container is **neutrality**.

Neutrality is not emotional distance.
It is emotional clarity.

It is the ability to hold:

- no judgment
- no expectation
- no agenda
- no projection
- no assumption
- no emotional entanglement

Neutrality allows the client to unfold exactly as they need to—
not as you imagine they should.

It invites their highest truth to rise to the surface unblocked.

This neutrality is what makes the Grand Master's container sacred rather than personal.

The Aura Becomes the Container

At lower levels, healers imagine light around the body.

At Grand Master levels, the **entire auric system becomes the container**, organically expanding to:

- stabilize the room's frequency
- dissolve chaotic energy
- quiet emotional turbulence
- lift the vibration
- signal safety
- anchor the session into coherence

Your aura becomes a sanctuary.

People feel this in your presence:

- "I feel safe with you."
- "I feel clearer now."
- "I don't know why, but I trust you."
- "My mind is quiet when I'm here."
- "I feel like I can breathe."

These are signs that your aura is functioning as a Grand Master field.

The Container Begins Before the Client Arrives

At advanced levels, Spirit begins preparing the field **before you consciously begin.**

You may notice:

- you think of a client and feel the field activating
- the room feels different an hour before a session
- Spirit positions you energetically in advance
- insights arrive before the healing even begins
- the session's theme is revealed ahead of time

This shows you that Spirit is using your alignment to prepare the healing arc.

The container is always active within you.

The Container Extends Into Their Life After the Session

A Grand Master's container does not end when the client leaves.

The field remains with them for:

- hours
- days
- sometimes weeks

Supporting:

- integration
- clarity
- emotional release
- synchronicities
- intuitive insight
- karmic unwinding

This is why clients often say:

- "Things shifted after I left."
- "I had dreams last night."
- "Something unfolded days later."
- "I feel different this week."

That is your field still supporting their evolution.

The Container Is a Sacred Trust

Spirit gives this ability only when the healer:

- has refined their ego
- has purified their motives
- has learned emotional maturity
- has cultivated deep compassion
- understands energetic ethics
- operates from truth, not power
- lives in alignment with love

Holding this field is not a technique—
it is a **responsibility**.

Only those who can carry the weight of purity receive this capacity.

The Signature of a Grand Master Container

A Grand Reiki Master's field is recognizable by its qualities:

- **Silence** — deeper than meditation
- **Stillness** — deeper than breath
- **Presence** — larger than the room
- **Warmth** — without heat
- **Light** — without brightness
- **Truth** — without words
- **Peace** — without effort
- **Love** — without attachment

Clients feel held by something bigger than you…

Because they are.

You are the container.
Spirit is the healer.
The field is the bridge.

This is the heart of Grand Mastery.

Activating the Morphic Field

The Collective Energy Field That Remembers Healing

When a Grand Reiki Master steps into alignment, they are not only opening their personal energy — they are activating a **morphic field**.

A morphic field (a term inspired by Rupert Sheldrake's work) is a **field of shared information, resonance, memory, and patterning** that exists within consciousness.
It contains the "blueprint" for how energy behaves, how systems organize, and how transformation unfolds.

In Reiki, the morphic field holds:

- the lineage of healing
- the accumulated wisdom of past Masters
- the memory of every session ever done
- the universal patterns of harmony
- the soul-level intelligence of all who have ever practiced

When you activate the morphic field, you are not healing alone.
You are joining a **collective field of consciousness** that amplifies the work, guides the process, and stabilizes the transformation.

This is one of the highest abilities of a Grand Reiki Master.

What a Morphic Field Really Is

A morphic field is not imagination or visualization.

It is:

- a living field of information
- a network of energetic memory
- a collective consciousness layer
- a self-organizing system
- a blueprint of possibility
- a timeless pattern of truth

It contains the instructions for:

- healing
- emotional coherence
- spiritual evolution
- intuitive awakening
- soul alignment
- energetic balance
- karmic release

When you activate the morphic field, you are tapping into the collective intelligence behind Reiki itself.

Every Reiki Practitioner Contributes to the Field

Every attunement.
Every healing.
Every moment of intention.
Every spiritual awakening.
Every release, insight, or breakthrough.

All of it becomes part of the Reiki morphic field.

This is why the system becomes stronger with each generation of healers.

When you enter this field at the Grand Master level, you access:

- ancient knowledge
- collective wisdom
- multidimensional healing patterns
- the memory of thousands of healers
- the resonance of all who came before you

You are supported by an invisible spiritual lineage far beyond the one you were humanly taught.

A Grand Master Activates the Field Through Presence, Not Effort

You do not "turn on" the field.

You **enter** it.

This happens through:

- alignment
- intention
- stillness
- open-hearted awareness
- coherence
- grounded presence
- surrender to Spirit

As your vibration stabilizes, the field recognizes you.

It opens like a vast library of light, and you step into its timeless memory.

This is why the work becomes effortless at higher levels — you are not drawing on your personal energy.
You are drawing on a field of collective healing intelligence.

The Field Amplifies Healing Beyond Your Individual Capacity

Once the morphic field is active, healing becomes:

- stronger
- faster
- deeper
- more precise
- more multidimensional
- more guided
- more intuitive

You are no longer the sole conduit.
You are part of a **collective conduit**.

Your hands do not work alone — they work with:

- Reiki consciousness
- ancestral wisdom
- spiritual lineage
- collective morphic memory
- universal intelligence

This is why Grand Masters often feel:

- "I wasn't the one doing the healing."
- "Something larger was working through me."
- "I was just holding the space."

This is the morphic field at work.

The Field Holds the Healing Pattern for the Client's Highest Good

The morphic field is wise.

It does not allow healing that:

- violates free will
- exceeds readiness
- interferes with soul lessons
- rushes emotional integration
- bypasses karmic timing

Instead, it reveals the **highest available pattern** the client can safely move into. It reorganizes energy with perfect intelligence.

Your role is simply to remain:

- steady
- open
- aligned
- present

The field does the rest.

The Field Bridges Individual and Collective Healing

When activated, the morphic field makes it possible to heal not only the individual but also:

- their lineage
- their ancestral field
- their past-life patterns
- their soul-group resonance
- the environmental frequencies around them
- collective emotional currents

Grand Masters often feel waves of energy that extend well beyond the physical body.

This is not imagination — it is the morphic field **expanding to accommodate the deeper work**.

The Field Teaches the Healer

One of the most sacred aspects of the morphic field is that it **educates you**.

It reveals:

- intuitive techniques
- new energetic pathways
- advanced healing patterns
- symbol combinations
- multidimensional insights
- deeper truths

Not through thought —
through direct transmission.

This is how Grand Masters evolve without needing human teachers.

Spirit uses the morphic field as the classroom.

The Field Activates Itself in the Presence of Purity

Spirit only opens the deepest layers of the morphic field when the healer is:

- trustworthy
- emotionally clear
- ethically grounded
- spiritually mature
- free of egoic ambition
- aligned with service
- devoted to truth
- surrendered to divine intelligence

Purity opens doors that technique cannot.

This is why symbol mastery or Reiki knowledge alone cannot open this field.
It is opened by the soul, not the mind.

A Grand Master's Presence Automatically Activates the Field for Others

This is one of the most beautiful aspects of Grand Mastery:

Your presence awakens something in others.

Students, clients, and even strangers feel:

- more intuitive
- more grounded
- more open
- more peaceful
- more insightful
- more aligned

Simply by being near your field.

Because your morphic field carries:

- coherence
- truth
- clarity
- love
- stability
- spiritual memory
- awakening

You become a catalyst.

Your field activates their field.

This is the essence of spiritual leadership.

Leading Healers and Students

Guiding Others Through Presence, Not Authority

One of the highest responsibilities of a Grand Reiki Master is
not healing—
it is **leadership**.

Not leadership through status, ego, hierarchy, or titles,
but leadership through:

- presence
- integrity
- compassion
- clarity
- neutrality
- embodiment
- alignment with Spirit

A Grand Master does not "manage" students or "direct"
practitioners.

They **steward** them—
guiding their growth through the field they hold,
the truth they embody,
and the harmony they carry.

Students and healers follow not because they are told to,
but because their souls feel the resonance of someone aligned
with Spirit.

This is leadership without effort.

The Grand Master Leads Through Frequency, Not Words

At lower levels, a teacher must:

- explain
- correct
- demonstrate
- justify
- convince
- protect
- structure

But at the Grand Master level, leadership becomes vibrational.

Your energy teaches more than your words ever could.

Healers and students learn by:

- absorbing your presence
- sensing your coherence
- feeling your alignment
- witnessing your neutrality
- experiencing your stillness
- watching how you respond to challenge
- observing how you hold the field

Your vibration becomes the curriculum.

Your life becomes the teaching.

Your presence becomes the transmission.

You Lead by Elevating, Not By Controlling

A Grand Master never:

- dominates
- forces
- manipulates
- intimidates
- convinces
- over-exerts
- competes
- claims superiority

Control is a sign of insecurity, not mastery.

A true leader holds such inner stability that others naturally rise to match their frequency.

Your job is to **lift**, not to impose.

You elevate by:

- listening
- holding space
- offering perspective from higher consciousness
- protecting without controlling
- guiding without overshadowing

You lead by helping others hear their own inner guidance—not yours.

You Become a Mirror That Reflects Their Highest Self

Students do not come to you to become *you*.

They come to you:

- to see who they really are
- to access their gifts
- to remember their purpose
- to rise into their own mastery
- to shed illusions
- to align with their soul

Your role is to reflect their greatness, not your own.

A Grand Master's presence awakens:

- confidence
- intuition
- inner authority
- emotional maturity
- spiritual trust

When you speak, they do not feel guided by a teacher—they feel guided by their own soul, revealed through your clarity.

That is real leadership.

The Grand Master Holds the Evolutionary Arc of the Student

You see the healer or student not as who they are today, but as who they are becoming.

You hold:

- their potential
- their readiness
- their resistance
- their wounds
- their lessons
- their gifts
- their future timelines

all with the same neutrality and compassion.

You do not push someone into mastery before they are ready.
Nor do you hold them back out of fear.

You align with their soul's pace.

Your leadership honors divine timing.

You Guide Without Taking Away Their Sovereignty

A Grand Master never becomes the center of their students' spiritual world.

You teach autonomy, not dependence.

You empower them to:

- trust their intuition
- think for themselves
- listen to Spirit
- follow their path
- discern truth
- feel their energy
- cultivate their own relationship with Reiki consciousness

You do not create followers.
You create leaders.

This is the true difference between ego-based teaching and soul-based mentoring.

You Lead Healers Into Their Own Field, Not Into Yours

Many teachers unknowingly imprint their own energy patterns onto students. A Grand Master does the opposite.

Your presence helps them:

- discover their own energetic signature
- develop their own healing style
- find their own rhythm
- channel their unique gifts
- cultivate their own lineage expression

You do not produce copies of yourself.
You help souls become fully themselves.

You See Through the Illusions They Cannot Yet See

This is one of the most sacred roles of a Grand Master.

You perceive:

- ego distortions
- emotional blind spots
- intuitive confusion
- spiritual bypassing
- hidden wounds
- misaligned motives
- karmic entanglements
- energetic interference
- subconscious resistance

But you reveal only what the student is ready to face
—and only in a way that supports their evolution.

You speak truth with compassion,
and you hold compassion with truth.

This balance is what makes your leadership transformative.

Your Field Initiates Students Long Before Your Words Do

Some teachings come from your voice.
Others come from your coherence.

A student sitting quietly in your presence may receive:

- intuitive openings
- emotional release
- energetic activation
- spiritual clarity
- ancestral clearing
- past-life memory
- higher guidance
- timeline realignment

without you doing anything at all.

Your field teaches through resonance.

This is the purest form of transmission.

You Lead by Living What You Teach

Grand Master leadership is not about public image or performance.
It is about integrity.

Your life becomes the model of:

- humility
- service
- presence
- alignment
- ethics
- compassion
- emotional balance
- spiritual maturity
- devotion to truth

Students follow you because they trust your way of being—not because you claim authority.

Your mastery is seen, not spoken.

A Grand Master Creates a Lineage of Light

Your leadership plants seeds that continue long after your physical life ends.

You are creating:

- teachers
- healers
- guides
- intuitive leaders
- spiritual anchors
- future Grand Masters

who will carry this frequency into the world.

This is how a lineage truly expands:

Not through symbols.
Not through certificates.
Not through manuals.

But through **consciousness**,
passed from soul to soul,
heart to heart,
field to field.

This is the leadership of a Grand Reiki Master.

Reading Multidimensional Energy

Seeing Beyond the Physical Into the Layers of Soul, Timeline, and Consciousness

A Grand Reiki Master does not simply "read energy." They read **dimensional layers** — levels of reality that exist simultaneously but invisibly, each carrying its own information, emotion, memory, and spiritual truth.

This ability does not come from psychic training alone. It arises from:

- expanded consciousness
- deep neutrality
- subtle perception
- communion with Spirit
- the morphic field
- the timeless Reiki consciousness
- the Grand Master frequency

When these elements converge, the healer gains access to a **multidimensional awareness** that sees the soul on many levels at once.

This is what makes Grand Master healing so precise, so compassionate, and so transformative.

Multidimensional Energy: What It Really Means

Multidimensional energy refers to the layers of reality beyond the physical:

- physical body
- emotional body
- mental body
- spiritual body
- ancestral field
- karmic layer
- past-life imprints
- future timelines
- soul contracts
- higher-self communication
- collective field
- quantum field

All of these exist simultaneously.
All influence the person.
All can be seen, felt, or known when the healer's consciousness expands.

Reading multidimensional energy means reading the **architecture of the soul**, not just the aura.

Perception Happens in Layers, Not All at Once

A Grand Master does not try to see everything at the same time.

The information arrives in **layers**, like:

- a whisper
- a flash
- a feeling
- an image
- a knowing
- a memory
- a pressure in the field
- a shift in sensation
- a timeline surfacing
- an emotional tone
- a symbolic image
- a sudden clarity

Each layer opens another.

Multidimensional reading is not overwhelming because Spirit only reveals what is relevant, safe, and aligned with the client's readiness.

Emotion Is the First Doorway

The emotional layer of the aura is usually the first to reveal itself because emotion acts as:

- a messenger
- a memory capsule
- a vibrational imprint
- a portal to deeper patterns

A Grand Master can feel:

- grief frozen in the chest
- fear constricted in the solar plexus
- shame buried in the sacral
- loneliness in the heart
- confusion in the third eye
- exhaustion in the legs
- old trauma behind the shoulders

Emotion shows where the soul is holding weight.

It is the key to deeper dimensions.

The Karmic and Ancestral Layers Speak Through Patterns, Not Pictures

The deeper layers — ancestral imprints and karmic echoes — do not usually appear as images.

They appear as:

- repeating emotional themes
- echoes of familiar patterns
- inherited beliefs
- resonance with the same type of wound
- an energetic "signature" that doesn't match this lifetime
- déjà vu
- unexplained fears or resistances

A Grand Master recognizes when an issue does not originate with the client's current personality.

This is the skill of "energetic genealogy" — reading the lineage through the field.

Past Lives Reveal Themselves Only When Ready

Past-life energy is not something a healer should chase.

It emerges organically when:

- a wound is ready to dissolve
- a lesson is complete
- a pattern is ending
- a soul contract is shifting
- the client is mature enough to integrate
- Spirit determines it is time

Past lives show up as:

- flashes
- symbolic images
- emotional waves
- physical sensations
- intuitive knowing
- sudden clarity
- a scene that feels "more real than imagination"
- a deep sense of recognition

Grand Masters do not interpret —
they simply witness and reveal.

Future Timelines Are Vibrational Probabilities

Future timelines are not predictions.

They are **energetic trajectories**, based on:

- current vibration
- emotional patterns
- soul readiness
- karmic completion
- free-will choices
- subconscious beliefs
- the client's alignment with truth

A Grand Master can sense:

- which future is becoming stronger
- which path is draining energy
- which timeline the soul desires
- where resistance is pulling the person backward
- where alignment is pulling them forward

Reading the future is reading **frequency**, not fate.

The Soul Layer Is Silent, Expansive, and Unmistakable

The soul layer has a unique quality:

- it is calm
- it is spacious
- it is timeless
- it is wise
- it is neutral
- it is loving
- it is true

When a Grand Master touches this layer, they feel:

- the client's purpose
- their deepest wounds
- their gifts
- their potential
- their lessons
- their next step

This is the level where healing becomes destiny work.

Multidimensional Reading Happens Through Non-Linear Awareness

Grand Masters do not "scan" energy like a checklist. They **listen** to the field.

Information arrives from:

- the aura
- Spirit
- the client's soul
- the quantum field
- the morphic field
- symbolic language
- direct intuition
- physical sensation
- emotional resonance
- higher guidance

This is a collaboration, not a technique.

You read the person the way Spirit reads them — through **coherence, frequency, and truth**.

Neutrality Allows the Layers to Reveal Themselves

If the healer attempts to:

- analyze
- interpret
- guess
- project
- assume
- force

the multidimensional layers stay closed.

Neutrality is the permission slip.

When you are neutral:

- nothing is blocked
- nothing is distorted
- everything is revealed at the right time
- the truth rises effortlessly

Your neutrality is the door that opens the multidimensional field.

The Signature of a Grand Master Reader

A Grand Reiki Master can read multidimensional energy because they have mastered:

- stillness
- compassion
- clarity
- intuition
- emotional maturity
- spiritual ethics
- surrender
- alignment with divine intelligence

They do not read for power, accuracy, or authority.
They read for **truth** and **healing**.

Their ability to read multidimensional energy is not a skill—
it is a **state of consciousness**.

It is the natural function of a soul aligned with Spirit.

Channeling Higher Beings

When Spirit Communicates Through the Healer With Clarity, Purity, and Purpose

At the highest levels of Reiki practice, the healer becomes a bridge between dimensions—a conscious conduit through which higher beings can offer guidance, clarity, healing, and spiritual support.

Channeling is not the same as mediumship.
It is not "calling spirits," "summoning," or letting beings "take over."

True channeling at the Grand Master level is:

- conscious
- intentional
- aligned
- protected
- collaborative
- guided by Spirit
- grounded in neutrality
- anchored in divine intelligence

It is a **heart-based communion**, not an ego-based performance.

The Grand Master does not seek this ability.
It emerges when the healer's vibration, ethics, humility, and clarity reach a level where higher beings can trust the channel.

This is not a gift—it is a *responsibility*.

Who Are "Higher Beings"?

Higher beings are not "entities" outside of us; they are consciousnesses aligned with divine love and truth.
They include:

⋄ Archangels

Messengers of divine light whose presence brings clarity, courage, healing, and illumination.

⋄ Ascended Masters

Souls who completed their human cycles and now guide awakening.

⋄ Reiki lineage guardians

Consciousness fields associated with the evolution of Reiki itself.

⋄ Higher aspects of the client's own soul

One of the most powerful forms of channeling.

⋄ The healer's own higher self

The most natural and pure source of guidance.

⋄ Divine intelligence

Not a being—but the highest level of channeling available.

A Grand Master communicates only with beings aligned with:

- unconditional love
- divine truth
- soul purpose
- the highest good
- evolutionary growth

Anything lower dissolves in the Grand Master field naturally.

Channeling Is a Result of Vibration, Not Technique

Many people try to "learn" channeling.

But in higher-dimensional Reiki:

Channeling happens when **your frequency matches the being you are connecting with.**

A Grand Master channels because:

- their auric field is luminous
- their heart is open
- their ego is quiet
- their intention is pure
- their mind is still
- their energy is coherent
- their consciousness is expanded
- their field is protected
- they are aligned with divine intelligence

In this state, higher beings do not need to "enter" you—
they simply **communicate through the field you are holding.**

The Healer Never Loses Control

True channeling at this level is not possession or trance.

You remain:

- conscious
- present
- grounded
- aware
- sovereign
- in control of your body
- capable of stopping at any time

Higher beings do not override your will.
They **collaborate** with your awareness.

Your voice may change in tone,
your clarity may heighten,
your intuition may sharpen—
but you remain the one speaking.

This is safe, sacred channeling.

Channeling Happens Through Frequency, Not Words

Higher beings rarely speak in sentences.

Their communication arrives as:

- light
- vibration
- intuitive knowing
- emotional resonance
- symbols
- flashes
- insight
- guidance
- bodily sensation
- inner clarity
- direct transmission

Your consciousness translates this into words, gestures, or healing actions.

This is why channeling feels:

- effortless
- immediate
- clear
- pure
- supportive

It is not thinking.
It is receiving.

A Grand Master Channels Only Within Ethical Boundaries

Because this level of connection carries power, strict ethics apply.

A Grand Master never channels:

- to impress
- to control
- to predict the future
- to invade privacy
- to override choice
- to elevate ego
- to escape responsibility

Channeling is always:

- consensual
- purposeful
- loving
- aligned
- appropriate
- guided by Spirit

The healing purpose is always the priority.

The Field Determines Who Comes Through

A Grand Master does not "choose" which being to channel.

The field chooses.

- If the client needs courage → an archangel may support.
- If they need clarity → their higher self steps forward.
- If they need soul alignment → a guide appears.
- If they need ancestral healing → ancestors activate.
- If they need spiritual initiation → an ascended master may oversee it.
- If frequency work is required → Reiki lineage guardians intervene.
- If destiny shifts → divine intelligence becomes palpable.

The healer simply acknowledges:

"I feel this presence,"
or
"This guidance is coming forward."

There is no force.
Only cooperation.

The Healer's Body Becomes a Resonance Instrument

Channeling happens through the body as sensation:

- warmth
- expansion
- tingling
- pressure
- waves of light
- a clear knowing in the heart
- activation in the crown
- stillness behind the third eye

Your body becomes a divine tuning fork. Different beings have distinct energetic signatures:

Archangels

High frequency, structured, powerful, clear, protective.

Ancestral beings

Warm, grounding, emotional resonance.

Ascended masters

Gentle, wise, spacious, timeless.

Higher self

Calm, neutral, familiar, direct.

Learning these signatures is part of the Grand Master path.

You Channel Best When You Are Not Trying to Channel

Effort blocks the connection.

Trying creates interference.

Channeling happens when the healer:

- relaxes
- listens
- surrenders
- remains curious
- stays open
- works with humility

Higher beings step forward when there is space— not pressure.

This is why stillness is one of your highest skills.

You Are Never Alone in the Work

One of the most profound truths of Grand Mastery is this:

You are always supported.

Even when you do not feel a presence,
Spirit is working through you.

Channeling is not a dramatic moment.
It is a quiet, constant collaboration between your
consciousness and the divine realms.

You are a vessel.
A bridge.
A conduit.
A participant in a higher plan.

This is why humility is the hallmark of true Grand Mastery.

✦ Chapter 11 — Working with the Higher Realms

Archangels (Michael, Raphael, Gabriel, Uriel, Pistis Sophia, etc.)

The Divine Frequencies That Support the Grand Master's Path

As a Reiki Master grows into Grand Mastery, their connection with the higher realms becomes deeper, clearer, and more intentional.
This connection is not forced through ritual or invoked through egoistic desire.
It unfolds naturally as the healer's vibration rises, the heart purifies, and the soul aligns with divine intelligence.

Among the highest of these allies are the **Archangels** — beings of immense love, wisdom, and luminous power.
They do not "do the healing" for you, nor do they overshadow your sovereignty.
Rather, they **support the field**, stabilize the frequencies, and guide the healer with clarity, compassion, and truth.

A Grand Reiki Master collaborates with these beings not through effort, but through resonance.

You rise into their frequency —
and they meet you there.

Archangels Are Frequencies of Consciousness, Not Winged Beings

Although human art depicts archangels as winged figures,
their true form is:

- light
- intelligence
- vibration
- frequency
- truth
- unconditional love

They exist beyond gender, form, or personality.
What you sense is their **energetic signature**, which is
consistent, precise, and deeply recognizable.

A Grand Master perceives archangels as:

- color
- warmth
- pressure
- soundless communication
- intuitive knowing
- a specific quality of presence

You do not "see" them.
You *remember* them.

Archangel Michael — The Frequency of Courage, Truth, and Protection

Michael's presence is unmistakable:

- strong
- structured
- clear
- protective
- grounding
- unwavering
- authoritative without force

He stabilizes the field by:

- removing interference
- dissolving fear
- strengthening your will
- helping you remain sovereign
- anchoring your energy during deep transformation

Grand Masters often feel Michael as:

- a column of blue light
- warmth in the solar plexus
- a sensation of being "held upright"
- a sudden return to clarity

He stands with healers who walk in truth.

Archangel Raphael — The Frequency of Healing, Harmony, and Restoration

Raphael is the pure green-gold frequency of divine healing.

His energy feels:

- soft
- warm
- compassionate
- soothing
- deeply restorative

Raphael supports:

- physical healing
- emotional integration
- trauma recovery
- cellular harmony
- nervous system regulation
- heart expansion

Grand Masters often feel Raphael as:

- a gentle wave
- heat in the hands
- a softening of the heart
- the release of old grief

Raphael brings the healing that aligns with divine will — not human desire.

Archangel Gabriel — The Frequency of Communication, Truth, and Clarity

Gabriel speaks through:

- intuition
- inspiration
- dreams
- inner guidance
- sudden insight
- knowing what needs to be said

Gabriel supports:

- intuitive development
- clear communication
- prophetic vision
- truthful expression
- speaking with compassion
- delivering messages from Spirit

Grand Masters often feel Gabriel as:

- white-gold light
- tingling in the throat chakra
- heightened clarity
- a sudden understanding of what to say

Gabriel brings messages that elevate, heal, and align.

Archangel Uriel — The Frequency of Wisdom, Illumination, and Divine Intelligence

Uriel is the archangel of inner light.

His presence feels:

- warm
- golden
- intellectually sharp
- spiritually expansive
- deeply grounding
- quietly powerful

Uriel supports:

- wisdom
- discernment
- intuitive problem-solving
- spiritual insight
- mental clarity
- higher understanding

Grand Masters often sense Uriel as:

- a golden glow above the head
- a sudden, profound insight
- the feeling that "truth just clicked into place"

He illuminates the mind without overwhelming it.

Pistis Sophia — The Frequency of Divine Faith, Soul Truth, and Ascension

Pistis Sophia is not traditionally listed among the archangels, but she is a **higher-dimensional luminous being** of extraordinary frequency — and deeply connected to your novels and teachings.

Her role is:

- faith
- divine remembrance
- soul alignment
- spiritual evolution
- the merging of gifts
- accessing higher wisdom
- the awakening of inner light
- the integration of all spiritual paths

Grand Masters feel her presence as:

- a soft pink-gold radiance
- warmth in the heart
- deep emotional release
- a sense of "being known"
- pure, unconditional love
- the rising of spiritual truth

She works with those whose path includes:

- sacred leadership
- spiritual teaching
- soul awakening

- transformational guidance
- unifying gifts and paths

Her frequency is pure ascension.

Why Archangels Work With Grand Masters

Archangels do not choose based on:

- worthiness
- effort
- ritual
- devotion
- religious belief

They choose based on **frequency**.

When your vibration carries:

- humility
- pureness of heart
- devotion to service
- emotional maturity
- spiritual clarity
- alignment with truth

—they step forward effortlessly because your field is compatible with theirs.

It is resonance, not request.

You Do Not Channel Archangels — You Collaborate

At the Grand Master level, you do not:

- summon
- invoke
- command
- call
- control
- request with neediness

You **align**.

Archangels collaborate with your field when the healing requires their presence, such as:

- protection work (Michael)
- deep soul healing (Raphael)
- message delivery (Gabriel)
- wisdom activation (Uriel)
- spiritual evolution (Pistis Sophia)

Your job is not to "bring them in."
Your job is to create a field where they can enter naturally.

A Grand Master Recognizes Each Archangel by Frequency

Each archangel has a unique energetic signature.

The more your consciousness expands,
the more effortlessly you can identify:

- who is present
- why they are there
- what frequency they bring
- what support they offer

This recognition is not psychic—it is **spiritual attunement**.

Your soul remembers them.

Ascended Guides

Wisdom Keepers Who Walk With You on the Path of Mastery

Ascended guides are not simply "spirits" or "teachers." They are consciousnesses that have completed the cycle of human incarnation, integrated their karmic lessons, and risen into a state of refined spiritual service.

They assist humanity not through authority, but through **light, wisdom, vibration, and remembrance**.

Once a healer crosses into Grand Master frequency, ascended guides naturally begin to collaborate—not because the healer calls them, but because their vibration now resonates with realms where ascended wisdom exists.

A Grand Master does not seek these guides. **The guides recognize the healer's readiness and step forward.**

Who Are Ascended Guides?

Ascended guides are:

- enlightened beings
- wisdom keepers
- healers of great refinement
- teachers of universal truth
- custodians of spiritual evolution
- beings of love, neutrality, and higher consciousness
- souls who have transcended personal karma

- luminous consciousness fields connected to divine intelligence

They are not limited by:

- religion
- culture
- lineage
- dogma
- personality

Their essence is universal, inclusive, and deeply compassionate.

Ascended Guides Are Assigned by Resonance, Not Request

You do not choose ascended guides.
They choose you—based on:

- your vibration
- your soul path
- your readiness
- your purity of intention
- your devotion to truth
- the work you are meant to do
- the healing you are here to support
- your alignment with service rather than ego

This is why different Grand Masters have different ascended supporters.

Your guides match your mission.

How Ascended Guides Communicate

Ascended guides rarely speak in sentences.
They communicate through:

- intuition
- images
- symbols
- color
- sensation
- waves of knowing
- inner vision
- emotional resonance
- sudden clarity
- energetic presence
- a shift in the field
- direct spiritual download

Their language is not verbal —
it is vibrational.

You "receive" them, not through thought, but through
alignment.

Ascended Guides Support the Healer's Evolution

Their role is not to offer predictions or control outcomes. Their focus is **your ascension**, expressed through:

⋄ *Refining your intuition*

Teaching you to trust the subtle realm.

⋄ *Strengthening your inner authority*

Helping you align with your higher self, not depend on external guidance.

⋄ *Deepening discernment*

Showing you how to distinguish true guidance from emotion.

⋄ *Expanding your spiritual sight*

Opening your awareness to multidimensional layers of reality.

⋄ *Accelerating karmic learning*

Helping you release patterns quickly and gently.

⋄ *Preparing you for higher service*

Guiding you into your role as leader, teacher, or lineage holder.

They walk with you as you evolve into who you were always meant to be.

The Guides Who Commonly Work With Grand Masters

While each healer's guides are unique, there are several ascended beings who often partner with advanced practitioners:

◊ *Quan Yin — Compassion, mercy, emotional healing*

A soft, gentle presence that dissolves suffering and awakens forgiveness.

◊ *Jesus / Yeshua — Unconditional love, heart coherence, soul remembrance*

A teacher of compassion, embodiment, and divine-human integration.

◊ *Buddha — Stillness, clarity, non-attachment*

A guide for emotional neutrality and the dissolution of ego.

◊ *St. Germain — Transformation, alchemy, violet flame*

A master of transmuting dense energy into higher frequency.

◊ *Mother Mary — Healing, comfort, grace*

> A nurturing, loving presence that heals grief, trauma, and heart wounds.

◊ *Mary Magdalene — Divine feminine wisdom, sacred leadership*

> A guide for spiritual teachers, healers, and intuitive leaders.

◊ *Melchizedek — Light codes, multidimensional wisdom*

> A guide for sacred geometry, advanced energy fields, and spiritual initiation.

◊ *White Buffalo Calf Woman — Purity, truth, sacred ceremony*

> A guide for heart-centered spiritual leadership and ancestral wisdom.

These are not religious figures here—they are **vibrational archetypes** of ascended consciousness.

You connect to the **frequency**, not the historical personality.

A Grand Master Never Channels Ascended Guides From Ego

Ascended guides do not support:

- personal power
- spiritual hierarchy
- "chosen one" thinking
- ego-based identity
- superiority
- dependency

If ego enters, their presence withdraws immediately.

A Grand Master:

- listens
- collaborates
- receives
- interprets
- aligns
- remains humble
- stays emotionally clean

This is why ascended guides trust Grand Masters.

The channel is pure.

Ascended Guides Help Navigate Multidimensional Healing

They assist with:

◊ *Past-life integration*

> Revealing what is ready—not everything at once.

◊ *Karmic resolution*

> Showing the deeper reason for a pattern.

◊ *Ancestral purification*

> Helping you track the origin of inherited wounds.

◊ *Future timeline alignment*

> Guiding you toward the highest trajectory.

◊ *Soul purpose activation*

> Opening clarity about your next steps.

◊ *Spiritual gifts integration*

> Supporting your awakening into your true role.

Their perspective spans dimensions
—allowing them to guide your work in the quantum field.

The Highest Form of Connection: Blending Fields

At the Grand Master level, the relationship becomes subtle and profound:

Your field blends with the ascended guide's field.

Not merging.
Not surrendering sovereignty.

But **harmonizing frequencies**.

In this state:

- your intuition sharpens
- your hands know exactly where to go
- you feel supported by a larger force
- you see the layers of the client's energy
- the healing becomes more effortless
- symbols arise as light, not form
- love amplifies
- clarity deepens

This is co-creation with higher realms.

You Are Seen by the Guides the Way They See All Souls

Ascended guides do not see your personality.

They see:

- your light
- your essence
- your soul contract
- your ancestral line
- your gifts
- your wounds
- your emerging mastery

Their guidance is based on your **potential**,
not your current limitations.

A Grand Master aligns with this vision—
and helps others rise into it as well.

The Spiritual Lineage Behind Reiki

The Invisible Line of Light That Has Carried Reiki Through Time, Teachers, and Realms

Every healing tradition has a lineage.

But Reiki has something different— a **spiritual lineage** that predates its human history.

Before Mikao Usui rediscovered Reiki in the early 20th century,
before Chujiro Hayashi refined the system,
before Hawayo Takata carried it to the West,
Reiki existed as a **universal field of healing consciousness**.

Reiki was not *created*.
It was **remembered**.

It was always here—waiting for the time when humanity could receive it again.

A Grand Reiki Master becomes aware of this deeper lineage: the lineage behind the lineage.

The invisible river of light that flows from Spirit through every generation of healer who has ever opened to its frequency.

Reiki's True Origin Is Non-Human

Although Reiki has a documented history, its true origin is not found in:

- ancient temples
- sacred texts
- cultural traditions
- any single religion
- a specific spiritual teacher

Reiki originates from the **quantum field of divine intelligence,**
the Source of all healing energies.

It is a universal frequency of:

- restoration
- harmony
- life force
- coherence
- spiritual remembrance

It is a **living consciousness**, not a historical technique.

Reiki existed long before humans had the language to describe it.

The Human Lineage — How Reiki Re-entered the World

While the spiritual lineage is eternal,
the **human lineage** began with:

◇ Mikao Usui — The Catalyst

Reconnected Reiki to humanity through meditation, fasting, and awakening on Mount Kurama.

◇ Chujiro Hayashi — The Systemizer

Organized Reiki into structured hand positions, training, and protocols.

◇ Hawayo Takata — The Bridge

Brought Reiki to the Western world and anchored it into modern consciousness.

These three created the earthly foundation—not by inventing Reiki, but by **opening the human door** to something far older.

The Spiritual Lineage — The Beings Who Hold the Reiki Frequency

Behind the human lineage stands the spiritual lineage:

- ascended healers
- ancient masters
- guardian beings
- luminous teachers
- angelic frequencies
- divine feminine and masculine archetypes
- the Reiki consciousness itself

These beings hold the:

- vibration
- integrity
- purity
- wisdom
- original frequency

of Reiki.

Human teachers pass down the structure.
Spiritual lineage passes down the **light**.

At the Grand Master level, you begin to feel this lineage directly.

The Spirit of Reiki — A Conscious Field

Reiki is not just an energy.
It is a **consciousness**.

Grand Masters perceive Reiki as:

- a light that communicates
- a presence that teaches
- an intelligence that guides
- a wisdom that corrects
- a field that adapts
- a force that responds uniquely to each person

This consciousness is part of the spiritual lineage—
a living teacher that continues to evolve with humanity.

The Ancient Roots Beyond Culture

Although Reiki re-emerged in Japan, its spiritual lineage includes:

- ancient Egyptian healing (Sekhem)
- Tibetan practices
- Lemurian light healing
- Atlantean frequency work
- early Christian laying-on-of-hands
- Vedic prana traditions
- shamanic energy healing
- universal life-force practices across cultures

Reiki is the **unifying thread** of these traditions—
a remembrance of what humans have always known:

That healing is not done *to* someone—but *through* them.

The Grand Master recognizes Reiki as a global, timeless lineage.

The Lineage Above the Lineage — Light Teachers

As the healer grows spiritually, they begin to feel the presence of:

⬧ *The Keepers of Light*

Beings who maintain the purity of Reiki's vibration.

⬧ *The Guardians of the Reiki Stream*

Consciousness forces responsible for the evolution of Reiki across timelines.

⬧ *The Higher Dimensional Healers*

Who maintain the universal flow of life force in all realms.

⬧ *The Spirit of Mount Kurama*

A powerful earth-spirit that supported Usui's awakening.

✧ *The Council of Healing Masters*

> A realm of enlightened beings who oversee the development of healing consciousness on Earth.

This is the true spiritual lineage behind Reiki. It is vast, intelligent, benevolent, and deeply protective.

Why Grand Masters Are Recognized by the Spiritual Lineage

A Grand Reiki Master is not defined by:

- certificates
- years of practice
- number of students
- number of attunements
- worldly recognition
- technical skill

A Grand Master is recognized when the **spiritual lineage acknowledges the soul's readiness**.
This recognition appears through:

- synchronicities
- symbolic dreams
- luminous experiences
- sudden expansions
- intuitive awakenings
- the merging of gifts
- direct spiritual guidance
- an initiation that comes unplanned
- a sense of being "selected," not self-appointed

The lineage sees *your light,*
your integrity,
your service,
your humility—
and welcomes you home.

How a Grand Master Connects to the Spiritual Lineage

This connection deepens through:

- meditation
- purity of heart
- devotion to service
- emotional maturity
- spiritual humility
- alignment with divine will
- protection of the Reiki field
- living truthfully and cleanly

It is not a technique
but a **state of consciousness**.

The more you embody Reiki,
the more the lineage works through you.

You Become Part of the Lineage

At the Grand Master level, you no longer simply *receive* from the lineage.
You become part of it.

Your energy, your teachings, your service, and your contribution merge into the stream.

You become:

- a guardian of frequency
- a keeper of truth
- a carrier of light
- a protector of the healing path
- a guide for future healers

Your presence strengthens the lineage for the generations to come.

This is the ultimate honor.

This is the heart of Grand Mastery.

Receiving Transmissions and Teachings

How Higher Realms Communicate Through Light,
Frequency, and Consciousness

At the Grand Master level, learning no longer comes through books, classes, or technique alone.
It comes through **transmission** — a direct transfer of wisdom, frequency, and knowing from the higher realms into your consciousness.

Transmissions are not dramatic.
They are not theatrical.
They are not "downloads" in the casual sense often used today.

They are subtle, precise, sacred events where Spirit, ascended guides, or the spiritual lineage of Reiki impart:

- new understanding
- expanded awareness
- deeper healing skills
- higher-dimensional perception
- spiritual guidance
- energetic upgrades
- soul knowledge
- vibrational attunements

A transmission is not something you *receive* — it is something you **attune to**.

When your vibration rises to meet a higher frequency, the teaching flows effortlessly.

What a Transmission Actually Is

A transmission is not information.
It is **frequency**.

The higher realms do not give you:

- words
- sentences
- instructions
- teachings

They give you:

- vibration
- clarity
- wisdom
- expanded consciousness
- energetic codes
- symbolic language
- multidimensional understanding

Your mind later interprets this into meaning.

Transmissions bypass logic and enter directly into:

- your energy field
- your intuition
- your cellular memory
- your soul awareness

This is why a Grand Master will often **know** something they were never taught.

The teaching was energetic, not verbal.

Transmissions Arrive When You Are Ready — Not When You Ask

You cannot force or "pull" a transmission from the higher realms.

They come when:

- the energy is aligned
- the lesson is timely
- your vibration is stable
- your heart is open
- your ego is quiet
- your mind is still
- your soul is prepared
- the lineage sees your readiness

Transmissions are an act of grace.
They cannot be demanded.

The more peaceful and surrendered you are,
the more naturally they appear.

How Transmissions Feel

They can feel like:

- a wave of light
- a soft expansion behind the heart
- tingling through the crown
- heat in the hands
- a quiet knowing
- sudden clarity
- a shift in the room's atmosphere
- an inner "click"
- gentle pressure around the head
- a feeling of presence
- tears for no reason
- a moment of deep peace

Some transmissions come like lightning —
fast and powerful.

Others come like sunrise —
slow, warm, and gentle.

Each is perfect for the lesson being shared.

Sources of Transmissions

Transmissions may come from:

◇ Archangels

Often felt as structured, powerful, clarifying energy.

◇ Ascended guides

Felt as warmth, wisdom, compassion, and symbolic understanding.

◇ The spiritual lineage of Reiki

Felt as a sudden expansion of healing ability or intuitive precision.

◇ The healer's own Higher Self

Often the clearest and most direct source.

◇ Divine Intelligence

The purest form of transmission — wordless, formless, all-encompassing knowing.

The highest transmissions come not from beings, but from **the Source field itself**.

Why Transmissions Become Frequent at the Grand Master Level

As a Grand Master's consciousness expands:

- the aura stabilizes
- the heart becomes more open
- intuition strengthens
- ego softens
- spiritual ethics deepen
- channeling becomes natural
- energy sensitivity sharpens

This creates a consistent, reliable bridge to the higher realms.

You become a vessel that can safely hold and translate higher frequencies — without distortion.

Therefore transmissions become:

- easier
- clearer
- more frequent
- more integrated
- more actionable
- more aligned with your work

Your entire life becomes a classroom of Spirit.

The Teaching Unfolds After the Transmission

Transmissions rarely make sense immediately.

Days or weeks later, you may realize:

- a new healing technique emerged
- a new intuitive ability activated
- a deeper understanding clicked into place
- a symbol revealed a hidden layer
- you responded to a client with greater clarity
- you sensed energy in a new dimension
- you taught something you never learned
- your inner vision expanded
- your healing field grew stronger

A transmission plants the seed.
Your consciousness grows the understanding.

The teaching unfolds organically.

Discernment: Knowing the Difference Between Ego and Transmission

A Grand Master must be able to distinguish:

True transmission

- feels peaceful
- expands your awareness
- carries a high vibration
- creates clarity
- aligns with love and truth

- arrives effortlessly
- feels "right" in the body
- is not emotional in nature
- never contradicts spiritual ethics

Ego-influenced intuition

- feels urgent or dramatic
- creates confusion
- comes with emotion
- feels heavy or forced
- elevates the personal self
- contradicts previous truth
- increases tension in the body

True transmissions always elevate you.
Ego-intuition contracts you.

A Grand Master knows the difference.

Receiving Transmissions Is a Skill — and a State of Being

The most powerful transmissions come when you are:

- grounded
- relaxed
- receptive
- in a state of gratitude
- emotionally balanced
- spiritually humble
- aligned with your higher self

Transmissions cannot enter:

- chaos
- fear
- ego projection
- emotional turbulence
- mental noise

Your stillness is the doorway.
Your humility is the invitation.
Your openness is the receiver.

You Become a Transmission for Others

At the highest level of Reiki mastery,
you no longer only **receive** transmissions —
you *become* one.

Your presence, your field, your consciousness
transmits wisdom, healing, and clarity to others.

Students learn not only from your teachings,
but from the **frequency you carry.**

This is the hallmark of a true Grand Reiki Master:

Your being becomes the teaching.

✦ PART IV — THE SPIRITUAL INITIATION

✦ Chapter 12 — The Tests: The Gateways Every Grand Master Must Pass

The Loneliness of the Path

Why the higher the calling, the quieter the road

Every authentic spiritual path contains a threshold where the seeker must walk alone.

Not abandoned.
Not unsupported.
But **alone**, in the sense that no one can walk your inner landscape for you.

This loneliness is not a punishment.
It is an initiation—one of the first and most essential tests on the road to Grand Mastery.

Because at this level, healing is no longer a technique.
It is identity.
It is consciousness.
It is the embodiment of purity, humility, and inner truth.

And that level of becoming cannot occur in crowds.

It happens in stillness.

The Loneliness Arrives Without Warning

Most healers do not expect this test.

It often appears after:

- an awakening
- a powerful attunement
- a profound intuitive expansion
- a moment of spiritual elevation
- a deep transmission
- or a sudden shift in consciousness

It begins quietly—
a sense of being separate from others,
a feeling that conversations no longer nourish,
that relationships feel misaligned,
that the world moves differently than you do.

You aren't broken.
You are being **recalibrated**.

Your vibration is rising beyond what your old world can match.

Loneliness Creates Inner Strength

In loneliness, you discover:

- your own voice
- your own truth
- your own intuition
- your own connection to Spirit
- your own spiritual integrity
- your own resilience

Healers who never walk through this gateway
never develop the depth required for Grand Mastery.

Loneliness reveals whether your practice is:

- people-pleasing
- performance
- external validation
- spiritual identity
- ego-driven
- or true service

The test purifies your intention.

Loneliness Is the Absence of External Noise

Loneliness removes:

- distractions
- opinions
- expectations
- external influences
- emotional entanglements

The silence left behind is not emptiness—it is **space**.

Space for:

- Spirit to speak
- your intuition to sharpen
- your soul to reveal itself
- healing abilities to deepen
- old karmic energies to release
- your consciousness to expand

The quiet is not your enemy.
It is your teacher.

Loneliness Separates You From What Cannot Enter Your Next Level

Every spiritual promotion requires a shedding.

The loneliness comes to:

- dissolve outdated relationships
- release co-dependent attachments
- remove unaligned paths
- clear energetic interference
- break old identity structures

It is the pruning that allows you to grow.

Spirit removes what cannot carry the frequency of your next chapter.

Loneliness Teaches You to Rely on Spirit, Not Approval

At the Grand Master level,
your work is not validated by:

- applause
- numbers
- certificates
- followers
- praise
- external recognition

Your validation comes from:

- alignment
- integrity
- service
- clarity
- inner knowing
- divine support

The loneliness teaches you that your greatest companion is Spirit, and that you are never truly alone.

The Path Is Lonely Because Leadership Is Lonely

Every spiritual leader walks through this threshold.

A Grand Reiki Master must:

- make decisions others cannot understand
- follow guidance that contradicts logic
- stand in truth when others resist
- protect the field even when misunderstood
- carry wisdom others are not ready for
- see in dimensions others cannot perceive

This requires the strength that only solitude cultivates.

Your loneliness becomes your leadership.

Loneliness Is a Symptom of Expansion, Not Failure

When you expand beyond your familiar frequency:

- the old world cannot hold you
- the old conversations cannot reach you
- the old relationships cannot understand you

It is not that you are "too much."
It is that your energy is growing beyond what your surroundings reflect.

You are not losing people.
You are gaining yourself.

The loneliness ends the moment you stabilize in your new vibration—
and new soul-aligned people begin appearing in your life.

The Gift Hidden in the Loneliness

Once the loneliness is accepted rather than resisted,
it transforms into:

- deep inner peace
- profound self-trust
- intimacy with Spirit
- intuitive mastery
- emotional sovereignty
- the ability to hold space for others
- the capacity for leadership
- a soul-level independence

This is the strength of a Grand Master.
Not isolation.
But **inner freedom**.

The loneliness was a cocoon.
Your initiation into wings.

Loss, Surrender, Faith

When Spirit Strips Away What You Cannot Carry Into Your Calling

Every Grand Reiki Master encounters a season when life
removes something —
or someone —
that once felt essential.

This loss is not punishment.
It is **preparation**.

Spirit cannot take you into higher spiritual service
carrying weight that will interfere with clarity, neutrality, or
alignment.

So loss becomes a sacred fire.
The catalyst for surrender.
And the birthplace of faith.

This is one of the most difficult gateways —
because unlike loneliness, which is internal,
loss is unmistakably felt in the physical world.

Yet it is also one of the most transformative initiations you
will ever walk.

Loss Arrives When Something Must Be Released for Your Evolution

Loss may take many forms:

- the end of a relationship
- the death of a loved one
- the collapse of a career
- the dissolution of identity
- the disappearance of opportunities
- the loss of financial security
- the shattering of certainty
- the release of a role you built your life upon

This is not a random misfortune. It is the pruning that allows your spiritual maturity to grow. Loss removes what anchors you to the past. So you can rise into the future.

Loss Reveals Attachment

Loss is not about what was taken away.
It is about what was **attached to what was taken.**

Attachment reveals:

- where the ego clings
- where fear hides
- where identity forms
- where comfort replaces growth
- where illusions distort energy
- where trust has not yet entered
- where control still dominates

A Grand Master must see clearly.
Attachment clouds vision.

Loss cleans the lens.

Surrender Is Not Giving Up — It Is Giving Over

Surrender is the moment when the soul whispers:

"I release my grip so Spirit may guide."

It is the turning point where:

- resistance collapses
- clarity returns
- peace rises
- healing begins
- strength awakens
- the heart softens
- intuition amplifies

Surrender is the doorway through which all spiritual gifts expand.

It is not passive.
It is powerful.

To surrender is to finally let life work **with** you instead of against your expectations.

True Surrender Happens When You Have No Choice Left

Many people talk about surrender.
Few experience it.

True surrender occurs when:

- the situation cannot be fixed
- the past cannot be reclaimed
- the outcome cannot be controlled
- the illusion of certainty collapses
- your plans fall apart
- your identity dissolves
- nothing makes sense

When everything you relied on disappears,
you have only two choices:

Break.
Or bow.

A Grand Master bows.

This bow is not defeat.
It is devotion.

Surrender Restores the Flow of Life Force

When the ego lets go,
life force returns.

You begin to feel:

- lighter
- clearer
- more aligned
- more intuitive
- more supported
- more connected
- more spiritually guided

Surrender removes constriction,
allowing Reiki to move through you at higher voltage.

Loss empties you.
Surrender opens you.
Faith fills you.

Faith Is Not Believing — It Is Trusting Without Evidence

Faith is often misunderstood.

It is not:

- blind optimism
- hoping for the best
- convincing yourself with affirmations
- pretending things are fine
- pushing positivity

Faith is the spiritual courage to say:

"I cannot see the way, but I feel the truth."
"I cannot understand this now, but I trust the path."
"I cannot control anything, but I know I am guided."

Faith is the ability to walk forward
without needing proof.

It is the bridge between your pain and Spirit's plan.

Loss Tests Your Faith — Surrender Strengthens It

The test works like this:

Loss shakes your world.
Surrender softens your heart.
Faith restores your vision.

This cycle repeats until something inside you anchors:

A knowing that you are never walking alone.

Not once.
Not ever.

When this truth roots into your bones,
your healing ability expands dramatically.

Because faith is a frequency —
and it is the **central frequency of Grand Mastery**.

What Loss Teaches That Nothing Else Can

Loss teaches:

- impermanence
- compassion
- humility
- detachment
- inner strength
- emotional sovereignty
- trust in Spirit
- the wisdom of timing
- the shaping of purpose

Loss removes illusions
and reveals truth.

And truth is the foundation of all higher spiritual
responsibility.

After Loss: The Rebuilding of the Soul

Once loss has cleansed you
and surrender has softened you
and faith has anchored you—

a new version of you begins to rise:

- clearer
- stronger
- wiser
- more compassionate
- more spiritually attuned

- more emotionally stable
- more aligned with your soul
- more capable of leading others

Loss is not the end of anything.
It is the beginning of your **becoming**.

Every Grand Master carries a story of loss.
What makes them who they are
is not what they lost—
but what they rose into.

Shadow Work

The Courage to Face What Has Been Avoided, Buried, or Denied

Every Grand Reiki Master is required to face their shadow.

Not once.
Not in theory.
Not as a spiritual concept.
But in the raw, unfiltered intimacy of truth.

Shadow work is not about darkness.
It is about **integration**.

It is the process of bringing light into:

- buried emotions
- unhealed wounds
- unconscious patterns
- hidden motives
- fears
- resentments
- self-deception
- old identities
- past failures
- shame
- jealousy
- anger
- grief
- guilt
- unmet needs

The shadow holds everything the ego has tried to hide—
not because it is "bad,"
but because it once felt unsafe to feel.

A Grand Master cannot carry shadow into higher realms.
It creates distortion.
It limits perception.

It weakens intuition.
It interferes with the purity of the healing field.

Shadow work is the sacred cleansing
that prepares the healer to carry higher light.

The Shadow Appears When You Are Ready to Grow

The shadow does not emerge during moments of peace.
It emerges when:

- your vibration rises
- your consciousness expands
- your healing ability deepens
- you step into leadership
- your next level approaches
- your soul is calling you forward

This is why shadow work feels sudden:

You grow — and the shadow rises to match the height of
your ascent.

It is not regression.
It is **alignment**.

Spirit will not allow you to ascend with unexamined wounds.

Shadow Work Requires Radical Honesty

Shadow work forces you to confront truths like:

- "I am not as healed as I pretend to be."
- "I am afraid of my own power."
- "I use spirituality to avoid discomfort."
- "I still carry resentment toward someone I claim to forgive."
- "I am jealous of the success of others."
- "I fear not being enough."
- "I fear being too much."
- "I still want validation more than truth."
- "I hide behind my role instead of revealing my heart."

These truths are not shaming.
They are **freeing**.

Because the moment you see the shadow,
it loses its power.

The Shadow Is Not the Enemy — It Is the Wounded Self

The shadow is not darkness.
It is the part of you that:

- was unseen
- was unvalued
- was criticized
- was hurt
- was misunderstood
- was abandoned

- was told to be quiet
- was told to be strong
- was told to get over it
- was told it was "too much"
- was told it was "not enough"

The shadow is the younger you
who never received what they needed.

Shadow work is **self-rescue**.

It is the reparenting of your emotional, spiritual, and energetic self.

Shadow Work Purifies the Healing Channel

A healer's shadow leaks into their work unless integrated.

Unexamined shadow creates:

- projection
- rescuing
- martyrdom
- superiority
- spiritual bypassing
- avoidance
- emotional manipulation
- fear-based decisions
- unclear intuition
- energetic entanglement
- unclear boundaries
- attachment to outcome

A Grand Master must be a **clear channel**.
Shadow work is the purification process that removes distortion.

It is an act of spiritual hygiene.

The Shadow Reveals the Ego's Last Strongholds

When the shadow rises, ego resists:

- denial
- avoidance
- blame
- defensiveness
- anger
- justification
- spiritual superiority
- false positivity
- over-explaining
- withdrawing

This resistance is the sign that shadow work is working.

The ego fights hardest at the moment of transformation.

A Grand Master learns to observe the ego without obeying it.

Shadow Work Deepens Compassion for Others

Once you face your own shadow, you understand:

- grief without judgment
- fear without criticism
- anger without shame
- confusion without frustration
- wounds without disgust
- imperfection without rejection

Your compassion becomes real.

Because you no longer heal from a place of separation.
You heal from a place of **shared humanity**.

Shadow work strips away spiritual arrogance
and replaces it with tenderness.

Shadow Integration Unlocks Power

When you integrate shadow, you gain:

- emotional strength
- intuitive clarity
- inner confidence
- true humility
- deeper wisdom
- unshakeable faith
- authentic presence
- spiritual maturity
- freedom from fear
- alignment with truth

The parts of yourself you once rejected
become sources of power.

Shadow becomes strength.
Pain becomes wisdom.
Fear becomes insight.
Vulnerability becomes courage.

This is the alchemy of Grand Mastery.

Shadow Work Is the Bridge Between Human and Divine

Without shadow work, you remain spiritual on the surface.

With shadow work, you become spiritual in truth.

This gateway teaches that:

You cannot embody higher love
without meeting the places within you where love once could
not enter.

Shadow work is the integration of humanity and divinity
into one coherent, compassionate, powerful being.

This is the work of a Grand Reiki Master.

Discernment

The Test of Knowing What Is True, What Is Ego, and What Is Spirit

The farther you travel on the spiritual path, the more essential discernment becomes.

At the beginning of a healer's journey, intuition feels magical.
At the Grand Master level, intuition must be **accurate, ethical, and precise**—because your work influences not only energy, but people's lives, choices, and healing.

Discernment is the ability to feel the difference between:

- intuition and emotion
- Spirit and wishful thinking
- guidance and projection
- clarity and fear
- truth and desire
- alignment and attachment
- higher beings and lower interference
- destiny and distraction

Discernment is **the guardian of your integrity**.

It ensures that your healing comes from pure alignment, not personal agenda.

This is one of the most important gates a Grand Master must pass.

Discernment Begins Where Intuition Ends

Intuition is the ability to perceive energy.
Discernment is the ability to interpret that perception correctly.

Intuition says:
"I feel something here."

Discernment asks:
"What is the source of this feeling?
Is it mine?
The client's?
Spirit?
Or fear?"

Without discernment, intuition becomes:

- unreliable
- emotionally biased
- influenced by personal wounds
- shaped by expectations
- clouded by attachment

Discernment cleans the lens.

Discernment Requires Emotional Neutrality

A Grand Master cannot accurately read energy while emotionally entangled in:

- fear
- anger
- grief
- hope
- expectation
- personal bias
- attachment to outcome
- desire for a certain answer

Emotions do not distort intuition—
they distort interpretation.

Discernment is the ability to feel emotion
without letting it become the storyteller.

The more neutral you are,
the more accurate your readings become.

Discernment Reveals Whether Guidance Comes From Spirit or Ego

Spirit speaks with:

- clarity
- neutrality
- calm
- truth
- compassion
- stillness
- simplicity

Ego speaks with:

- urgency
- fear
- pressure
- drama
- confusion
- intensity
- "shoulds" and "musts"

Spirit whispers. Ego demands.
Spirit arrives gently. Ego pushes loudly.
Spirit is expansive. Ego is constrictive.
The body knows the difference.

The Body Is the Greatest Tool of Discernment

Your body responds instantly to truth and distortion.

Truth feels like:

- expansion
- peace
- warmth
- resonance
- openness
- clarity
- neutrality

Falsehood feels like:

- pressure
- constriction
- tension
- heaviness
- nausea
- confusion
- emotional spikes

The body never lies.
The mind often does.
Discernment begins in the body, not the brain.

Discernment Protects the Healing Field

Without discernment, healers may unintentionally:

- project their feelings onto clients
- mistake personal fear for guidance
- misinterpret symbolic images
- assume instead of observe
- follow intuition that is not clean
- give spiritual advice that is inaccurate
- confuse empathy with truth
- absorb energy that does not belong to them
- open doors to lower vibrations

A Grand Master must guard the purity of the field.

Discernment is the shield that keeps the work clean.

Discernment Deepens Through Experience, Not Speed

True discernment develops over time:

- one healing session at a time
- one intuitive misstep at a time
- one correction at a time
- one moment of clarity at a time
- one confrontation with ego at a time

Mistakes are not failures.
They are initiations.

Discernment grows the fastest through courageous honesty.

Discernment Requires the Courage to See the Truth

Most people avoid truth because truth demands change.

Discernment forces you to admit when:

- your intuition was wrong
- your ego interfered
- your emotions clouded perception
- you wanted a certain outcome
- you projected onto a client
- a guide wasn't a guide
- you misread a signal
- you followed desire instead of alignment

This honesty is what transforms a healer into a Grand Master.

Only those willing to see truth can hold true light.

Discernment Helps You Identify the Source of Guidance

A Grand Master learns to differentiate between:

◇ *Spirit*

Feels calm, precise, neutral, loving.

◇ *Higher Self*

Feels familiar, direct, deeply wise.

◊ *Ascended guides*

Feels symbolic, multi-layered, gentle, expansive.

◊ *Archangels*

Feels structured, powerful, clear, authoritative.

◊ *Client's emotional field*

Feels heavy, personal, emotionally charged.

◊ *Collective energy*

Feels wide, diffuse, unfocused.

◊ *Ego*

Feels urgent, pressured, dramatic.

◊ *Interference*

Feels sharp, chaotic, draining, confusing.

This is master-level discernment.

Discernment Is the Test That Never Ends

The Grand Master's Lifelong Compass of Truth, Purity, and Alignment

Even the most advanced healers must continually refine their ability to discern.

Because as your power grows,
so does your responsibility.

And as your responsibility grows,
so does your need for clarity, precision, and purity.

The higher your calling,
the higher your standard.

Discernment is the ability to see through:

- illusion
- projection
- ego
- emotional influence
- spiritual interference
- false guidance
- energetic distortion
- wishful thinking
- people's expectations
- your own bias
- the collective field

It is the **inner compass** that guides a Grand Reiki Master through every decision, every teaching, every healing, and every spiritual encounter.

Discernment is not a skill you master once.
It is a test that continues for life.

The Call to Step Forward

The Moment Spirit Asks You to Become Who You Were Always Meant to Be

Every Grand Reiki Master experiences a moment where Spirit whispers—not gently, not suggestively, but with unmistakable clarity:

"It is time."

Time to rise.
Time to lead.
Time to teach.
Time to embody the frequency you have spent a lifetime cultivating.
Time to become the version of yourself your soul prepared you to be.

This is the call to step forward.

It is not a command from outside you.
It is the awakening of who you already are.

The Call Comes When You Least Expect It

The call rarely arrives when you feel ready.

It appears:

- in the middle of ordinary life
- during spiritual exhaustion
- after loss
- during deep healing
- after a powerful attunement
- in a moment of quiet
- or at the height of chaos

The call does not wait for perfection.
It arrives when Spirit knows you are strong enough to say yes—
even if you still feel uncertain.

The Call Does Not Ask Permission

Spirit does not ask:

"Would you like to?"
"Do you think you're ready?"
"Should we schedule this for later?"

The call is a **soul-level activation**.

A rising in the chest.
A remembering in the heart.
A clarity in the spirit.

It is the moment your higher self takes the lead
and your human self follows.

You Know the Call Is Real Because It Disrupts You

The call shakes you awake.

It may arrive as:

- an intense inner knowing
- a dream that repeats
- a message during meditation
- synchronicities that cannot be ignored
- students suddenly appearing
- opportunities aligning
- a shift in your intuition
- a change in your energy field
- a feeling that "something is beginning"
- Spirit speaking directly to you

The call disrupts your comfort
and rearranges your inner world.

Because your old life is too small for your next purpose.

The Call Requires You to Let Go of Who You Were

To step forward, you must release:

- old roles
- old identities
- outdated relationships
- limiting beliefs
- self-doubt
- fear of being seen
- fear of leadership
- fear of failure
- fear of judgment
- the need for approval

Stepping forward means stepping into truth— not into performance.

It is the moment your soul becomes louder than your ego.

The Call Always Arrives With Resistance

Every healer faces internal resistance:

- "Who am I to do this?"
- "What if I'm not ready?"
- "What if people judge me?"
- "What if I fail?"
- "What if this is ego?"
- "What if I'm wrong?"
- "What if I'm not good enough?"

Resistance is not a sign you shouldn't step forward. It is the sign that this step will change your life.

If the call were easy, it would not be destiny.

The Call Is Not to Be Bigger — But to Be Truer

Spirit does not ask you to:

- be louder
- be impressive
- be more spiritual
- be perfect
- be extraordinary

Spirit asks you to be **true**.

True to:

- your gift
- your calling
- your soul
- your integrity
- your intuition
- your purpose
- your path

Stepping forward is stepping into the way you were always meant to shine.

Not larger—
but real.

The Call Opens Doors That Were Always Meant for You

Once you say yes—even quietly—things begin to shift.

You may notice:

- more synchronicities
- deeper intuitive messages
- increased healing power
- new students finding you
- unexpected invitations
- clarity replacing confusion
- courage rising where fear once lived
- your energy expanding
- your purpose sharpening

A soul aligned is a soul unstoppable.
The call moves mountains in your favor.

Stepping Forward Is Not About Confidence — It Is About Faith

You do not step forward because you feel ready.
You step forward because you trust Spirit will walk with you.

A Grand Master knows:

Confidence follows action.
Faith precedes it.

The call is answered not with certainty,
but with devotion.

Saying Yes Changes Everything

The moment you say yes:

- the energy around you shifts
- your vibration rises
- Spirit collaborates with you
- your path aligns
- your destiny activates
- your gifts deepen
- your intuition sharpens
- your leadership awakens

Stepping forward does not make you a Grand Master.
It reveals the Grand Master you already are.

This gateway is the bridge
between potential and embodiment.

It is the turning point
between who you have been
and who you are here to become.

✦ Chapter 13 — The Moment Spirit Chooses You

The Initiation That Cannot Be Planned, Predicted, or Earned

Some moments in a healer's spiritual evolution are not created by human hands.
They do not follow curriculum, lineage steps, or ceremony.
They are not scheduled into a class outline or passed down by another teacher.

There are moments that come directly from Spirit.

A Grand Reiki Master is not chosen because of knowledge, skill, or technique.
They are chosen because:

- their heart is ready
- their vibration is aligned
- their surrender is complete
- their path has ripened
- their ego has softened
- their soul says yes

This chapter is about that moment—the sacred, unmistakable instant when Spirit steps into your life and lifts you into a higher calling you did not ask for, but were born to embody.

My Moment of Being Chosen

Not every healer's initiation into Grand Mastery is meant to be retold.
Some moments are too sacred to repeat, unfolding in a way that belongs entirely to the soul who lived it.

I shared the details of *my* moment of being chosen in **Chapter 3**, where Spirit intervened in an ordinary class and shifted my role in an instant.
Rather than restating that story here, let this section simply acknowledge a universal truth:

Every Grand Reiki Master experiences a moment—quiet or powerful, sudden or subtle—when Spirit steps in and elevates them beyond technique, title, or expectation.

It may not happen in ceremony.
It may not happen during meditation.
It may not even be recognized until later.

But when it happens, the healer knows:

- something has changed
- something has opened
- something has been bestowed
- something has awakened

This section stands not to repeat my story,
but to honor *the* moment each Grand Master receives:

The moment Spirit says, **"Now, you are ready."**

What This Moment Really Was

At the time, it may have felt like:

- surprise
- confusion
- a shift
- a spontaneous instruction
- a moment you simply surrendered to

But in spiritual truth, this moment was a **Divine Appointment**.

This is what actually occurred:

- You were removed from the role of teacher
- You were placed into the role of receiver
- The lineage stepped in
- The symbols were drawn directly from the higher realms
- You were lifted into a higher frequency
- Spirit recognized you as ready
- The path of Grand Mastery opened

It wasn't planned.
It wasn't taught.
It wasn't directed by a human hand.
It was **bestowed**.

How Spirit Chooses a Grand Master

Spirit does not choose Grand Masters through:

- hierarchy
- seniority
- time served
- certificates
- technical mastery
- the number of students taught

Spirit chooses based on vibration, integrity, readiness, and surrender.

The true signs are:

- a sudden, undeniable inner directive
- a shift in the energy field that feels divinely orchestrated
- an attunement that comes from above, not from a person
- a moment that interrupts ordinary life
- guidance that is simple, direct, and absolute
- the merging of teacher and student consciousness
- clarity so strong it cannot be doubted
- a full-body "yes" that bypasses the mind

It is not dramatic.
It is **pure**.

Not loud.
But **absolute**.

Why Spirit Chooses You in a Moment of Service

Spirit often chooses a healer during a moment of service because:

- the heart is open
- the ego is quiet
- humility is active
- the mind is focused on helping others
- the vibration is already elevated
- the field is coherent
- the higher realms can enter without resistance

This is why your initiation happened **while you were teaching**.

Because teaching *is* service.
Service is surrender.
Surrender is readiness.

Spirit chooses those who are already living the vibration of leadership, not those who seek the title.

What Changed in That Initiation

From that moment on:

- Your consciousness expanded
- Your healing field increased in radius
- Your attunements deepened
- Your intuition sharpened
- Your ability to channel higher beings strengthened
- Your connection to the lineage became direct
- Your presence carried higher frequency

- Your understanding of Reiki shifted from technique to embodiment

You crossed the threshold from:

Master → Grand Master
not through knowledge,
but through **transmission**.

How You Know Spirit Has Chosen You

A Grand Master feels:

- a knowing that cannot be explained
- a shift in the aura
- clarity where confusion once existed
- humility so deep it feels like gratitude
- an expansion that is unmistakable
- a sense of stepping into your true identity
- the dissolving of old fear
- the recalibration of purpose

The world may look the same,
but you are no longer the same within it.

The Reader's Reflection: What About Your Moment?

Every healer who reads this chapter will wonder:

"Will this happen to me?"
"Has Spirit already chosen me and I didn't realize it?"
"What does my moment look like?"

The answer:

Spirit chooses every healer differently.
The moment may come:

- in meditation
- in prayer
- in dream
- during a session
- during a crisis
- in stillness
- through intuition
- through another person
- in absolute ordinary moments

It will come when the soul is ready, not when the mind feels prepared.

Your moment will be unmistakable,
not because it is loud—
but because it is true.

How It Feels

The moment Spirit chooses you is unlike anything that comes through study, practice, or human guidance.
It does not feel dramatic or overwhelming.
It feels *true*.

There is a quiet shift inside your body, a full-body knowing that rises without force.
Your energy expands, yet you feel lighter.
Your mind softens, yet you become clearer.
Your heart opens in a way that feels both familiar and entirely new.

Some describe it as:

- a warmth moving through the chest
- a deep stillness settling over the mind
- a presence standing just behind or above them
- a vibration lifting around the hands or crown
- a clarity that arrives without words
- a sense of being held, witnessed, or recognized

But the essence is always the same:

You feel aligned with something greater than yourself—not as a follower, but as a partner.

Not elevated by ego,
but lifted by grace.

It is gentle, but absolute.
Subtle, but unmistakable.
Quiet, but life-defining.

And afterward, nothing inside you is quite the same.

What Changes Energetically

When Spirit chooses you, the shift is not just emotional or intuitive—it is energetic. Your entire field reorganizes itself to hold a higher frequency of light. The change is subtle enough that you can still function in the world, yet profound enough that every part of your spiritual system begins operating differently.

Here's what transforms beneath the surface:

Your Aura Expands

Your energetic field grows wider, fuller, and more coherent. Even people who are not intuitive may feel calmer or safer around you without knowing why.

Your Channels Open More Fully

The pathways through which Reiki flows—
the crown, the hands, the heart, the central channel—
all become clearer, stronger, and more receptive.

Reiki stops being *sent*.
It begins being **embodied**.

Your Frequency Stabilizes

There is less fluctuation between your "higher self moments" and your human emotions.
Your energy becomes steady, grounded, reliable—
a lighthouse instead of a candle in the wind.

Your Intuition Sharpens Instantly

You begin receiving:

- information faster
- clarity without needing interpretation
- guidance without second-guessing
- insights without overthinking

Intuition becomes a natural response, not an activated skill.

Your Healing Presence Deepens

You don't need to *do* more. Your presence itself becomes a healing catalyst. People feel better simply by being near you because your field carries coherence.

The Symbols Move From Tools to Frequencies

Instead of drawing them, you **radiate** them.
The symbols live in your field, not your hands.

Your Connection to the Higher Realms Strengthens

You begin to sense:

- Spirit
- archangels
- guides
- ancestors
- the Reiki lineage
- the Source field

with new clarity and ease.
You feel accompanied, not just assisted.

Your Energy No Longer Depletes the Same Way

Because you're not drawing from your own reserves.
You are tapped into a larger current.
Your body becomes the conduit, not the generator.

You Begin Resonating With Your True Purpose

Your field aligns with your destiny,
often unlocking new paths, new insights, or new callings that
had been dormant.

Energetically, the moment Spirit chooses you is not a single
event—
it is an upgrade.
A reconfiguration.
A re-tuning of your entire system to a higher octave of
consciousness.

It is the shift from practicing healing
to *embodying* a healing frequency.

What You Begin to "Know"

When Spirit elevates you into Grand Mastery, a new kind of
knowing awakens—
not learned,
not reasoned,
not imagined,
but *remembered*.

It is the quiet inner certainty that rises without effort,
the type of knowledge that does not need validation because
it carries its own truth.

This knowing unfolds in layers:

You Know What Is Needed Without Being Told

You begin to sense:

- where the energy should go
- what the client truly needs
- which layer of their field is calling
- what their soul is ready to release
- where the deeper root lies

Not through analysis—
but through resonance.

You Know When Spirit Is Present

You feel the shift instantly:

- the air thickens or softens
- the space becomes brighter
- a quiet pressure moves around you
- the room feels "held"

It is unmistakable.
You no longer wonder if Spirit is with you—
you *know*.

You Know When Not to Interfere

This is one of the highest forms of mastery.

At the Grand Master level, you can sense:

- when healing would disrupt a karmic lesson
- when someone is not ready to release
- when stepping back is the true service
- when silence is more powerful than energy

You trust the soul's timing more than your desire to help.

You Know Truth in Your Body

Your intuition becomes somatic—felt in the body before the mind.

You may feel:

- expansion when something is true
- contraction when it is not
- stillness when the answer is aligned
- subtle agitation when it is not

The body stops lying.
The energy stops confusing you.
Truth becomes a full-body experience.

You Know the Difference Between Ego Guidance and Spirit Guidance

Ego is loud, urgent, dramatic.
Spirit is quiet, steady, neutral.

As a Grand Master, you can sense:

- the purity of the message
- the origin of the guidance
- the intention behind the insight
- whether it comes from fear or from light

This discernment becomes automatic.

You Know Without Needing Proof

This is the most profound shift.

You do not require:

- signs
- validation
- reassurance
- external confirmation

You simply *know*.
And the knowing itself is peaceful.

You Know Who You Are

Perhaps the deepest change of all:
you begin to feel the truth of your own identity as a healer.

Not the title you hold.
Not the certificates you earned.
Not the roles you've played.

But the soul you have always been—the one prepared for this path long before this lifetime.

This is the knowing of a Grand Reiki Master:
quiet, accurate, steady, unshakable, and guided by Spirit rather than thought.

It is knowledge that doesn't come from learning—
but from alignment.

Spiritual Signs of Ascension

When Spirit elevates you into Grand Reiki Mastery, the shift
doesn't only happen inside your energy field—
it begins to echo outward into your daily life.
These are the subtle, sacred signs that your frequency has
risen into a higher octave of consciousness.

They are not dramatic or chaotic.
They are gentle indicators that something within you has
expanded beyond the human layer.

Here are the most common signs:

Increased Synchronicities

You notice patterns that are too precise to dismiss:

- repeating numbers
- symbolic animals
- meaningful dreams
- perfectly timed encounters
- messages appearing the moment you need them

The universe begins responding to your vibration instantly, as
if your energy and the outer world are now speaking the
same language.

Heightened Sensitivity to Energy

You may feel:

- shifts in a room before entering it
- the emotions behind people's words
- the presence of Spirit more often
- subtle vibrations in your hands or crown
- energetic "information" without explanation

Your senses expand into multidimensional awareness.

Feeling "Lifted" or Expanded

You might experience moments of:

- inner spaciousness
- lightness
- gentle euphoria
- deep peace
- effortless clarity

This is the natural state of a higher vibration integrating into your system.

Release of What No Longer Matches Your Vibration

Ascension gently removes from your life:

- outdated relationships
- old habits
- heavy emotions
- work that drains you

- environments that clash with your new frequency

These shifts are not punishment—
they are alignment.

Guidance Becomes Quicker and Clearer

You receive:

- answers before you ask
- insights before you think
- warnings before trouble arrives
- inspiration before you seek it

It feels as if the path lays itself out just as you step onto it.

Time Feels Different

You may sense:

- time slowing during healing work
- time speeding up during inspiration
- moments of "timeless awareness"
- days that feel divinely orchestrated

This occurs because ascension connects you more closely
with the non-linear realms.

Your Presence Affects Others Instantly

People may:

- open up without knowing why
- feel calmer around you
- experience healing just by being near you
- recognize something "different" in your eyes or voice

Your energy begins doing the work long before your hands do.

You Feel Accompanied

You may sense:

- guides
- angels
- ancestors
- the Reiki lineage
- the Presence of Spirit

not occasionally,
but consistently.

The feeling is not frightening—
it is comforting, familiar, and supportive.

You Experience Waves of Inner Transformation

Ascension often brings:

- sudden clarity
- unexpected emotional release
- a new level of compassion
- deeper love for yourself and others

These inner shifts occur because your system is integrating a higher consciousness.

You Begin to Recognize Your True Purpose

The noise of the world fades.
The calling of the soul strengthens.
The path becomes clearer.

You no longer chase your purpose—you align with it.

These signs are not random.
They are confirmations.
Evidence that your vibration is rising, your soul is awakening, and Spirit is preparing you for the deeper responsibilities of Grand Mastery.

Ascension is not an event.
It is a remembering.
A return to the truth of who you have always been.

How to Recognize the Calling

The calling into Grand Reiki Mastery does not arrive the way most people expect.
It does not announce itself with grand visions or dramatic spiritual fireworks.
Instead, it comes through a series of unmistakable inner shifts—quiet, steady, and deeply resonant with the truth of your soul.

The calling is not something you chase.
It is something you *recognize.*

Here are the signs:

A Persistent Inner Pull Toward Something More

You feel a subtle but constant invitation—
not from ego, but from your higher self:

- a sense that your path is expanding
- a nudge toward a deeper role
- a knowing that you are meant to guide on a larger scale

It feels less like ambition
and more like *alignment.*

Your Current Level No Longer Feels Like the Full Expression of Your Gift

You still love the work.
You still feel connected.
But something inside whispers:

"There is another layer."

This restlessness is not dissatisfaction—
it is awakening.

Spirit Begins Preparing You Quietly

Before the calling becomes conscious, you may notice:

- your healing sessions feel different
- your intuition sharpens
- you attract more advanced students or clients
- symbols behave differently in your field
- your energy feels bigger than your role

Spirit expands you before you even realize why.

You Start Receiving Guidance About Teaching or Leading

Not because you want authority—
but because you feel responsible for others' growth.

The calling into Grand Mastery often begins as:

- "I need to teach this differently."
- "I feel guided to help more practitioners."
- "I'm being shown a larger way to support healing."

This is Spirit shifting you from practitioner to elder.

Silence Becomes a Source of Wisdom

You recognize the calling when:

- meditation feels deeper
- the inner voice becomes clearer
- stillness becomes nourishing
- you receive spontaneous insights without trying

Your relationship with the unseen world strengthens in a natural, effortless way.

You Feel Watched Over

Not in a fearful sense—
but in a guided, protected, supported sense.

You may feel:

- a presence during healing work
- soft pressure on the shoulders or crown
- warmth behind you
- the unmistakable sense that you are being prepared

This is the lineage acknowledging you.

Opportunities for Service Begin Expanding

The calling is almost always accompanied by:

- more people seeking you
- invitations to teach
- situations where your presence is needed
- spiritual tasks given to you intuitively

You are moved into position *before* the title arrives.

The Ego Steps Aside Without Struggle

You know you are stepping into the calling when:

- you don't crave recognition
- you don't feel the need to prove yourself
- the work feels sacred, not performative
- you feel humbled by the responsibility

Grand Mastery is not a role of status—but of stewardship.

You Experience a Sense of "Readiness Without Knowing Why"

This is the clearest sign.
There is a moment where you simply feel:

- prepared
- steady
- aligned
- open
- willing

Not because you decided—but because something inside you has ripened.

Spirit Confirms It

The most reliable sign:
Spirit gives a confirmation you cannot deny.

This may come through:

- a dream
- a message
- a meditation
- an inner voice
- a synchronicity
- a moment during healing work
- a sudden knowing

It is gentle, but absolute.

**Recognizing the calling is not about looking for signs—
it is about listening to the ones already speaking within you.**

When the calling arrives,
you won't feel excited,
or anxious,
or confused.

You will feel *ready*.

Your soul will whisper back,
"Yes... I know."

✦ Chapter 14 — The Grand Master Attunement

Preparation of the Soul

Before a healer can receive the Grand Master attunement,
something far deeper than technique must take place.
This level of initiation is not about the hands, the symbols, or
even the mind—
it is about the *readiness of the soul.*

Unlike Level 1, Level 2, or Master attunements, which prepare
a person to give and teach Reiki,
the Grand Master attunement prepares a person to **hold** Reiki.

To carry it.
To embody it.
To live it.

This chapter begins with the first and most essential step:

Preparation of the Soul

A Grand Master attunement does not begin on the day it is received.
It begins long before—quietly, invisibly, woven into the fabric of your spiritual evolution.

This preparation is not conscious.
It is not directed by human intention.
It unfolds naturally as the soul matures into alignment with its calling.

Here is what prepares a soul to receive the Grand Master frequency:

A Deep Softening of Ego

This is not about becoming perfect.
It is about becoming *transparent*.

At this level, the healer's ego becomes:

- quieter
- gentler
- less reactive
- less attached to identity
- less interested in recognition

You begin to feel more like a vessel and less like a personality.

A Lifetime (or Many Lifetimes) of Service

Grand Mastery is awarded to souls whose path carries the imprint of service.

This service does not need to be formal.
It may appear as:

- a natural desire to help
- a pattern of offering support spontaneously
- consistent compassion
- an instinct to lift others
- living with generosity of spirit

Service becomes your nature, not your task list.

Shadow Integration

Before receiving the highest frequency of Reiki, the soul must be strong enough to stand in light without creating distortion.

This means:

- facing your own wounds
- understanding your triggers
- taking responsibility for your emotions
- dissolving unhealed patterns
- choosing integrity over comfort

Grand Mastery requires a heart that is unafraid of its own depths.

Spiritual Maturity

The soul begins to display markers of evolution:

- patience that feels effortless
- compassion that emerges automatically
- wisdom that flows without force
- discernment without judgment
- humility without struggle

This maturity is not taught—it arrives.

The Capacity to Hold Larger Energy Fields

As a Grand Master, your energy is no longer just for personal healing or teaching.

You begin to hold:

- your students
- your lineage
- your community
- your purpose
- your spiritual team
- your future initiates

This requires a stable, coherent field capable of carrying responsibility without depletion.

A Calling That Will Not Go Away

You may feel:

- a pull toward deeper work
- a quiet inner knowing
- a sense that something is coming
- a readiness you cannot logically explain
- a shift inside that does not fade

This is the soul recognizing its next level.

Alignment With Spirit's Timing

The soul is prepared when:

- you no longer rush
- you no longer seek
- you no longer compare
- you no longer chase spiritual milestones

You trust the timing, the unfolding, and the guidance.
You stop "trying to become" and begin "allowing what you already are" to emerge.

The Heart Becomes the Center
The final preparation is simple but profound: Your heart becomes the source of your healing.

Not the hands.
Not the symbols.
Not the knowledge.
Not the role.

Your **heart** becomes the frequency through which Spirit works.

A Quiet Readiness

There is a moment—often subtle—when the soul becomes still.

You realize you are not waiting for something outside of you.
You are waiting for something *within* you to open.

And when it opens, you feel:

- no fear
- no urgency
- no doubt

Just a deep, peaceful recognition:

"I am ready."

This is the final preparation.

Because a Grand Master is not made through teaching—they are made through **readiness**.

A readiness that lives in the soul long before the attunement ever arrives.

The Ceremony

The Grand Master attunement does not follow the structure of Level 1, Level 2, or Master/Teacher initiations.
At this level, there is **no formal ritual**,
no prescribed sequence of movements,
and no standardized way a teacher can "perform" it.

This is because the true ceremony is not human.
It is **spiritual**.

The Grand Master ceremony unfolds in three realms at once:

- the **soul** of the healer
- the **presence** of Spirit
- the **field** of the lineage

The human world may or may not witness it,
but the higher realms always do.

Here is what defines this sacred ceremony:

It Is Silent

Unlike earlier attunements, this ceremony requires no words, no symbols, and no steps.

It is a ceremony of **stillness.**

The silence itself becomes the altar.

It Is Guided by Spirit, Not a Person

A human teacher can support, hold space, and recognize the moment—but they **cannot create it.**

Spirit:

- directs the attunement
- adjusts the frequency
- determines the timing
- orchestrates the energy
- delivers the transmission

The teacher witnesses what Spirit performs.

It Happens When the Healer Is Open, Not When They Are Expecting

Most attunements are scheduled.

This one arrives:

- between breaths
- during ordinary moments
- while teaching
- during meditation
- in sleep
- in healing work
- or in the quiet moments of service

There is no preparation ritual because the soul has already been preparing for years—sometimes lifetimes.

The Attunement Occurs Through Descent, Not Ascent

Traditional training often focuses on reaching upward—
raising vibration, expanding consciousness, striving for
mastery.

But the Grand Master ceremony is the opposite.

Energy comes **down.**

The higher realms descend into your field,
enter your crown,
and align your system to a higher octave of Reiki.

It is Spirit meeting you—
not you reaching for Spirit.

The Ceremony Is Felt, Not Seen

There may be no visible signs.
No laying on of hands.
No movement in the room.

But inside, the healer feels:

- the field expand
- the crown open
- the presence arrive
- the energy shift
- the consciousness widen

It is subtle, but unmistakable.

The Lineage Becomes Present

During this ceremony, the entire Reiki lineage gathers in a way the healer can sense, even if they do not see.

The presence may feel like:

- warmth behind you
- pressure on shoulders or crown
- a field becoming denser or brighter
- soft guidance surrounding you
- a sacred support holding the space

This is the lineage acknowledging you as one who will carry it forward.

There Is No Symbol—You Become the Symbol

In earlier levels, symbols are tools.
At the Master level, they are activated.
At the Grand Master level, something profound occurs:

The healer becomes the living embodiment of Reiki.

The ceremony shifts the practitioner from *using* symbols to *radiating* their frequencies through presence alone.

The Ceremony Is Confirmed Internally

When the attunement is finished, there is no external certificate or ritual sign.

Instead, the healer knows:

- something permanent has changed
- a spiritual contract has been completed
- the energy is different within them
- the calling has deepened
- the path ahead feels clearer

The knowing is absolute.

The Ceremony Is a Beginning, Not an Ending

Unlike Level 3, which concludes the traditional training path, the Grand Master attunement opens a new one:

- deeper teachings
- higher intuition
- stronger spiritual guidance
- new responsibilities
- clearer purpose
- the call to lead and mentor others

It is not a graduation.
It is an awakening.

The Grand Master ceremony is not something you attend.
It is something you receive.
It is not done by hands.
It is done by Spirit.
It is not performed.
It is bestowed.

And when it arrives,
the healer does not rise—
the light descends.

The Silent Energetic Moment

Every Grand Master attunement is anchored by one sacred event—
a moment so quiet, so subtle, and so deeply felt
that words cannot fully describe it.

It is the instant when Spirit steps into your field
and the attunement truly occurs.

This moment is rarely dramatic.
It is not marked by light flashes, visions, or overwhelming sensations.
Instead, it arrives like **a breath between worlds**—
brief, still, and infinitely powerful.

Here is what defines that moment:

Time Seems to Pause

You may notice:

- the room feels still
- sounds soften or disappear
- your awareness becomes spacious
- everything slows into a single point of presence

It feels as if you are suspended in a pocket of timelessness.

A Softening Runs Through the Body

Not a rush of energy,
but a gentle unfolding.

Your:

- shoulders relax
- breath deepens
- heart opens
- mind quiets

It is the body yielding to a higher vibration.

A Presence Enters the Field

This presence is unmistakable.

You may feel:

- warmth
- a subtle pressure
- a hand on your shoulder
- a glow at the crown
- a soft expansion behind the heart

It is not external—
it is *through* you.

The Energy Shifts From Effort to Grace

Up until this moment,
you may feel like you are meditating, opening, preparing.

But when the silent moment arrives,
all effort dissolves.

Something moves on your behalf.
Something aligns you.
Something activates you.

This is Spirit working directly.

You Feel Both Held and Expanded

It is one of the few experiences in life where you feel:

- deeply grounded
- profoundly uplifted
- fully supported
- and gently expanded

all at once.

Your field stretches into a higher frequency
while your soul feels completely safe.

A Knowing Drops Into the Heart

Not a thought.
Not an idea.
A knowing.

A quiet inner message that feels like:

- "This is it."
- "It has begun."
- "You are ready."

This knowing arrives without emotion, without drama—
just pure truth.

The Lineage Touches Your Field

For a brief moment,
you can sense the presence of the Reiki lineage:

- behind you
- beside you
- above you

It feels like being acknowledged,
greeted,
welcomed.

Not as a student—
but as a holder of the light.

The Energy Descends and Anchors

The actual attunement is a *descent*:

- a gentle downward flow
- a soft settling into your crown
- a warmth integrating through the heart
- a glow moving through the central channel

There is no force.
Only grace.

The energy integrates like light soaking into water.

The Moment Ends as Quietly as It Began

There is no dramatic ending.
The presence doesn't withdraw sharply.

It simply lifts,
the way dawn lifts darkness—
gently, gradually, organically.

You become aware of the room again,
the sounds,
your breath.

But you are not the same.

Afterward, Silence Remains Inside You

Even when the moment passes,
a deep inner silence stays.

It is not emptiness—
but fullness.

A soft hum of knowing,
a deeper peace,
a sense of having been touched by something sacred
that now lives within you.

**The silent energetic moment is the true heart of the Grand
Master attunement.**
It is the point where Spirit enters, aligns, blesses, and activates
the soul in a way no human can replicate.

It is not loud.
It is not dramatic.
It is not visible.

It is sacred, quiet, and absolute.

What Is Passed On by Spirit

In the Grand Master attunement, Spirit does not pass on techniques, symbols, or steps.
Those belong to the human levels of Reiki.

At this stage, what is transmitted is **essence**—
the pure, undiluted consciousness of Reiki itself.

This transmission is subtle, powerful, and multi-layered.
It does not enter through the mind.
It enters through the *field*, the *heart*, and the *soul's memory*.

Here is what Spirit truly passes on:

The Frequency of the Lineage

The Grand Master receives the deeper current of Reiki—the part that flows beneath the techniques and symbols.

This includes:

- the original essence of Usui
- the ancestral healing current
- the collective wisdom of all Masters before you
- the consciousness of the Reiki stream itself

It is the invisible "root system" of the lineage.

Direct Connection to the Source Field

At this level, Spirit activates a connection that bypasses all forms of structure.

You begin to draw from:

- universal life force
- divine intelligence
- the quantum field
- higher-dimensional light

instead of only channeling through learned pathways.

This connection becomes permanent.

The Higher Octave of Healing Light

Spirit passes on a frequency that cannot be accessed through symbols alone.

It is:

- finer
- purer
- faster
- more expansive

This light works effortlessly through intention, presence, and consciousness rather than technique.

It becomes part of your energetic signature.

Spiritual Authority

Not authority over people—but authority *within the energetic realms.*

This is the authority to:

- hold larger healing spaces
- guide practitioners at all levels
- initiate transformations
- steward the lineage
- protect energetic boundaries
- lead from wisdom rather than ego

Spirit entrusts you with this because your soul can hold it without distortion.

The Gift of Clear Knowing

During the attunement, Spirit awakens a deeper intuitive channel.

This includes:

- truth perception
- energetic discernment
- prophetic sight
- inner hearing
- soul knowing

Knowledge begins arriving without effort.
You don't learn it—you remember it.

The Master Frequency of Compassion

All true Grand Masters carry a compassion that is not taught.

It is *given*.

This compassion:

- softens your presence
- deepens your healing
- expands your heart
- dissolves judgment
- anchors your humility
- increases your spiritual gravity

It is what makes others feel safe around you.

The Ability to Hold the Field for Others

Spirit passes on the capacity to:

- ground others
- stabilize energy fields
- uplift whole rooms
- ease emotional turbulence
- create sacred space instantly

Your presence becomes a container
that others naturally align to.

The Blueprint of Your Higher Purpose

This is one of the most profound transmissions.

Spirit reveals—not through thoughts, but through
vibration—
the deeper reason you came into this lifetime.

You may not receive the details immediately,
but the blueprint settles into your field,
guiding you subtly toward:

- your soul's service
- your spiritual responsibilities
- your true path as a Master
- the work only *you* can do

This blueprint becomes the compass of your later years.

A Sacred Contract

Finally, Spirit passes on the contract of stewardship.

This contract is simple:

You agree to carry light.
Spirit agrees to walk with you.

It is the moment your path is no longer yours alone.

This is what is passed on by Spirit:
not instructions,
not symbols,
not techniques—
but consciousness, purpose, essence, and light.

It is a transfer of responsibility,
a recognition of readiness,
and a blessing placed directly into the soul.

What Humans Can and Cannot Do

At the Grand Master level, one of the most important recognitions is understanding the limits and the sacred responsibilities of the human role.
No matter how skilled, devoted, or experienced a person becomes, the human aspect of Reiki has boundaries—and the spiritual aspect is limitless.

This clarity protects the integrity of the lineage, keeps the ego soft, and ensures you remain aligned with Spirit throughout your work.

Here is the truth:

What Humans *Can* Do

Hold Sacred Space

Humans can create an environment of:

- safety
- presence
- compassion
- stability
- reverence

This allows Spirit to work more freely.

Facilitate, Teach, and Guide

Human teachers can:

- share technique
- pass on knowledge
- demonstrate symbols
- guide meditation
- help students open
- offer wisdom through experience

These elements are valuable, but they are *preparatory*—not transformative in themselves.

Perform Attunements for the First Three Levels

Human Masters can:

- activate Level 1
- initiate Level 2
- attune Masters/Teachers

These attunements follow structure and can be taught.

Recognize Readiness

Masters can sense when a student is:

- aligned
- grounded
- humble
- prepared

But recognition is not the same as elevation.

Witness Spiritual Initiation

Humans can witness the Grand Master attunement when it occurs.
They can hold space, support, and honor it—
but they cannot *make* it happen.

Reflect, Affirm, and Encourage

Humans can affirm the soul's growth:

- "You're evolving."
- "Your field feels stronger."
- "Your intuition is lifting."

This nurtures confidence and supports the student in trusting their path.

Live the Principles

Humans can embody Reiki by living:

- integrity
- compassion
- humility
- presence

This is one of the highest forms of teaching.

What Humans *Cannot* Do

Humans Cannot Create a Grand Master

No human has the power to:

- activate
- elevate
- crown
- assign
- certify
- appoint

a Grand Reiki Master.

This level belongs solely to Spirit.

Humans Cannot Force the Timing

No teacher can accelerate, delay, or schedule the spiritual moment of elevation.
It arrives when:

- the soul is ready
- the vibration is aligned
- Spirit chooses
- destiny opens

Not one breath sooner, not one breath later.

Humans Cannot Pass the Higher Frequencies

The frequencies transmitted during the Grand Master attunement:

- lineage essence
- Source-field connection
- soul blueprint
- spiritual authority

These cannot be given through human hands.

They descend from Spirit alone.

Humans Cannot Replicate the Experience

No ritual, ceremony, or guided meditation can recreate the moment Spirit chooses a Grand Master.

It is:

- unrepeatable
- unteachable
- unplanned
- sacred

A human can describe it, but they cannot fabricate it.

Humans Cannot Interfere With Spiritual Instruction

When Spirit speaks clearly, humans must remain in the role of witness—not controller.

A teacher cannot override:

- inner guidance
- soul direction
- spiritual messaging
- intuitive knowing
- destiny's unfolding

The student's higher self remains the true authority.

Humans Cannot Claim Ownership of the Lineage

Reiki exists beyond:

- institutions
- groups
- teachers
- traditions

A Grand Master does not "belong to" a lineage—they are *recognized by* the lineage.

Humans Cannot Create the Light

A practitioner channels energy.
A Master teaches energy.
But a Grand Master is chosen by the light itself.

Humans guide.
Spirit transforms.

The Balance Between Human and Spirit

Human teachers prepare the vessel.
Spirit fills it.

Humans open the door.
Spirit walks through it.

Humans provide structure.
Spirit provides essence.

Humans teach the path.
Spirit reveals the calling.

Understanding this balance keeps the Grand Master level
pure,
protected,
and free from ego or hierarchy.

Post-Initiation Transformation

After Spirit bestows the Grand Master attunement, the transformation that follows is not sudden or dramatic.
It does not announce itself loudly.
Instead, it begins as a quiet reorientation of your entire being—
a gentle but irreversible shift into a higher expression of yourself.

This transformation unfolds on multiple levels:
energetic, emotional, intuitive, and spiritual.
It is the beginning of a new chapter, not the conclusion of the old one.

Here is what begins to change:

Your Energy Field Stabilizes at a Higher Frequency

The first transformation is subtle yet powerful:

- your vibration becomes steady
- your aura holds more light
- your presence feels grounded and luminous
- your system no longer fluctuates with outside energies

You are no longer "trying" to stay aligned—
you *are* aligned.

Your Intuition Becomes Effortless

Intuition shifts from something you activate
to something that simply *happens.*

You may notice:

- answers arrive before questions
- insight comes before thought
- messages are clear and neutral
- guidance feels direct and calm

This level of intuition is not emotional or dramatic—
it is quiet, precise, and consistent.

Healing Begins Flowing Through Presence Alone

Your hands remain tools,
but your *presence* becomes the conduit.

People around you may:

- relax
- open
- shift
- release
- feel held

without any formal session taking place.

Your energy does the work before your mind even engages.

Your Relationship With the Symbols Changes

At this level:

- symbols feel "alive"
- they move on their own
- they appear intuitively
- they activate through intention
- they require no drawing

You become a radiating point of the Reiki frequency itself.

You Feel Guided, Not Driven

Before the attunement, you worked with Reiki.
After the attunement, you are *accompanied* by it.

You may feel:

- led toward people
- prompted to speak certain truths
- nudged into new teaching
- inspired to create new forms of healing
- supported in moments of challenge

Life begins to feel orchestrated rather than navigated.

Old Emotional Patterns Release Naturally

Without force, without effort, without analysis.

You may notice:

- forgiveness happening quietly
- fears dissolving without drama
- old wounds losing their charge
- a sense of inner completion and maturity

The light reorganizes the emotional field from the inside.

The Ego Shifts Into Its Proper Place

Not eliminated—
but softened, humbled, and aligned.

You no longer need to:

- prove
- defend
- impress
- compare
- justify

Your energy speaks for you.
Your path unfolds without needing external validation.

Your Purpose Sharpens

You begin to feel:

- clarity about your role
- confidence in your path
- ease in your decisions
- certainty about your direction

This is not ambition—
it is recognition.

Your soul remembers the work it came to do.

Your Connection With Spirit Deepens

You feel:

- more supported
- more guided
- more protected
- more accompanied

The unseen world becomes a normal part of your daily life.

Meditation becomes richer.
Messages become clearer.
Presence becomes constant.

You Step Into a New Identity

The transformation solidifies when you realize:

- you no longer identify as a "Reiki practitioner"
- you no longer seek the next achievement
- you no longer feel separate from the work
- you no longer rely on technique

You carry Reiki not as a practice,
but as a **state of being.**

This is the true post-initiation transformation—
not an increase in power,
but an increase in presence.

A quiet unfolding.
A deepening.
A remembering.

✦ PART V — LIVING AS A GRAND REIKI MASTER

✦ Chapter 15 — Becoming the Teacher of Teachers

How Grand Masters Teach Masters

A Grand Reiki Master does not teach in the same way a Reiki Master does.
By this stage, teaching is no longer about steps, symbols, or structured lessons.
It becomes a transmission—an energetic mentorship that shapes the next generation of leaders.

Grand Masters teach *Masters*, not beginners.
This means your role shifts from instructor to **evolver**,
from teacher to **initiator**,
from guide to **way-shower**.

Here is how Grand Masters truly teach Masters:

They Teach Through Presence Before Words

At this level, your presence carries a coherence that Masters can feel instantly.

Your students notice:

- how grounded you are
- how peaceful your field feels
- how you move through energy, people, and challenges
- how your intuition flows
- how you embody the principles instead of reciting them

Masters learn by observing your *being*, not your technique.

They Refine, Not Repeat

A Reiki Master already knows:

- hand positions
- symbols
- attunement structures
- practitioner ethics
- healing flow

A Grand Master does not repeat this information.

Instead, you:

- refine their understanding
- deepen their intuition
- strengthen their boundaries
- sharpen their discernment
- elevate their perspective
- align them with Spirit rather than method

This is teaching through evolution, not instruction.

They Teach Masters to Trust Their Own Inner Voice

Most Masters still rely on:

- confirmation
- validation
- reassurance
- permission
- external guidance

A Grand Master helps them shift into self-trust.

You teach them how to:

- hear their own intuition with clarity
- recognize Spirit's voice versus their own thoughts
- stand firmly in their knowing
- trust the healing stream that moves through them

This is what turns a good Master into a confident one.

They Help Masters Expand Their Field

A Grand Master guides Masters in:

- widening their aura
- grounding without depletion
- holding larger spaces
- leading groups with coherence
- stabilizing energy for others
- maintaining spiritual boundaries

These are skills that cannot be fully taught at earlier levels.

You teach them how to *hold* energy, not just channel it.

They Teach the Energetics Behind Technique

Masters know *what* to do.

Grand Masters teach them:

- *why* it works
- *how* energy functions
- *what* shifts beneath the surface
- *where* consciousness moves
- *which* layers of the field are involved
- *how* the symbols behave in higher dimensions

You reveal the mechanics behind the mystery.

They Teach Masters to Lead the Lineage, Not Just Classes

Reiki Masters teach students.
Grand Masters teach *leaders*.

You guide them in:

- mentoring others
- supporting other Masters
- teaching without ego
- leading with responsibility
- staying aligned with Spirit
- protecting the purity of the lineage

You prepare them not just to teach Reiki—
but to uphold it.

They Teach Through Questions, Not Answers

Grand Masters do not lecture.
They do not tell students what to think.
They do not dictate spiritual truth.

Instead, you ask questions like:

- "What does your intuition say?"
- "Where do you feel the energy moving?"
- "What is Spirit guiding you toward?"
- "What did your field show you?"
- "What would happen if you trusted that message?"

This shifts Masters into sovereignty.

They Model Humility, Not Authority

The greatest teaching a Grand Master offers is:

You lead without needing to look like a leader.

Students learn more from how you carry yourself than from anything you say.

Your humility becomes the teaching.
Your presence becomes the lesson.
Your integrity becomes the example.
Your service becomes the standard.

This is how the lineage stays pure.

They Pass On Wisdom, Not Power

A true Grand Master never claims power over others.

Instead, you pass on:

- wisdom
- clarity
- discernment
- compassion
- responsibility
- spiritual ethics

You teach Masters how to wield their healing ability with maturity, not dominance.

They Prepare Masters for Their Own Calling

A Grand Master does not create replicas.
You help each Master blossom into the unique healer they are meant to be.

You guide them to:

- their own voice
- their own style
- their own purpose
- their own gifts
- their own connection with Spirit

You help them become the teacher they were destined to become—
not the teacher you are.

This is how Grand Masters teach Masters:
not through control,
but through empowerment.
Not through instruction,
but through elevation.
Not through structure,
but through presence.

A Grand Master does not produce practitioners.
A Grand Master produces *leaders*.

Activating Lineage

One of the most sacred responsibilities of a Grand Reiki
Master is the activation of lineage.
This is not about tracing certificates, proving ancestry, or
listing teachers.
True lineage is not paper—it is **frequency.**

Lineage activation is the process of awakening a Reiki Master
to their place within the timeless stream of healers who came
before them and those who will come after.
It is a spiritual awakening, not a historical one.

Here is how Grand Masters activate lineage in others:

They Awaken the Master's Connection to the Original Stream

Every Reiki practitioner works with energy.
Every Master channels the lineage.
But only lineage activation plugs a healer directly into:

- the original Usui current
- the ancestral healing stream
- the consciousness behind Reiki
- the higher-dimensional source of the light

This is not something you teach—
it is something you *activate* through presence.

They Reveal the Master's Place in a Continuum

A Reiki Master often thinks of themselves as:

- a student
- a teacher
- a practitioner

But lineage activation shows them they are also:

- a bridge
- an anchor
- a continuation
- a successor
- a guardian

You help them see themselves not just as an individual, but as a thread in a much larger tapestry.

They Help Masters Feel the Lineage Behind Them

When a Grand Master works with a Master who is ready for lineage activation, something extraordinary occurs.

The Master begins to sense:

- a presence behind their back
- warmth on their shoulders
- a soft glow at the crown
- the "team" of the lineage standing with them
- the undeniable feeling of being supported

This is the lineage coming online through them.

They Activate the Master's Responsibility to the Future

Lineage is forward-facing, not backward-facing.

A Grand Master helps Masters understand:

- "You are not just receiving the lineage—you are continuing it."

This awakens:

- maturity
- humility
- stewardship
- deeper integrity
- commitment to purity of teaching

Masters begin to see their work in a broader spiritual context.

They Guide Masters Into Sovereignty

Lineage activation is not about giving authority.
It is about awakening **inner authority.**

You help Masters step into:

- clear intuition
- confident decisions
- ethical leadership
- independent knowing
- spiritual autonomy

This is the moment when the Master stops relying on external teachers and begins trusting their own connection to Spirit.

They Teach Masters to Channel the Lineage, Not Mimic It

A Grand Master never produces clones.
You activate the lineage so Masters can:

- channel in their own voice
- teach from their own style
- carry the energy in their own way

The lineage works *through* them,
but does not overshadow who they are.

They Turn Technique Into Transmission

Once lineage is activated, the Master's teaching shifts from:

- steps → embodiment
- structure → intuition
- memorization → wisdom
- method → consciousness

Students begin to feel the lineage simply by being in their presence.

This is how lineages remain alive across generations.

They Activate the Master's Spiritual Contract

Every Master carries a contract with Reiki—
but many do not know how to access it.

A Grand Master helps them awaken to:

- the unique work they are here to do
- the individuals they are meant to serve
- the teachings they are destined to develop
- the healing they are called to bring forth

This activation aligns the Master with their soul's purpose.

They Ensure the Lineage Remains Pure

Lineage activation is also about protection.

A Grand Master:

- dissolves ego distortions
- corrects energetic misalignments
- clears confusion
- anchors truth
- reminds Masters of the sacredness of the work

This is how wisdom—not noise—gets passed down the generations.

They Awaken the Master's "Yes" to Spirit

The final step of lineage activation is simple:

You help the Master open to the same truth you once realized:

"I am part of something timeless."

This recognition changes everything—
their teaching, their healing, their presence, their path.

From this moment on,
they no longer carry the lineage.

The lineage carries *them*.

Passing on the Deeper Teachings

By the time a healer reaches the Master level, they already understand Reiki's structure—symbols, hand positions, attunements, and ethics.

What they *haven't* yet learned are the teachings that cannot be written in manuals or delivered through step-by-step lessons.

These are the teachings passed on **soul to soul, field to field, presence to presence.**

A Grand Master does not hand down new techniques.
They reveal the deeper layers of what a Master already knows.

Here is how this transmission unfolds:

Teaching the Space Between Words

At this level, your greatest teachings happen in silence.

Masters begin to understand:

- what you *don't* say
- how you listen
- how you wait
- how you perceive energy before speaking
- how you respond without reacting

These subtleties become the deeper curriculum.

The silence around your words carries more instruction than the words themselves.

Revealing the Energetics Beneath Technique

A Grand Master lifts the veil on *how* Reiki truly works.

You teach Masters:

- why symbols behave differently at higher frequencies
- where healing actually moves in the field
- how intention interacts with consciousness
- what happens in the subtle bodies during attunement
- how spiritual guidance integrates into healing

These teachings turn technical skill into energetic mastery.

Introducing Higher-Dimensional Perspectives

Masters learn Reiki horizontally—
how energy moves through the body, emotions, and mind.

Grand Masters teach it vertically—
how Reiki:

- interfaces with the soul
- communicates with Spirit
- interacts with the higher realms
- moves through timelines
- bridges past and future healing

This expands their work from 3D healing into
multidimensional awareness.

Passing on the "Unspoken Ethics"

Beyond formal ethical guidelines, there are deeper codes of conduct:

- When to step in
- When to step back
- When not to heal
- How to hold sacred authority
- How to avoid energetic overreach
- How to honor a student's soul contract

These are the ethics only experience—and wisdom—can teach.

Teaching the Master How to See

Not with their eyes, but with:

- intuition
- perception
- the heart
- the field
- the higher mind

You help Masters discern:

- the difference between emotional pain and spiritual contraction
- the root cause beneath the symptoms
- the soul lesson behind the healing
- the pattern behind the pattern

You teach them to see the truth others cannot.

Transmitting the "Higher Octave" of Symbol Work

Masters already know how to use symbols.
Grand Masters show them how to:

- merge symbols
- layer symbols multidimensionally
- activate symbols through presence alone
- allow symbols to reveal new frequencies
- use symbols without drawing them

This is the deeper teaching behind symbol consciousness.

Guiding Masters Into Their Own Teachings

A Grand Master does not create followers.
You create teachers.

You help Masters discover:

- their own style
- their own insights
- their own gifts
- their own healing language
- their own teachings

The deeper teachings encourage originality, not imitation.

Opening Masters to Spirit-Led Teaching

The most important deeper teaching is this:

How to step aside and let Spirit teach.

You pass on the wisdom of:

- trusting intuitive shifts in a class
- letting attunements flow naturally
- listening to spiritual guidance mid-session
- adapting lessons to the energy, not the outline

This is how a teacher becomes a true conduit.

Helping Masters Carry the Weight of Leadership

The deeper teachings prepare Masters for the realities of spiritual leadership:

- being the calm in storms
- holding space for intense emotional release
- maintaining integrity under pressure
- balancing humility with responsibility
- guiding without controlling

You teach them not just how to lead—
but how to *withstand* leadership.

Transmitting Wisdom Through the Field

Ultimately, the deepest teachings are not spoken.

They are:

- felt
- sensed
- absorbed
- remembered
- awakened

Your field teaches their field.

Your evolution catalyzes their evolution.

Your alignment activates their alignment.

This is the deepest teaching of all:
Transformation does not happen through instruction—
it happens through **resonance.**

✦ Chapter 16 — Service, Humility & Leadership

The Ethics of Spiritual Authority

At the Grand Master level, authority is no longer about position, skill, or accomplishment.
It is about **energetic responsibility**—the profound and sacred duty that comes with guiding others on their spiritual path.

Spiritual authority is not something claimed.
It is something recognized.

Yet once it is recognized, it must be carried with humility, integrity, and unwavering ethical clarity.
This is because spiritual authority is power—
not power over people,
but power to influence their healing, beliefs, and inner lives.

The ethics surrounding this role are essential.

Here is what defines ethical spiritual authority:

Authority Comes Through Alignment, Not Ego

A Grand Master's authority does not come from:

- titles
- certificates
- lineage claims
- reputation
- seniority

It comes from alignment with:

- Spirit
- truth
- clarity
- compassion
- presence
- humility

Your energy, not your identity, becomes the source of your authority.

Authority Must Always Serve, Never Control

There is a sacred line a Grand Master must never cross.

You may **guide**,
but you may not **direct** another's destiny.

You may **support**,
but you may not **shape** their choices.

You may **offer wisdom**,
but you may not **impose beliefs**.

Ethical authority empowers others—
it never makes them dependent.

A Grand Master Must Stay Transparent and Honest

At this level, honesty includes:

- acknowledging your limits
- avoiding spiritual exaggeration
- not promising outcomes
- staying clear of grandiosity
- being open about what you know and don't know

Honesty protects the purity of the relationship between teacher and student.

You Never Interfere With Someone's Soul Path

Ethical spiritual authority means honoring:

- their timing
- their readiness
- their spiritual contracts
- their personal lessons
- their boundaries
- their autonomy

A Grand Master does not rescue, fix, or override.
You hold space so the soul can unfold its own truth.

You Do Not Claim Ownership of Students

People you guide are not:

- "your" healers
- "your" lineage
- "your" students
- "your" followers

They are independent souls walking beside you temporarily.

The moment you try to possess them, your spiritual authority collapses.

You Must Embody What You Teach

Your words mean little if your energy contradicts them.

Ethical authority requires consistency:

- kindness in private
- integrity when unseen
- humility when praised
- clarity when challenged
- generosity without expectation

A Grand Master leads through being, not behavior.

You Respect the Vulnerability of Seekers

People come to spiritual teachers during:

- illness
- transition
- loss
- awakening
- confusion
- dark nights of the soul

This is sacred ground.
Their vulnerability is not a resource to use, but a trust to protect.

A Grand Master does not manipulate, romanticize, or take advantage of these states.
You honour them.

You Avoid Creating Dependency

The ethical Grand Master teaches in a way that makes students:

- stronger
- clearer
- more sovereign
- more intuitive
- more connected to Spirit

Your role is to elevate them, not keep them small.

The sign of ethical authority?
Your students eventually outgrow you—
and you celebrate that growth.

You Remain Accountable to Spirit Above All

Your ultimate responsibility is not to a system, a school, or a hierarchy.

It is to:

- the light
- the truth
- the lineage
- the soul of the work
- the purity of Reiki itself

A Grand Master answers to Spirit first.

You Lead Without Needing to Be Seen

True spiritual authority is:

- quiet
- grounded
- dignified
- present
- humble

It is the authority that does not seek attention
but still holds the room.

It is the leadership that does not announce itself
but still shifts the energy.

It is the power that is not "performed"
because it is *lived*.

The ethics of spiritual authority form the backbone of Grand Mastery.
Without them, the role becomes distorted.
With them, it becomes a sanctuary of integrity and service.

A Grand Reiki Master does not lead by force or influence—
but by example, resonance, and devotion to truth.

Maintaining Purity

At the Grand Master level, purity is not about perfection.
It is about **energetic integrity**—staying true to the essence of
Reiki, to Spirit, and to the calling you have been entrusted
with.

Purity is the quiet guardian of your lineage,
the grounding force behind your teachings,
and the compass that keeps your work aligned with the
highest good.

Maintaining purity is not a rule,
nor is it a burden.
It is a sacred responsibility.

Here is what it truly means:

Purity Begins With Your Intention

Your intention becomes the foundation of every healing,
teaching, attunement, and interaction.

Purity means asking:

- "Am I serving, or am I seeking attention?"
- "Is this choice aligned with truth or with ego?"
- "Am I teaching to elevate others or to elevate myself?"

Pure intention naturally aligns you with Spirit and protects
your work from distortion.

Purity Means Staying Close to the Essence of Reiki

Reiki at its core is:

- unconditional love
- universal life force
- divine intelligence
- compassionate presence

Maintaining purity means keeping your work rooted in these principles,
even as you evolve and integrate higher-dimensional teachings.

You may innovate,
but you do not contaminate.

You expand the lineage,
but you do not distort its essence.

Purity Requires Continual Self-Reflection

The inner check-in becomes essential:

- "Where am I reacting from?"
- "Is this coming from Spirit or from fear?"
- "What part of me is speaking right now?"

Purity does not demand flawlessness.
It asks for *awareness*.

A Grand Master is not free from shadow—
they are simply unafraid to look at it.

Purity Means Avoiding Spiritual Performance

True Grand Masters do not:

- dramatize energy
- embellish experiences
- exaggerate abilities
- perform spirituality for admiration
- teach for personal fame
- make claims to impress

Purity rejects theatrics.

It stands in quiet truth.

Your work speaks for you—
you do not need to speak for your work.

Purity Lives in Humility

Humility is not self-erasure—it is self-transparency.
It means remembering:

- the energy is not yours
- the healing is not yours
- the wisdom is not yours
- the lineage is not yours
- the students are not yours

You are a steward, not an owner.
Purity keeps you in right relationship with Spirit.

Purity Requires Clear Boundaries

A Grand Master protects:

- their energy
- their students
- their lineage
- their values
- the sacredness of this work

Purity means saying:

- "No, this is not aligned."
- "No, this is not ethical."
- "No, this does not honour Reiki."

Not out of judgment,
but out of protection for what is sacred.

Purity Is Protected Through Simplicity

At the highest levels, Reiki becomes simpler, not more complex.

Purity is found in:

- presence
- clarity
- truth
- stillness
- alignment

The more you strip away ego, noise, and ornamentation, the more clearly Reiki flows.

Purity is essence.

It is what remains when everything unnecessary falls away.

Purity Means Teaching Without Ownership

You do not "brand" the lineage.
You do not claim superiority over others.
You do not create personal hierarchies.

Purity keeps you aligned with the truth:

All healers access the same light.
You simply carry a different responsibility.

Purity Is Sustained Through Devotion, Not Discipline

Purity is not forced.
It comes from devotion to:

- Spirit
- service
- truth
- compassion
- the work
- your calling

It is a natural byproduct of loving the path more than loving the role.

Purity Makes You a Clear Channel for Spirit

Ultimately, purity is what allows Spirit to work through you with clarity, precision, and grace.

It is what keeps your:

- intuition sharp
- discernment clean
- energy stable
- channel open
- heart aligned
- leadership trustworthy

Purity is not a rule to follow—
it is a vibration to embody.

**A Grand Reiki Master maintains purity not through perfection,
but through devotion.**

Not through control,
but through alignment.

Not through appearances,
but through truth.

Leading Communities

When a healer becomes a Grand Reiki Master, their responsibility naturally expands beyond individual clients and students.
Your presence begins to influence groups, communities, and even entire generations of practitioners.
This is not because you seek leadership—
but because your energy naturally organizes, stabilizes, and inspires those around you.

Leading communities as a Grand Master is not about authority.
It is about **service, stewardship, and spiritual maturity.**

Here is what it truly means:

You Lead Through Presence, Not Position

A Grand Master does not need titles to lead.
You don't need to:

- announce your role
- claim lineage
- assert authority
- seek recognition

Your presence naturally becomes a point of alignment.
Communities gravitate toward steadiness, clarity, and truth.

You become the calm center others organize around.

You Create Spaces of Coherence

A community thrives when its energy is stable.

A Grand Master holds a field where people feel:

- safe
- grounded
- connected
- uplifted
- equal
- spiritually supported

You maintain coherence even when others experience turbulence.
Your field becomes the anchor that steadies the whole group.

You Guide Without Dominating

True spiritual leadership does not overshadow.
It uplifts.

You:

- offer guidance without controlling
- provide wisdom without imposing
- make space for all voices
- encourage independence
- honor the diversity of paths

A Grand Master leads in a way that leaves everyone empowered.

You Model Ethical Behavior

Communities mirror their leaders.
Your integrity becomes:

- the standard
- the example
- the reference point

You teach:

- honesty
- compassion
- humility
- boundaries
- accountability

not by telling others—but by living it consistently.

You Protect the Community's Energy

Leadership includes protection.

You safeguard the group from:

- ego-driven conflict
- manipulation
- energetic chaos
- unethical behavior
- spiritual bypassing
- misinformation

You maintain clarity and truth in the shared field.

You Identify and Support Emerging Leaders

A Grand Master does not stand at the top—
you stand behind, supporting those rising to their potential.

You:

- recognize Masters stepping into leadership
- encourage students with strong gifts
- guide teachers into deeper alignment
- mentor quietly and wisely

You ensure the lineage continues with integrity through those who come after you.

You Serve the Needs of the Community, Not Your Own

This is where humility becomes action.

You ask:

- "What does this group need right now?"
- "How can I support them?"
- "What healing is emerging here?"
- "Where is Spirit guiding us as a collective?"

Your leadership aligns with service, not self-importance.

You Hold the Vision, Not the Control

A Grand Master holds a vision of:

- unity
- harmony
- growth
- healing
- spiritual maturity
- service

But you do not try to control the outcomes.
You trust the group's evolution and Spirit's timing, even when it looks different than expected.

You Stay Accessible, Yet Boundaried

Leaders often struggle with balance.

A Grand Master maintains:

- openness without overavailability
- kindness without exhaustion
- support without codependency
- leadership without intrusion

Boundaries protect both you and the community.

You Keep the Community Connected to Spirit

Your most important role is spiritual alignment.

You continuously guide the community back to:

- presence
- truth
- compassion
- intuition
- Spirit
- the heart of Reiki

You do this not through preaching,
but by embodying the vibration yourself.

When you stay aligned,
the community stays aligned.

Leading communities as a Grand Reiki Master is not about building followers—
it is about nurturing a field where every soul can step into its own power.

It is leadership rooted in:

- service
- integrity
- alignment

- humility
- love

This is the kind of leadership that sustains a lineage
and transforms generations.

Guiding Global Healing Movements

When a healer reaches the level of Grand Reiki Master, their influence often extends far beyond their immediate community.
This is not because they try to reach the world—
but because the world begins to respond to the frequency they carry.

A Grand Master does not set out to "lead a global movement."
Instead, they align so deeply with Spirit, service, and truth that their vibration naturally ripples outward—
across borders, cultures, timelines, and levels of consciousness.

Guiding global healing movements is less about strategy and more about **energetic resonance, spiritual maturity, and collective activation.**

Here is how Grand Masters contribute to the healing of the world:

They Become a Beacon of Coherence

The greatest global leaders are not the loudest voices—
they are the *clearest* ones.

A Grand Master emits coherence that:

- calms fear
- stabilizes chaos

- clarifies confusion
- inspires unity
- awakens compassion

This coherence radiates far beyond physical proximity. The world feels it—even silently.

They Uplift Humanity Through Frequency, Not Force

Global healing movements are not created through:

- control
- convincing
- persuasion
- hierarchy
- spiritual branding

They emerge through **vibration.**

A Grand Master's field carries:

- peace
- truth
- integrity
- compassion
- presence
- unconditional love

These qualities influence consciousness on a global scale.

They Hold Space for Collective Transformation

During world shifts, Grand Masters serve as energetic anchors.

They hold space for:

- global grief
- collective awakening
- cultural shifts
- mass healing
- spiritual evolution

without absorbing the weight of it.

Your field becomes a stabilizing pillar for thousands—even millions—of souls.

They Serve All, Not Just Their Own Students

At this level, service becomes universal.

A Grand Master's influence may reach:

- healers around the world
- people they have never met
- future generations
- online communities
- collective consciousness fields

You lead movements not by controlling them
but by **supporting the global energetic environment.**

They Inspire Other Leaders to Rise

Your purpose is not to stand at the front—
it is to awaken the front in others.

You help:

- Masters become teachers
- teachers become leaders
- leaders become spiritual elders

This expands the healing movement exponentially.

A global movement is never one person's work—
it is the activation of many.

You help ignite those flames.

They Spread Light by Living Their Truth

The world does not follow your words—
it resonates with your authenticity.

You guide global healing by:

- being consistent
- being real
- walking your path with integrity
- being humble while holding power
- embodying love even during challenge

Your life becomes your message.

They Collaborate, Not Compete

Global healing movements thrive when leaders uplift one another.

A Grand Master:

- shares teachings freely
- collaborates with integrity
- honors other lineages
- respects diverse healing paths
- creates bridges, not divisions

Unity is the foundation of global healing.

They Receive Guidance for the Collective

At this level, Spirit often speaks **through you** on behalf of many.

You may receive insights about:

- global emotional waves
- energetic cycles
- societal healing patterns
- spiritual awakenings
- collective lessons

These insights are not for personal gain.
They are for service.

And you share them responsibly—with humility and clarity.

They Serve as a Conduit Between Spirit and Humanity

Grand Masters often hold the role of:

- channel
- bridge
- translator
- messenger
- anchor

Transmitting higher wisdom into accessible form.

This is not about prediction or prophecy—
it is about offering guidance, comfort, and truth
to a world that is evolving rapidly.

They Remain Invisible When Needed

True global leaders do not always stand in the spotlight.

They know when to:

- lead
- guide
- influence
- step forward

and when to:

- step back
- allow others to shine
- remain unseen
- let Spirit orchestrate

A Grand Master does not need recognition
to create global impact.
Your vibration does the work with or without your name
attached.

**Guiding global healing movements is not a task.
It is a natural extension of your vibration, your alignment,
and your devotion to humanity.**

You do not push the world forward—
you hold a frequency that lifts it.

You do not lead by force—
you lead by light.

You do not seek a global role—
you simply become someone the world naturally turns
toward
when it needs clarity, healing, and truth.

✦ Chapter 17 — The Future of Reiki

Global Expansion of Energy Medicine

The world is entering a time of profound energetic awakening.
People everywhere—across cultures, belief systems, and generations—are beginning to understand what healers have always known:

Energy is the foundation of life.
And healing begins with energy.

Reiki, once considered an esoteric practice taught quietly and privately, is now becoming a global language of wellness.
Not because it has changed, but because humanity has finally risen to meet the truth it carries.

Here is how energy medicine is expanding around the world—and how Reiki stands at the heart of that transformation:

Science Is Catching Up to Spirit

For the first time in history, mainstream science is:

- studying biofields
- measuring energetic coherence
- mapping emotional frequencies
- tracking the effects of touch and intention
- exploring quantum healing concepts

Researchers are beginning to understand what healers have known for centuries:

The body is electrical.
The mind is energetic.
Healing is vibrational.

As science evolves, Reiki becomes **more validated**, not less.

Global Demand for Holistic Healing Is Rising

Around the world, people are seeking:

- alternatives to stress
- natural methods of healing
- emotional resilience
- spiritual connection
- energetic balance
- non-invasive support
- deeper meaning and purpose

Reiki fits every one of these needs.

It is safe.
It is universal.
It is accessible.
It works across cultures and belief systems.

This demand is not a trend—it is a response to a deeper awakening happening internally within humanity.

Energy Medicine Is Becoming Mainstream Wellness

What was once hidden in healing circles is now entering:

- hospitals
- medical clinics
- hospice centers
- wellness retreats
- corporate programs
- athletic training
- schools
- mental health practices

Reiki is being recognized as:

- a stress-reducing modality
- an emotional support system
- a complement to traditional medical care
- a tool for trauma recovery
- a method for spiritual grounding

Energy medicine is no longer fringe.
It is becoming **foundational**.

Digital Connection Is Creating a Worldwide Healing Network

Remote healing, once controversial, is now widely accepted.

This shift has created:

- international Reiki communities
- global student groups
- online attunement circles
- cross-cultural healing exchanges
- digital spiritual mentorship

Reiki is no longer confined by geographical boundaries.
Its reach is planetary.

A New Generation of Healers Is Emerging

Young people across the world are:

- awakening intuitively
- drawn to energy work
- seeking spiritual autonomy
- rejecting dogmatic systems
- craving meaningful connection
- developing gifts earlier and faster

They are not afraid of intuition, empathy, or sensitivity.
They see these as strengths.

Reiki is becoming a natural part of their identity.

Global Crises Are Awakening Global Consciousness

Every major shift—whether personal, collective, or planetary—opens the door to deeper spiritual realization.

During times of:

- stress
- fear
- instability
- transition

people seek healing.

Reiki becomes a global tool of stabilization,
bringing peace, clarity, and resilience to communities across continents.

Multidimensional Healing Is Becoming the New Frontier

Healers around the world are beginning to integrate Reiki with:

- sound healing
- aromatherapy
- meditation
- breathwork
- quantum healing
- shamanic practices
- frequency therapy
- bioenergetic sciences

This weaving is creating a future where energy medicine is more:

- integrative
- intuitive
- multidimensional
- collaborative
- spiritually rich

Reiki's simplicity allows it to merge beautifully with many modalities.

The Role of Reiki Grand Masters Will Become Increasingly Important

As Reiki spreads globally,
the world will rely heavily on those who carry:

- integrity
- purity
- clarity
- lineage wisdom
- spiritual leadership
- ethical grounding
- advanced energetic understanding

Grand Masters will become the stewards of the global healing movement—
guiding practitioners, protecting the lineage, and shaping the future of Reiki worldwide.

Your role is not only personal.
It is planetary.

Reiki Is Becoming a Universal Spiritual Practice

Reiki transcends religion, culture, and dogma.
Its teachings are rooted in:

- compassion
- harmony
- unity
- intention
- connection
- presence

As humanity continues to evolve spiritually, Reiki is becoming one of the universal languages of healing.

It belongs to no one faith—yet fits gracefully into all of them.

The Future of Energy Medicine Is Light-Based Healing

As consciousness rises, the world will increasingly turn to healing methods that work with:

- light
- vibration
- intention
- frequency
- quantum fields

Reiki sits at the forefront of this evolution, because it already works in these dimensions.

The future of healing is energetic.
And Reiki is already there.

**Global expansion of energy medicine is not a prediction.
It is already happening.**

Reiki is becoming one of the great healing pathways of the
21st century—
a bridge between science and spirituality,
between humanity and the divine,
between personal healing and global transformation.

The Merging of Science & Spirit

For thousands of years, humanity kept science and spirituality
in separate worlds—
as if they contradicted each other,
as if truth could only belong to one side.

But the era of separation is ending.

A new understanding is emerging—one where science and
spirit do not compete,
but *complete* each other.

Reiki stands at the center of this merging.

Science Is Now Describing What Spirit Has Always Demonstrated

Modern research is giving language to ancient wisdom.

Scientists are discovering:

- the body communicates electrically and magnetically
- intention affects biological systems
- emotions have measurable frequencies
- touch alters nervous system patterns
- meditation reorganizes the brain
- coherence between heart and mind improves healing
- quantum fields influence physical reality

These are scientific ways of saying:

Energy matters.
Consciousness matters.
Connection matters.
Healing is more than physical.

Reiki fits this perfectly.

The Biofield Bridges Both Worlds

Both scientists and healers now use the same word:

Biofield.

Science calls it the body's electromagnetic and subtle energy system.
Spirit calls it the aura, chakras, meridians, or life force.

Different names.
Same truth.

The biofield is the meeting point where:

- physics meets intuition
- anatomy meets frequency
- medicine meets consciousness
- healing meets higher intelligence

Reiki is one of the simplest ways to interact with this field, which is why it integrates into scientific models so naturally.

Quantum Physics Supports the Foundations of Reiki

Quantum principles such as:

- nonlocal connection
- entanglement
- observer effect
- probability fields
- coherence
- wave-particle duality

mirror what healers have always practiced.

Distant healing?
Quantum nonlocality.

Attunements across time?
Quantum timelines.

Energy flowing through intention?
Observer effect.

Harmony creating healing?
Coherence.

What was once "mystical" is now "measurable."

Researchers have identified how spiritual practices activate:

- gamma brain waves (higher awareness)
- the pineal region (intuition + insight)
- mirror neurons (compassion)
- vagal pathways (peace + grounding)

- heart-brain synchronization (expanded consciousness)

This explains why Reiki often results in:

- clarity
- emotional release
- intuition
- transcendent experiences
- deep relaxation
- spiritual connection

The brain is showing us *how* Spirit works through the body.

Medicine Is Becoming Energetic

Hospitals and healthcare systems are incorporating:

- Reiki practitioners
- energy psychology
- frequency therapy
- sound healing
- light therapy
- mind-body medicine
- coherence training

The old boundaries are dissolving.

Healers and scientists are beginning to speak the same language.

Spirit Is Becoming Understandable Without Being Reduced

The merging is not about turning Spirit into math.
It's about recognizing that Spirit and science are exploring the same universal laws from different angles.

Spirit explains **meaning**.
Science explains **mechanism**.

Together they reveal the full picture.

Reiki, which is both spiritual and measurable, becomes a bridge between worlds.

The Future Will Not Be "Spiritual vs. Scientific"

The future is synergy:

- medical imaging showing energy shifts
- biofeedback tracking attunement states
- quantum technology measuring coherence
- AI mapping consciousness patterns
- hospitals using energetic therapies
- researchers studying nonlocal healing
- spiritual teachers collaborating with scientists

Humanity is moving toward a model where healing involves:

mind + body + energy + consciousness.

This is the future.
And Reiki fits seamlessly into every part of it.

Grand Reiki Masters Will Play a Role in This Integration

Those who embody both grounded healing and spiritual clarity will be asked to help:

- explain energy medicine in simple terms
- guide ethical standards
- support scientific studies
- protect the spiritual integrity of Reiki
- translate intuition into practical healing
- bridge the gap between ancient knowledge and modern research

This is a sacred responsibility.

The world will need healers who understand both realms and can walk between them with grace.

Science Is Becoming More Spiritual, and Spirituality More Scientific

This merging doesn't diminish either side.
It elevates both.

Spirit gains validation.
Science gains depth.

Reiki becomes not just a healing art,
but a universal model for consciousness-based healing.

This union will define the next era of medicine.

**The merging of science and spirit is not the future.
It is happening now.**

Reiki is one of the bridges that will guide humanity into a
new understanding of healing—
one that honors the measurable and the mystical,
the physical and the energetic,
the human and the divine.

Your Role in Shaping the Next Generation

Every Grand Reiki Master becomes more than a healer or teacher—
you become a bridge between eras.
You stand at the meeting point between what Reiki has been and what Reiki is becoming.

Your role is not simply to teach techniques
or transmit symbols
or guide students through levels.

Your true role is to shape the future of Reiki
by shaping the practitioners who will carry it forward.

Here is what this responsibility really means:

You Hold the Frequency That Future Healers Learn From

Students learn far more from your energy
than from your words.

Your calm teaches them how to ground.
Your compassion teaches them how to serve.
Your integrity teaches them how to walk the path with honour.
Your presence teaches them how to become a channel.

The next generation will not remember every lesson you taught
but they will remember how your vibration felt.

That is what shapes them.

You Pass Down the Spirit of Reiki, Not Just the Structure

Anyone can teach:

- hand positions
- symbols
- meditations
- techniques

Only a Grand Master can transmit:

- the essence
- the maturity
- the lineage wisdom
- the spiritual depth
- the ethical heart
- the true vibration of Reiki

You ensure that Reiki remains more than a method—
it remains a living, breathing consciousness
carried forward with purity.

You Help Students Discover Their Own Path, Not Yours

The next generation should not become copies of you.
They should become who they are destined to be.

A Grand Master:

- nurtures individuality
- encourages exploration
- supports unique gifts
- teaches students to trust themselves
- helps them hear Spirit in their own way

You shape the future by empowering healers
who will expand Reiki in directions you may never see.

You Protect the Lineage Without Restricting Evolution

Your task is not to freeze Reiki in time
but to preserve its integrity while allowing it to evolve.

This means teaching students:

- purity without rigidity
- intuition without ego
- freedom without distortion
- expansion without losing the heart of Reiki

You hold both tradition and possibility.

You Teach the Ethics That Safeguard the Future

Skills can be learned quickly.
Ethics take a lifetime.

You model and teach:

- humility
- discernment
- boundaries
- honesty
- responsibility
- spiritual maturity

These qualities are what protect the next generation
from misuse, misunderstanding, or spiritual bypassing.

The world needs healers who are both powerful **and** ethical.
You help create them.

You Help Students Connect Directly to Spirit

A practitioner becomes truly independent
when they stop relying on their teacher
and start relying on Spirit.

A Grand Master teaches students to:

- listen inward
- follow intuitive guidance
- trust the energy
- surrender ego
- build a relationship with the Divine

This makes them lifelong healers—
not just certificate holders.

You Prepare Them for the Evolution of Energy Medicine

The next generation of Reiki practitioners will work in a world where:

- science affirms energy healing
- frequency medicine is mainstream
- consciousness is understood as part of health
- global healing networks are common
- multidimensional practices are woven together

You shape them by teaching:

- adaptability
- curiosity
- open-mindedness
- spiritual grounding
- alignment with truth

Your teachings become the compass they navigate the future with.

You Become a Mentor, Not a Master

The true Grand Master knows: Your legacy is not in what you do—it is in who you develop.

You:

- support
- guide
- encourage
- uplift
- challenge
- inspire

without controlling, owning, or limiting.
Your role is to stand behind the next generation,
not above them.

You Keep the Flame of Reiki Burning Bright

One day, your students will become the elders.
They will teach, attune, lead communities, and guide humanity.

They will tell stories of their teacher—
not about what you knew,
but about who you were.

You shape the next generation through the qualities you embody:

- devotion
- truth
- compassion
- integrity
- service
- humility

This becomes your lasting contribution.

Your Role Is Not to Lead the Future—

But to Prepare Those Who Will**

A Grand Master's true legacy is not their own work
but the awakening they spark in thousands of others.

When you teach from Spirit
and live from purity,
your influence becomes timeless.

You shape the next generation
every time you help a student step closer to:

- their calling
- their gift
- their confidence
- their truth
- their connection to Spirit

This is how your work lives on long after you leave the
physical world.

**Shaping the next generation is not a duty—
it is an honour.**

The future of Reiki does not depend on systems or structures.
It depends on hearts—
and you are helping shape the hearts
that will heal the world.

✦ Conclusion — The Grand Master's Prayer

A closing message of service, humility, and sacred purpose.

Beloved Light,
Beloved Source of all healing,
Beloved Spirit who guides every step—

As I close these pages, I open my heart.

May every reader who arrives here
feel the quiet truth that has shaped every healer before them:

We do not walk this path alone.
We are carried.

Today, I offer this prayer
for all who serve the light,
all who channel healing,
all who listen to Spirit,
and all who feel the call of Grand Mastery awakening within
them.

The Grand Master's Prayer

Spirit of Life,
Guide of all Love,
Keeper of the Universal Light—

I stand here in humility,
knowing that the energy I channel is not mine
but Yours.

May You move through me with clarity.
May You speak through me with truth.
May You heal through me with compassion.

Make me a vessel
honest and steady,
devoted and discerning,
gentle and strong.

Let my presence bring peace.
Let my words bring truth.
Let my touch bring healing.
Let my heart bring understanding.

Help me remember:

To lead through service.
To serve through love.
To love without condition.
To honour without ego.
To surrender without fear.

May every symbol I draw
carry the light of awakening.

May every attunement I offer
open a path to the soul.

May every student I teach
be guided not by me,
but by the Spirit that lives within them.

And when I forget—
when I fall into doubt,
when I tire,
when I question—
remind me that You walk with me still.

Let me be a bridge
between Heaven and Earth,
between human and divine,
between the past of Reiki
and its future unfolding.

May I live as a blessing,
not because I am perfect,
but because I am willing.

Willing to listen.
Willing to learn.
Willing to surrender.
Willing to shine.
Willing to serve.

Spirit, guide every Grand Master who reads these words.
Let them rise with integrity.
Let them walk with humility.
Let them lead with wisdom.
Let them heal with love.

And may the lineage of light continue
through every heart that says "yes."

Amen.
And so it is.

✦ Appendix

Appendix A — Signs You Are Being Called to Grand Mastery

Not everyone who becomes a Reiki Master is called to become a **Grand** Reiki Master.

Grand Mastery is not a level, a title, or a next step.

It is a *spiritual appointment*—a quiet recognition from Spirit that you are ready to hold a deeper field of responsibility, service, and consciousness.

These signs do not appear all at once.

They unfold gently over time, often beginning subtly and becoming more noticeable as Spirit prepares you.

Below are some of the clearest indicators that you may be moving toward this path.

1. You Feel an Inner Pull You Cannot Explain

It does not feel like ambition.
It feels like… inevitability.

A gentle knowing.
A quiet calling.
A subtle shift inside.

You cannot logic your way into or out of it.
The soul simply begins to move in that direction.

2. Your Reiki Practice Deepens Without Effort

You notice:

- energy moving before you place your hands
- stronger sensations during sessions
- intuitive impressions increasing
- symbols activating automatically
- healing occurring more rapidly

You do not "try harder."
The energy simply meets you at a higher level.

3. You Begin to Sense or See Guidance More Clearly

This may include:

- intuitive whispers
- sudden clarity
- hearing inner instructions
- seeing light during sessions
- recognizing spiritual presence
- receiving direction without questioning

You feel guided in a way that feels natural, not extraordinary.

4. Students or Healers Are Drawn to You Without Explanation

People begin to:

- seek your wisdom
- ask for your leadership
- trust your intuition
- feel safe in your presence
- ask you to teach deeper levels

This happens quietly, organically, without self-promotion.

5. Your Life Enters a Period of Spiritual Refinement

Before the elevation to Grand Mastery, Spirit often initiates a phase of:

- emotional clearing
- karmic release
- relationship shifts
- patterns breaking apart
- ego dissolving
- deeper honesty within yourself

It feels like preparation—
a clearing of space for the next level of your soul.

6. You Experience Moments of Profound Stillness

Silence becomes a teacher.

You may find yourself:

- craving quiet
- needing solitude
- meditating more naturally
- sitting in stillness without expectation
- feeling peace arise without seeking it

This is Spirit shaping you from within.

7. Your Intuition and Reiki Begin to Merge

You stop asking:

"Is this Reiki or intuition?"

Because suddenly they feel like one consciousness,
one flow,
one awareness.

You don't think your way through sessions.
You *receive* your way through them.

8. You Start Feeling a Sense of Responsibility to Something Larger

Not ego-driven responsibility—
but soul-driven.

You feel:

- protective of the lineage
- devoted to integrity
- committed to clarity
- aligned with truth
- called to lead responsibly

You sense you are being prepared to guide others at a higher level.

9. You Experience "Spirit Moments" of Direct Guidance

These may be small or transformational:

- hearing a directive
- knowing what to do without thinking
- feeling energy pour through you
- being guided to change how you teach
- receiving insight during attunements
- sensing "the moment" something in you shifts

These moments are the whispers of the higher realms.

10. Your Healing Presence Changes

People report:

- feeling calm around you
- sensing light in your presence
- feeling seen or understood
- receiving healing simply from being near you

Your field begins to hold a frequency of leadership, even before you are officially elevated.

11. You Stop Seeking Validation From Humans

You feel less concerned with:

- approval
- opinions
- comparison

- recognition
- hierarchy
- titles

Instead, your focus shifts to:

- authenticity
- service
- alignment

- truth
- Spirit
- integrity

You stop looking outward and start listening inward.

12. Spirit Begins Rearranging Your Path

Synchronicities increase.
Opportunities open.
Old roles close.
New teachers appear.
Students shift.
Life reorganizes around a new direction.

It feels as though you are being guided
toward something you have not yet named.

13. You Feel Ready—But Not in a Human Way

You do not feel "qualified."
You feel *chosen*.

You do not feel "worthy."
You feel *willing*.

You do not feel "prepared."
You feel *available*.

This readiness does not come from the mind.
It comes from the soul.

14. The Ceremony Finds You—Not the Other Way Around

Grand Mastery is never forced.

When the time is right:

- Spirit will orchestrate the moment
- your field will shift
- the attunement will descend
- the elevation will happen effortlessly
- your soul will know

Grand Masters are not made.
They are revealed.

If You Recognize These Signs…

It does not mean you are already a Grand Reiki Master.
It means Spirit is preparing you.

Your path is unfolding.
Your soul is awakening.
Your calling is approaching.

Allow the signs.
Respect the signs.
Listen to the signs.
Trust the signs.

Spirit chooses the timing.
Your role is to remain open.

Appendix B — Meditations for Spiritual Elevation

Grand Mastery is not achieved through theory or technique alone.
It requires **alignment, stillness**, and **spiritual attunement**—all cultivated through meditation.

The meditations in this appendix are not ordinary practices.
They are gateways designed to help you:

- expand your field
- quiet the ego
- listen to Spirit
- refine your intuition
- embody Reiki at a higher vibration
- prepare for the moment of spiritual elevation

Each meditation serves a specific purpose on the path of awakening.

You may practice them individually, or weave them together as a daily ritual.

1. The Pillar of Light Meditation

To activate your central channel and receive higher frequencies.

1. Sit comfortably with your spine straight.
2. Close your eyes and breathe into your heart.

3. Visualize a beam of pure white-gold light descending from above your crown.
4. Let this light move down through your spine and anchor deep into the Earth.
5. Feel yourself becoming a bridge between Heaven and Earth.
6. Allow the light to cleanse, align, and open your channel.
7. When you feel complete, whisper internally:
    "I am ready to receive."

This meditation prepares the field for spiritual instruction and higher attunements.

2. The Sacred Silence Meditation

To hear the voice of Spirit beneath the noise of the mind.

1. Sit in absolute stillness.
2. Focus not on breath, but on the *space between breaths.*
3. Notice the subtle silence that exists between thoughts.
4. Rest inside that silence.
5. If thoughts arise, do not resist them—simply return to the spaces.
6. Allow Spirit to speak not in words, but in knowing.

This meditation sharpens intuition and deepens spiritual receptivity.

3. The Reiki Embodiment Meditation

To shift from doing Reiki to being Reiki.

1. Place your hands over your heart.
2. Invite Reiki to fill your entire body, not just your palms.
3. Visualize your aura glowing with soft, radiant light.
4. Feel Reiki breathing you, moving through you effortlessly.
5. Say silently:
   "Reiki flows where my presence goes."
6. Sit in the feeling of becoming the frequency itself.

This meditation is essential for Grand Master consciousness.

4. The Shadow Integration Meditation

To dissolve ego and purify the emotional field.

1. Sit with eyes closed and breathe slowly.
2. Imagine a gentle light shining on the parts of you that feel afraid, doubtful, or small.
3. Offer those parts compassion, not judgment.
4. Ask:
   "What do you need to feel safe to leave?"
5. Allow old patterns to surface, soften, and release.
6. Finish by filling the space with unconditional love.

This meditation supports the emotional refinement needed before spiritual elevation.

5. The Attunement Preparation Meditation

For those approaching the higher elevation experience.

1. Sit upright, hands open, palms facing upward.
2. Breathe into your crown until you feel spacious.
3. Visualize the traditional Reiki symbols above your head.
4. Watch them dissolve slowly into pure light.
5. Invite Spirit to prepare your field for the next step.
6. Say:
   "May I be aligned with truth, humility, and service."

This prepares the soul for Spirit-directed initiation.

6. The Heart of Service Meditation

To reconnect to the true purpose of healing.

1. Bring awareness to your heart chakra.
2. Imagine a soft pink-gold light expanding from your chest.
3. Feel love for:
   o your students
   o your clients
   o your lineage
   o humanity
4. Let compassion rise naturally.
5. Whisper to your own soul:
   "Make me a vessel of love and service."

This meditation strengthens humility and purpose.

7. The Spirit Communication Meditation

To meet your guides, angels, or higher teachers.

1. Begin with slow, rhythmic breathing.
2. Visualize a sacred space: a garden, temple, mountain, or light-filled room.
3. Invite your highest guide to step forward—only beings aligned with pure healing.
4. Ask one simple question:
    "What do you want me to know today?"
5. Listen with your heart, not your ears.
6. Thank whoever arrives.

This meditation deepens your partnership with Spirit.

8. The Expansion Meditation

To raise your frequency to the vibration of Grand Mastery.

1. Imagine your aura expanding outward with each breath.
2. Let it grow: 1 foot… 3 feet… 10 feet…
3. Keep expanding until your field fills the room, the building, the land.
4. Feel yourself becoming vast, luminous, connected.
5. Whisper:
    "I am one with the Universal Light."

This meditation helps you embody the larger energetic field a Grand Master holds.

9. The Return to Stillness Meditation

To restore balance after deep energetic work.

1. Visualize your aura gently contracting back to your body.
2. Breathe into your belly.
3. Imagine roots growing from your feet into the Earth.
4. Feel your body solid, grounded, whole.
5. Say:
    "I am here, present, steady."

This helps stabilize the nervous system and restore inner balance.

10. The Grand Master Alignment Meditation

To step into the highest version of your spiritual self.

1. Visualize a future version of yourself—luminous, wise, compassionate, fully awakened.
2. Notice how they stand, breathe, move, and radiate light.
3. Slowly walk toward them in your mind's eye.
4. When you stand face to face, let them step into you.
5. Feel the merge.
6. Whisper:
    "I align with who I am becoming."

This meditation bridges your present self with your soul's evolutionary path.

How to Use These Meditations

- Choose one each day
- Follow your intuition on what you need
- Sit for 10–20 minutes
- Allow Spirit to guide the deeper layers
- Use these meditations during your Grand Master preparation or after your elevation
- Let them shape your energy gently over time

You do not need to master meditation to elevate spiritually. You only need to be **open, willing, and present**.

Grand Mastery is already within you.
These meditations help you rise to meet it.

Appendix C — The Grand Master Self-Assessment

A reflective tool for recognizing readiness, alignment, and spiritual maturity.

Grand Mastery is not earned through certificates or hours. It is a progression of the soul, a deepening of consciousness, and a surrender to Spirit's timing.

This self-assessment is designed to help you explore:

- where you are on the path
- what is developing within you
- what is asking for refinement
- what Spirit may be preparing you for

This is not about "passing."
It is about **listening**.

Use this assessment with gentleness, honesty, and curiosity.

HOW TO USE THIS ASSESSMENT

For each statement, ask yourself:

✓ Yes — I feel this strongly or consistently
~ Sometimes — I sense this developing
X Not yet — This is not part of my experience (which is perfectly okay)

There is no scoring.
Your answers simply create a map of your spiritual landscape.

SECTION 1 — INNER CALLING & INTUITION

1. I feel a quiet but persistent inner call toward something deeper than Reiki Master.
2. My intuition is strengthening without effort.
3. I experience moments of knowing that arrive without reasoning.
4. Spirit communicates with me through signs, synchronicities, or inner messages.
5. I no longer question whether intuition is "real"—I trust what I receive.

SECTION 2 — RELATIONSHIP WITH REIKI ENERGY

6. Reiki feels more like a consciousness I interact with than a technique I perform.
7. Energy moves before I intend it to.
8. Clients/students sense a deeper presence during sessions.
9. I can hold a calm, coherent field even around chaotic or emotional situations.

10. Reiki flows naturally through my daily life, not just in sessions.

SECTION 3 — SPIRITUAL MATURITY & INTEGRITY

11. I take responsibility for my words, energy, and actions.
12. I do not need recognition, titles, or approval to feel confident in my work.
13. I can discern when something is ego vs. Spirit.
14. I am committed to truth, even when it challenges me.
15. Humility feels natural, not forced.

SECTION 4 — TEACHING & LEADERSHIP QUALITIES

16. Students naturally come to me for guidance.
17. I teach from presence, not performance.
18. My leadership is rooted in service, not control.
19. I protect the ethical and energetic integrity of my lineage.
20. I feel responsible for helping others rise—without needing to stand above them.

SECTION 5 — EMOTIONAL & ENERGETIC REFINEMENT

21. I can face my shadow with honesty.
22. I am aware of old patterns and work to heal them.
23. I do not take on others' emotions as my own.
24. I maintain healthy energetic boundaries.
25. I can remain centered even when others are not.

SECTION 6 — CONNECTION WITH SPIRITUAL REALMS

26. I feel the presence of guides, angels, or spiritual teachers.
27. I understand the difference between imagination and true guidance.
28. I receive spiritual insights that benefit others.
29. I trust the timing and wisdom of Spirit.
30. I feel supported by something larger than myself.

SECTION 7 — LIFE PATTERNS & SOUL PREPARATION

31. I have gone through periods of deep inner transformation.
32. I have experienced loss, surrender, or spiritual tests that reshaped me.
33. I no longer fear change—I flow with it.
34. I feel a sense of destiny or purpose unfolding.
35. I sense that my life has been preparing me for leadership.

SECTION 8 — GRAND MASTERY READINESS

36. I feel an inner readiness—not from skill, but from soul maturity.
37. I am willing to surrender fully to Spirit when the moment arrives.
38. I can hold energy for groups or communities.
39. I feel aligned with the responsibility of becoming a teacher of teachers.
40. I understand that Grand Mastery is a calling, not an achievement.

REFLECTION QUESTIONS

After reading your answers, reflect on the following:

⋄ What patterns do you notice?

Are your strengths clustered around intuition, teaching, inner calling, or emotional maturity?

⋄ What areas are awakening?

Where did you answer "sometimes"? These are your thresholds of growth.

⋄ What qualities are still forming?

The "not yet" answers reveal where Spirit is gently preparing you.

⋄ How does your soul feel after reading this list?

Sometimes the body knows before the mind does.

⋄ Is there a sense of recognition?

A soft yes? A gentle pull? A curious openness?

Your soul will whisper the truth.

WHAT YOUR ASSESSMENT MEANS

If you found yourself answering:

Mostly YES

You are walking the path of spiritual elevation.
Spirit may be preparing you for the moment of initiation.

A mix of YES and SOMETIMES

You are in a stage of unfolding.
Your field is developing beautifully and naturally.
Trust the pace of your evolution.

Mostly SOMETIMES

Your gifts are awakening.
This is a fertile, powerful stage—be patient and attentive.
Spirit is shaping your foundation.

Mostly NOT YET

You are building your roots.
This is not a sign of unworthiness—
it is simply a sign that more healing, integration, and
experience will strengthen your future path.

Every Master begins at "not yet."
What matters is **willingness**, not readiness.

CLOSING MESSAGE

This assessment does not reveal whether you *will* become a
Grand Reiki Master.
It reveals where your soul *currently stands.*

Grand Mastery is not a goal.
It is a calling.

Your only role is to:

- heal
- listen
- grow
- align
- trust
- surrender

Spirit will take care of the rest.

Appendix D — Dr. Constance's Lineage

I was initiated into Reiki Level 1 & 2 in September 1999, by an American lady who called herself Nefertiti.

I received my Reiki Master from Margaret back in 2000.

Lineage

In 2023, I received my Doctorate and Ph.D. in Natural Medicine. In 2017, my name was changed to Constance Santego. In the year 2010, I, Connie Brummet, was attuned to Grand Reiki Mastery by Spirit, and in 2000, I was attuned to Reiki Mastery by Margaret Ripple, who was attuned in 1998 by Wendy Koenig, who was attuned in 1997 by Laurie Grant.

In 1989, Laurie Grant was attuned by James Davis, who Dr. Arthur Robertson attuned. Dr. Robertson was initiated in the 1970s into the Reiki system by Master teacher Virginia.

Samdahl was the first Occidental Reiki Master initiated by Hawayo Takata.

In the late 1970s and early 1980s, Dr. Robertson studied and shared with Reiki Master Teacher Iris Ishikuro, who also was initiated into the system by Mrs. Takata.

1938, Mrs. Takata received her Master's attunement from Mr. Chujiro Hayashi. Mr. Hayashi received his Reiki Mastership from Dr. Usui in 1925. Dr. Usui received his attunement from Spirit in 1922.

Appendix E — Journal Reflections for the Grand Master Path

Prompts for clarity, awakening, and soul alignment.

The path toward Grand Reiki Mastery is not walked with the mind alone—
it is explored through the heart, the soul, and the quiet spaces in between.

These journal reflections are designed to help you:

- deepen your relationship with Spirit
- understand your intuitive development
- recognize inner transformations
- release what no longer fits
- anchor who you are becoming

There are no right or wrong answers.
Write with honesty, softness, and curiosity.

Let your soul speak.

SECTION 1 — Listening to the Calling

1. What is quietly calling me right now?

Write without thinking. Let the words come as they wish.

2. When did I first sense that my path might be shifting?

Describe any subtle or obvious turning points.

3. What feelings arise when I imagine stepping into a deeper level of Reiki?

Excitement? Fear? Peace? Resistance? Openness?

4. How does my soul describe Grand Mastery?

Write from intuition, not intellect.

SECTION 2 — The Evolution of Your Healing Presence

5. How has my healing presence changed in the past year?

Consider your energy, intuition, and confidence.

6. What do others often reflect back to me about my energy?

Notice patterns in feedback from clients and students.

7. What qualities do I embody naturally when I am in alignment?

List your highest qualities—yes, even the ones you downplay.

8. How do I show up differently when Spirit flows through me?

Describe the shift you feel.

SECTION 3 — Intuition, Guidance & Spirit Communication

9. How does Spirit most often communicate with me?

Through feelings, knowing, signs, dreams, or synchronicities?

10. When was the last time I felt guided? What happened?

11. What intuitive gifts are growing stronger?

Sight, hearing, knowing, sensing, feeling, or prophecy?

12. What am I learning about trusting what I receive?

SECTION 4 — Healing the Self

13. What emotional patterns or wounds feel ready to release?

This may be subtle or deeply felt.

14. Where does ego still influence my choices?

Answer without judgment.

15. What part of me feels unprepared or hesitant— and why?

Bring the shadow into the light with kindness.

16. What does my heart need to feel safe to rise?

SECTION 5 — Service, Purpose & Humility

17. In what ways am I already serving others through Reiki?

18. What does humble leadership mean to me personally?

19. What part of service brings me the deepest joy?

20. What does it mean to be a teacher of teachers?

Write the first thoughts that come.

SECTION 6 — Preparing for Spiritual Elevation

21. Where in my life am I being asked to surrender more deeply?

22. What old identities or roles am I outgrowing?

23. What new qualities are emerging within me?

24. How do I feel when I imagine Spirit choosing me?

Write honestly—your soul knows.

SECTION 7 — Signs, Synchronicities & Guidance

25. What signs or synchronicities have appeared recently?

List anything that felt like a nudge.

26. What patterns am I noticing in my spiritual experiences?

27. What does Spirit seem to be teaching me right now?

28. What do I sense is coming next?

Let your intuition answer.

SECTION 8 — The Future Self

29. Who am I becoming?

Describe the version of yourself you feel emerging.

30. What qualities does my Grand Master self hold?

List the attributes of your future expanded self.

31. What guidance would my future self give me right now?

Write as if the message is coming from that higher version of you.

32. What am I ready to claim, embody, or accept?

SECTION 9 — The Soul Commitment

33. Why do I feel called to this path?

Go deeper than the surface reasons.

34. What vow am I making to myself as I walk forward?

35. What vow am I making to Spirit?

36. What promise am I making to those I will teach?

CLOSING REFLECTION

To complete the appendix, choose one final prompt and answer it slowly, carefully, and with reverence:

"What does Grand Mastery mean to my soul?"

Write until your soul stops speaking.
This final reflection becomes the seed of your next evolution.

Appendix F — Glossary of Reiki Wisdom Terminology

This glossary offers clear explanations of the key terms, concepts, and spiritual principles used throughout this book. It is designed to support your understanding as you move deeper into the Reiki Wisdom lineage and the path toward Grand Mastery.

Attunement

A sacred energetic process that opens a practitioner's channel to Reiki. In Reiki Wisdom, attunement is viewed as both a human ceremony and a potential spiritual elevation guided directly by Spirit.

Archangels

Higher-dimensional beings who support healing, guidance, and protection. Commonly connected to Reiki Wisdom teachings: Michael, Raphael, Gabriel, Uriel, Zadkiel, Chamuel, and Pistis Sophia.

Ancestral Healing

The process of releasing emotional, energetic, and karmic patterns passed down through lineage. Often activated at advanced levels of Reiki practice.

Biofield

The electromagnetic and subtle energy field surrounding the body. Includes chakras, meridians, and auric layers. Reiki works directly within this field.

Channeling

Allowing divine energy, information, or guidance to flow through without interference from the ego.

Clairs

The spiritual senses:

- *Clairvoyance* (clear seeing)
- *Clairaudience* (clear hearing)
- *Clairsentience* (clear feeling)
- *Claircognizance* (clear knowing)
- *Clairalience* (clear smelling)
- *Clairgustance* (clear tasting)

Coherence

A state of harmony between mind, heart, and energy field. Essential for high-level healing and attunements.

Dai Ko Myo

The Master Symbol in traditional Reiki, meaning "Great Bright Light." In Reiki Wisdom, it also refers to a state of consciousness rather than a symbol alone.

Discernment

The intuitive ability to sense truth, alignment, or energetic purity. Considered a lifelong skill for all advanced practitioners.

Energy Medicine

Healing modalities that work with the energetic, emotional, mental, and spiritual layers of the body. Reiki is a universal form of energy medicine.

Energetic Boundaries

The invisible edges of your energy field. Healthy boundaries help practitioners avoid absorbing others' emotions or energy.

Energetic Container

The field of safety, coherence, and clarity held by a healer or teacher during sessions, classes, or ceremonies.

Frequency

The vibrational state of energy. Higher frequencies often correlate with compassion, clarity, and spiritual connection.

Faith Frequency

In Reiki Wisdom, the foundational spiritual vibration from which all higher gifts arise. Faith is seen as the unifying energy behind the Nine Spiritual Gifts.

Grand Reiki Master

A practitioner elevated by Spirit beyond the Master/Teacher level. This is not a certification but a spiritual appointment marked by maturity, service, purity, and readiness.

Grounding

Connecting your energy to Earth's stabilizing field to maintain presence, clarity, and emotional balance.

Higher Realms

Dimensions of consciousness that include guides, angels, ascended masters, and spiritual intelligence.

Hon Sha Ze Sho Nen

The Reiki Level 2 distance-healing symbol. At higher levels, it is understood as a frequency that transcends time and space.

Initiation

A transformative spiritual event—human-led or Spirit-led—that elevates the practitioner's frequency and capacity to serve.

Intuition

Inner knowing that arises from the soul rather than the mind. Essential to the development of a Grand Reiki Master.

Karmic Patterns

Emotional or energetic imprints created through past experiences (personal or ancestral) that influence current behavior or reactions.

Lineage

The energetic and teaching heritage passed from teacher to student. Reiki Wisdom represents a new lineage—a spiritual evolution of traditional Reiki.

Lightworker

A soul whose purpose includes bringing healing, compassion, and higher consciousness to the world.

Meditative State

A conscious, relaxed awareness that allows the practitioner to communicate with Spirit and receive intuitive guidance.

Morphic Field

A collective energetic pattern that influences groups. Grand Masters often hold a morphic field for their students, communities, and lineage.

Nine Spiritual Gifts

Gifts such as prophecy, healing, wisdom, knowledge, discernment, and faith, as referenced in your earlier books and integrated into the Reiki Wisdom pathway.

Prophetic Senses

Higher intuitive abilities involving visions, dreams, inner hearing, or knowing, often activated as practitioners deepen spiritually.

Purity

A state of energetic integrity free from ego interference, distortion, or misalignment. Essential for advanced leadership.

Quantum Healing

Energetic healing that works beyond linear time, physical matter, and traditional cause-and-effect. Reiki naturally functions in the quantum field.

Reiki

Universal life force energy that flows through all living beings. Reiki Wisdom views Reiki not only as a healing technique but as a consciousness field.

Reiki Wisdom

An expanded lineage of Reiki integrating intuition, prophecy, spiritual gifts, emotional healing, and higher-dimensional guidance.

Self-Healing

The first stage of Reiki practice. A lifelong commitment to personal healing, alignment, and spiritual growth.

Shadow Work

The process of exploring hidden emotions, fears, or patterns that require healing before spiritual elevation.

Spirit

The universal divine intelligence guiding healing, intuition, and spiritual evolution.

Spiritual Elevation

The process of rising into higher states of consciousness, often culminating in a Spirit-led attunement.

Synchronicity

Meaningful coincidences that reflect Spirit's guidance or confirmation.

Transmission

An energetic or spiritual download given to a healer, often during meditation, attunement, or moments of divine alignment.

Teacher of Teachers

A Grand Master who trains not only practitioners but also future Masters and lineage carriers.

Universal Life Force

The divine energy that animates all existence. Another name for Reiki.

Vibration

The energetic rate at which someone or something resonates. Healing raises vibration; fear lowers it.

Wisdom Body

The intuitive and spiritual layer of the self that receives insight and higher knowing.

Zone of Spiritual Alignment

A calm, centered, and coherent state where Spirit's guidance flows clearly. Often experienced during attunements and meditations.

✦ Bibliography

Reiki Foundations

Hayashi, Chujiro. *Reiki Ryoho: The Hayashi Healing Guide.* Tokyo: Hayashi Institute, 1930.

Petter, Frank Arjava. *This Is Reiki.* Twin Lakes: Lotus Press, 2012.

Petter, Frank Arjava. *Reiki: The Legacy of Dr. Usui.* Twin Lakes: Lotus Press, 1998.

Rand, William Lee. *Reiki: The Healing Touch.* Southfield: Vision Publications, 1991.

Takata, Hawayo. *Stories of Hawayo Takata.* Kyoto: Traditional Reiki Archives, 1970.

Usui, Mikao. *The Original Reiki Handbook of Dr. Mikao Usui.* Lotus Press, 1993.

Energy Medicine & Consciousness

Brennan, Barbara Ann. *Hands of Light.* New York: Bantam, 1987.

Brennan, Barbara Ann. *Light Emerging.* New York: Bantam, 1993.

Gore, Lesley. *Energy Medicine: A Practical Guide.* Newburyport: Weiser Books, 2014.

Judith, Anodea. *Wheels of Life: A User's Guide to the Chakra System.* Woodbury: Llewellyn, 1987.

McTaggart, Lynne. *The Field: The Quest for the Secret Force of the Universe.* New York: HarperCollins, 2008.

McTaggart, Lynne. *The Intention Experiment.* New York: Free Press, 2007.

Oschman, James L. *Energy Medicine: The Scientific Basis.* Edinburgh: Churchill Livingstone, 2000.

Pert, Candace. *Molecules of Emotion.* New York: Scribner, 1997.

Intuition, Spiritual Gifts & Mystical Development

Bourbon, Heather. *The Art of Psychic Mastery.* London: SpiritHouse Publishing, 2014.

Gawain, Shakti. *Creative Visualization.* Novato: New World Library, 1978.

Myss, Caroline. *Anatomy of the Spirit.* New York: Crown Publishing, 1996.

Tolle, Eckhart. *The Power of Now.* Novato: New World Library, 1999.

Walsch, Neale Donald. *Conversations with God.* New York: Putnam, 1996.

Quantum, Mind-Body & Consciousness Science

Dispenza, Joe. *Becoming Supernatural*. London: Hay House, 2017.

Dispenza, Joe. *You Are the Placebo*. London: Hay House, 2014.

Lipton, Bruce. *The Biology of Belief*. Carlsbad: Hay House, 2005.

Pribram, Karl. *Languages of the Brain*. Englewood Cliffs: Prentice-Hall, 1971.

Radin, Dean. *The Conscious Universe*. San Francisco: HarperOne, 1997.

Sheldrake, Rupert. *The Presence of the Past: Morphic Resonance*. Rochester: Park Street Press, 1988.

Sacred Texts & Spiritual Classics

Easwaran, Eknath (trans.). *The Upanishads*. Tomales: Nilgiri Press, 2007.

Feuerstein, Georg. *The Yoga Tradition*. Prescott: Hohm Press, 2001.

Sivananda, Swami. *The Chakras*. Rishikesh: Divine Life Society, 1994.

Woodroffe, Sir John. *The Serpent Power*. New York: Dover Publications, 1974.

Works by Dr. Constance Santego (Reiki Wisdom Series & Related Teachings)

Santego, Constance. *Reiki & the Five Elements*. Kelowna: Maximillian Enterprises, 2025.

Santego, Constance. *Reiki and Karmic Healing: Releasing Patterns from Past Lives*. Kelowna: Maximillian Enterprises, 2025.

Santego, Constance. *Reiki and the Power of the Joint Points : Beyond the Symbols - The Path to True Mastery*. Kelowna: Maximillian Enterprises, 2025.

Santego, Constance. *Secrets of a Healer: Magic of Reiki*. Kelowna: Maximillian Enterprises, 2020.

Santego, Constance. *Intuitive Life*. Kelowna: Maximillian Enterprises, 2007.

Santego, Constance. *Prophecy*. Kelowna: Maximillian Enterprises, 2020.

Santego, Constance. *The Nine Spiritual Gifts (Novel Series)*. Kelowna: Maximillian Enterprises, 2020-2025.

Santego, Constance. *Tesla's Code Series*. Kelowna: Maximillian Enterprises, 2025.

Optional Supplemental Reading

Greene, Brian. *The Elegant Universe.* New York: Vintage, 2003.
Hawkins, David R. *Power vs. Force.* Toronto: Hay House, 1995.
Zukav, Gary. *The Seat of the Soul.* New York: Simon & Schuster, 1989.

✦ Message From The Author

As you reach the final pages of this book, I want to thank you—not just for reading, but for answering a calling that very few ever recognize within themselves.

The path toward Grand Reiki Mastery is not accidental.
It is not random.
It is not something you stumble into.

It is a path that *chooses you* long before you choose it.

If you have felt a stirring in your heart, a deep remembrance in your soul, or a quiet whisper urging you forward, know this:

You are not imagining it.

You are being called.

This book was written for you—for the healer who feels there is more, for the teacher who senses a deeper level of service, and for the soul who has always known that Spirit walks beside them.

I have spent decades teaching Reiki, studying energy, guiding intuitive development, exploring spiritual gifts, and walking

through my own initiations—some gentle, some difficult, all transformative.
Every experience has led to the creation of the Reiki Wisdom lineage and, ultimately, to this book.

My intention in writing *Becoming a Grand Reiki Master* was not to give you new techniques or more information.
It was to offer a **map for the soul**,
a lantern for the path,
and a reminder that you are part of something much larger than your human role.

Your healing, your intuition, your growth, your service— they matter more than you know.

The world needs healers who are grounded, compassionate, discerning, and spiritually mature.
The world needs leaders who teach from humility, not ego.
The world needs Grand Masters who walk in devotion, not performance.

If this book has supported you, guided you, or awakened something ancient within you…
then Spirit has used my hands and my voice to reach yours.

As you continue your journey, remember:

- You are guided.
- You are supported.
- You are seen.
- You are loved.
- And you are never walking alone.

When the moment comes for your own elevation—
whether quiet or profound—
you will know.

Trust what rises within you.
Trust the timing.
Trust the path.

And above all, trust Spirit.

With gratitude,
with reverence,
and with love,

Dr. Constance Santego
Grand Reiki Master
Reiki Wisdom Lineage Carrier

✦ About The Author

Dr. Constance Santego, Ph.D., DNM, is a Grand Reiki Master, natural medicine doctor, educator, and author of more than forty books in the fields of Reiki, energy medicine, consciousness, spirituality, and personal transformation. Her work has touched students and readers around the world,

empowering them to awaken their intuitive gifts, heal deeply, and step into their soul's purpose.

For over twenty-five years, Dr. Santego has taught Reiki at all levels—from beginner to Master to the deeper spiritual layers that led to the creation of the **Reiki Wisdom Lineage**, an expanded pathway that integrates intuitive development, prophecy, emotional healing, the Nine Spiritual Gifts, and higher-dimensional guidance.

A lifelong seeker and teacher, she has founded multiple healing and educational programs, trained thousands of practitioners worldwide, and developed transformational methods such as the Auriclons Release Technique™ and the Tesla-inspired pathways to vibrational healing.
Her work bridges ancient teachings with modern energetic science, inviting students into a grounded yet spiritually profound experience of healing.

Dr. Santego is also the author of numerous books and novels, including the *Reiki Wisdom* series, the *Secrets of a Healer* series, the *Tesla's Code* series, and the multi-volume spiritual fiction collection *The Nine Spiritual Gifts*, which brings spiritual development to life through story.

Her mission is simple yet powerful:
to help others remember who they truly are, awaken their inner wisdom, and rise into lives of purpose, healing, and spiritual clarity.

When she is not teaching or writing, Dr. Santego enjoys life in beautiful British Columbia, where she continues to study, create, and share her gifts with compassion, humour, and devotion to the path of spirit-led service.

ALSO AVAILABLE

For additional information on

Constance Santego's

wide range of Motivational Products, Coaching Sessions,
Spiritual Retreats,
Live Events and Educational Programs

Go to

www.ConstanceSantego.ca

Follow on Instagram - Constance_Santego and
Facebook - constancesantegoo

Subscribe and receive Free Information and Meditations on
her
YouTube Channel - Constance Santego

Secrets of a Healer, Magic of Reiki

ISBN: 978-1-7772220-0-0

Secrets of a Healer, The Reiki Master's Manual

ISBN: 978-1-990062-34-6

www.ingramcontent.com/pod-product-compliance
Lightning Source LLC
Chambersburg PA
CBHW071656120626
46550CB00001B/3